The Long Partition and the Making of Modern South Asia

CULTURES OF HISTORY

CULTURES OF HISTORY

NICHOLAS DIRKS, SERIES EDITOR

The death of history, reported at the end of the twentieth century, was clearly premature. It has become a hotly contested battleground in struggles over identity, citizenship, and claims of recognition and rights. Each new national history proclaims itself as ancient and universal, while the contingent character of its focus raises questions about the universality and objectivity of any historical tradition. Globalization and the American hegemony have created cultural, social, local, and national backlashes. Cultures of History is a new series of books that investigates the forms, understandings, genres, and histories of history, taking history as the primary text of modern life and the foundational basis for state, society, and nation.

Shail Mayaram, *Against History, Against State: Counterperspectives from the Margins*

Tapati Guha-Thakurta, *Monuments, Objects, Histories: Institutions of Art in Colonial and Postcolonial India*

Charles Hirschkind, *The Ethical Soundscape: Cassette Sermons and Islamic Counterpublics*

Ahmad H. Sa'di and Lila Abu-Lughod, editors, *Nakba: Palestine, 1948, and the Claims of Memory*

Prachi Deshpande, *Creative Pasts: Historical Memory and Identity in Western India, 1700–1960*

Laura Bear, *Lines of the Nation: Indian Railway Workers, Bureaucracy, and the Intimate Historical Self*

The Long Partition and the Making of Modern South Asia

REFUGEES, BOUNDARIES, HISTORIES

Vazira Fazila-Yacoobali Zamindar

Columbia University Press *New York*

COLUMBIA UNIVERSITY PRESS

Publishers Since 1893

New York Chichester, West Sussex

Paperback edition, 2010

Library of Congress Cataloging-in-Publication Data

Zamindar, Vazira Fazila-Yacoobali.

The long partition and the making of modern South Asia /

Vazira Fazila-Yacoobali Zamindar.

p. cm. — (Cultures of history)

Includes bibliographical references and index.

ISBN 978-0-231-13846-8 (cloth : alk. paper) — ISBN 978-0-231-13847-5 (pbk. : alk. paper) — ISBN 978-0-231-51101-8 (electronic)

1. India—History—Partition, 1947. 2. Refugees—India. 3. Refugess—Pakistan.

4. India—Borders—Pakistan. 5. Pakistan—Borders—India.

I. Title. II. Series.

DS480.842Z37 2007

954.04'2—dc22 2007012702

Columbia University Press books are printed on permanent and durable acid-free paper.

Printed in the United States of America

Designed by Audrey Smith

For all our divided families,
and most specially for my mother

Contents

In Conclusion

List of Illustrations

PLATES

MAPS

TABLES

Acknowledgments

This book is most indebted to all the Indo-Pak divided families that shared their lives and stories with me each time I showed up at their doorstep. Their hospitality and warmth made the often difficult interviews a shared journey of aligning memories into history, although I am certain the one I have written will surprise them as much as it did me.

The research and writing of this book took place in many different countries across three continents. As I crisscrossed the map of the world, I became acutely aware of my privileges as a scholar, and the extraordinary generosity of family, friends, and strangers that have enabled and sustained sometimes seemingly impossible border-crossings.

For a peripatetic project of this kind, with no geographically contained community or single archive to go to, I had to rely on networks of old friends, scholars, and acquaintances who enabled its research in astonishing ways. To give just one example from a chest full of stories: a school friend's mother's former colleague in Karachi gave me the name of his childhood friend in Delhi, who received me as if I were a member of his own family, and introduced me to his students, who in turn took me home and befriended me as their own. My debts are so numerous, and I think in part because Partition is still so close to so many of our hearts, that I can only account for a part of my interlocutors. In Karachi, Sarwar, and Abida Abidi,

Iftikhar Ahmad, Khalid Ahmad, Mehr Alavi, Nisreen Azhar, Naushaba Burney, Arif Hasan, Lala Hayat, Begum Kadiruddin, Syed Hashim Reza, Ahmad Salim, Hasan Zaidi, Mussarat Zaidi, and all the Dilliwallas in my printmaking class; and in Delhi, Muzaffar Alam, Urvashi Butalia, Mushirul Hasan, Ritu Menon, Vimla Rajan, Sharib Rudaulvi, and Mohammad Talib made time to talk to me, introduced me to friends and families, and helped locate records or simply negotiate logistics. I would also like to thank M. S. Karnik, as well as Papan and Mohan Punjabi, for sharing their memories of Karachi with me, which provided valuable insight for writing the section on the Hindu exodus from Karachi. Anuradha Roy and Rukun Advani not only provided me with my first introduction to Delhi, but became my anchors there every time I showed up on short notice, and comforted me through grueling Delhi summers. Research in old Delhi would not have been possible without Attia Rais' support, friendship, and the warmth of her entire family. I thank them for their enduring affections.

In Pakistan, individuals almost mattered more than institutions in reading any kind of written record, and so the personal help and cups of tea I received more than tempered the lonely task of archival research there. I would like to thank in particular Khwaja Razi Haider at the Quaid-e-Azam Academy, Malahat Kaleem Sherwani at Karachi University, Mr. Kachelo at the Sind Archives, and Mr. Salimullah Khan and Khalid Ahmad at the National Documentation Center. Mahmood Sham, the editor of *Jang*, allowed me to read and use the materials from their archive, and Salimullah Siddiqui not only put up with me for months in his tiny microfilm office, but followed my research with leads, insights, and a great deal of technical help. In India, Pradeep Mehendiratta of the American Institute of Indian Studies was an invaluable help, and the staff at the Nehru Memorial Museum and Library, the National Archives of India, and the Delhi State Archives assisted me in finding records, speedy photocopying, cups of tea, affection, and good humor, especially when I was under stress or running out of time.

Research for this book was supported by fellowships from the Social Science Research Council, the American Institute for Pakistan Studies, the Council for American Overseas Research Centers, the Center for Historical Social Sciences at Columbia University, and the Mary Elvira Traveling Fellowship.

I have carried this project with me to a number of academic locations in both the United States and the Netherlands, which became my home for a productive six years. From the Interdepartmental Program in History and Anthropology at the University of Michigan, Ann Arbor, where I began my first musings, to the Department of Anthropology and the Center for Historical Social Sciences at Columbia University, the Amsterdam School of Social Science Research and the now-defunct Belle van Zuylen Institute at the University of Amsterdam, the International Institute for the Study of Islam in the Modern World in Leiden, and finally to the History Department at Brown University, each has supported my transnational existence, and provided me with an intellectual community where I received valuable feedback on early proposals and various drafts of writing on this project. I would like to thank Janaki Bakhle, Partha Chatterjee, Deborah Cohen, Juan I. Cole, Frederick Cooper, E. Valentine Daniels, Nicholas B. Dirks, Francis Gouda, Ashok Koul, Muhammad Khalid Masud, Brinkley Messick, Birgit Meyer, Anneliese Moors, Amir Mufti, Tara Nummedal, Gyanendra Pandey, Peter Pels, Thangam Ravindranathan, Seth Rockman, Willem van Schendel, Robert Self, Naoko Shibusawa, Ann Stoler, Mark Swislocki, Thomas Trautmann, and Peter van der Veer. Nick Dirks in particular made me follow my heart on this project and supported it over the years with belief even when my own faltered, while Peter van der Veer and Anneliese Moors mentored me through my years in the Netherlands. Brinkley Messick and Partha Chatterjee's ever-thoughtful comments reshaped it in important ways. Willem van Schendel generously read and commented on the entire manuscript.

Beth Notar has served as a remarkable guide from a distance, and Omar Khalidi and John Torpey generously sent me their writings to assist my own. Akbar Zaidi, Kamran Asdar Ali, and David Gilmartin's insightful comments encouraged the sharpening of my arguments in the final drafting of the book. I would like to thank David Magier, Mary Beth Bryson, Jonathan Sidhu, and Laura Molton for help with the details of the manuscript, and Anne Routon and Ron Harris for their supportive editorial transformation of my manuscript into a book.

Both Eqbal Ahmad and Hamza Alavi mentored different moments of my intellectual career, and cannot go unmentioned, for toward the end of their lives, as scholars-cum-activists, they were concerned in different ways with Partition and its historiography, the folding of the past into shoddy imperatives of nation. I hope this work in some way repays my debts to them for their enormous generosity and affection. They have been an inspiration for thinking about a different South Asia.

My own immediate and extended family on both sides of the divide, as well as childhood friends and neighbors, actively participated in this research. I interviewed them all, asked them the difficult questions that I could not sometimes ask of others, and they in turn excavated materials to help me. Although I did not use any of the interviews with my own family here, they shadowed the project in unquantifiable ways. My parents and Yusuf Khalo in particular took part in my research as collaborators, assistants, and interlocutors, and my father's daily newspaper cuttings continue to give me an archive to think and argue with.

I have done most of my writing around the births of my two sons, and this would have been impossible without an extraordinary mother who stepped in with sustained encouragement and indispensable help. In addition, my father and Markus Berger extended and overextended themselves to grant me those hours of writing and seemingly endless rewriting. My brother Naeem, and all my Amsterdam friends (including Irfan Ahmad, Mohammad Amer, Miriyam Auroagh, Nandini Bedi, Franya Chilova, Julia Hornberger, Anouk de Koning, Marina de Regt, and Indra Silar) read drafts, helped out with the boys, and argued and listened whenever I needed it most. Markus has been such a gracious companion through all these years, and Kabir and Elyas, with their joyous and tumultuous presence, have thankfully forced me to bring this work to a close.

Translations / Transliterations

The oral histories were conducted in Urdu, and I have retained the original Urdu in the quoted excerpts to retain some of the emotional tenor of the spoken language. In the case of quotations from Urdu newspapers, I have mostly only given the English translations, though I have retained the Urdu original in some places where the wording in Urdu captured a particular nuance. All translations from the Urdu are my own.

For the sake of readability, I have kept the use of diacritical marks to a minimum in the transliterations into Roman, and used the most comon Roman forms for common use words, like *muhajir*, *dada*, *khala*, and so on. The following diacritics are used to distinguish:

a	ā
i	ī
t	ṭ
d	ḍ
r	ṛ
ʻain appears as	ʻ

Word-final *h* is indicated only when it is pronounced, and izā*fat* is indicated by adding *-e*. I have followed English rules of capitalization for sentences, proper names, titles, etc.

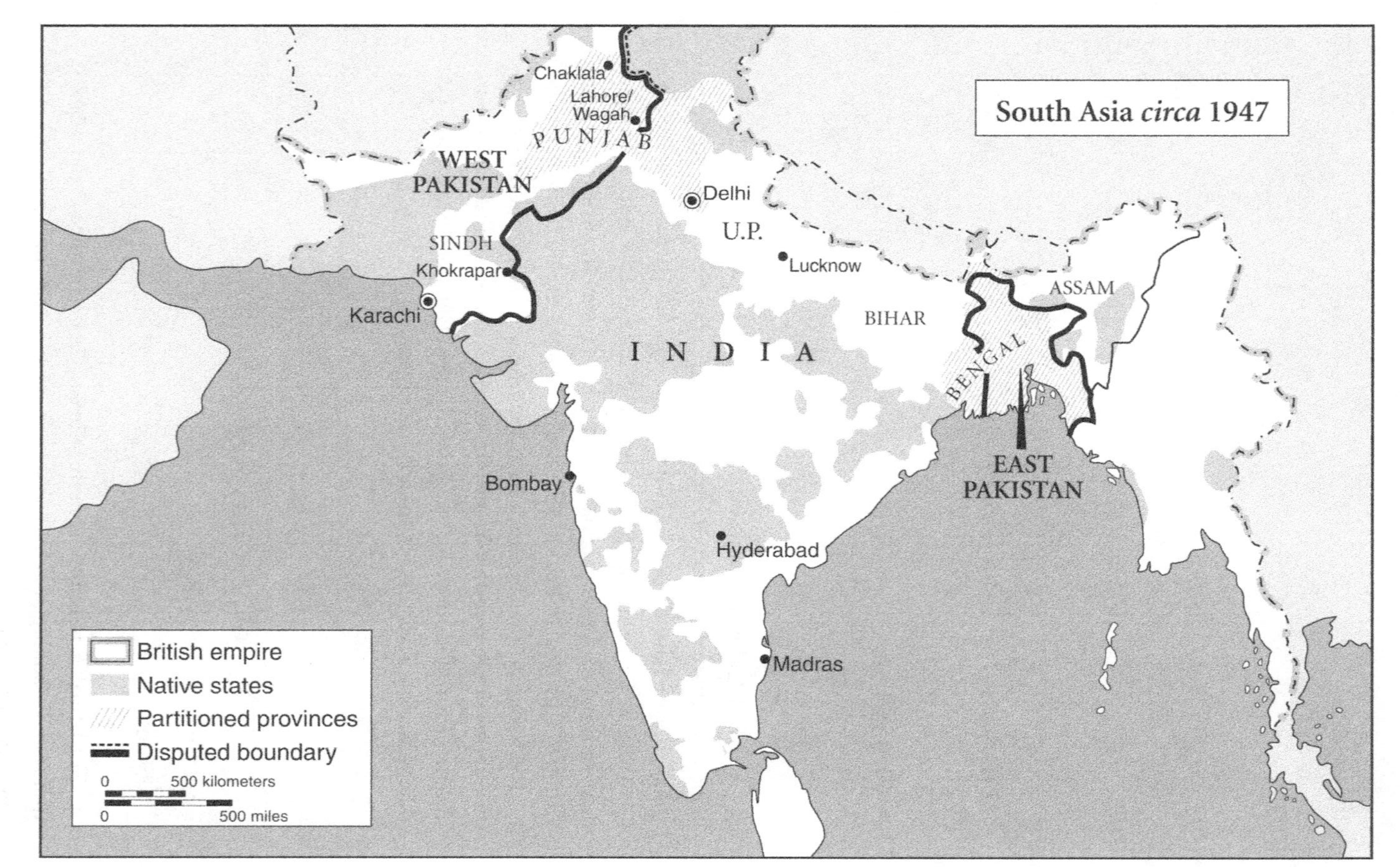
South Asia *circa* 1947
Chaklala
Lahore/
Wagah
PUNJAB
WEST
PAKISTAN
Delhi
U.P.
SINDH
Khokrapar
Lucknow
Karachi
ASSAM
BIHAR
INDIA
BENGAL
EAST
PAKISTAN
Bombay
Hyderabad
Madras
British empire
Native states
Partitioned provinces
Disputed boundary
0
500 kilometers
0
500 miles

Introduction: The Place of Partition

There behind barbed wire, on one side, lay India and behind more barbed wire, on the other side, lay Pakistan. In between, on a bit of earth which had no name, lay Toba Tek Singh.[1]

In our maps of the world the bit of earth with no name simply disappears. It folds into a black, impenetrable line. Let me begin with Ghulam Ali's story as a way of unfolding this history, drawing out lives from lines, untended margins from marked places.

Ghulam Ali was a subaltern officer in the British Indian Army, an *havildar,* who had been sent to receive technical training in artificial-limb making in Britain during the closing years of the Second World War. When he returned, he was posted at the military workshops in Chaklala, near Rawalpindi. On June 3, 1947, a partition of the Indian subcontinent was announced, concomitant with the coming end of almost two centuries of colonial rule, and a Partition Council began the exacting task of counting and dividing the vast machinery of colonial statecraft into two—everything from tables and chairs, weather instruments and military hardware, to railway engineers and office clerks. All those in government and military service were asked to choose which post-independence nation-state they wanted to serve—India or Pakistan.

Ghulam Ali "opted" for the Indian Army since his familial home was in Lucknow. But before post-independence maps could be drawn up that would show Lucknow in a new India and Chaklala in a new Pakistan, genocidal violence engulfed Rawalpindi and war broke out between the two nascent states over Kashmir. Prevented from returning to India, Ghulam Ali was forced to work for the fledgling Pakistan Army. Eventually in 1950 the Pakistan Army discharged him on the grounds that he had opted for the Indian Army. The limb maker was taken to the Pakistani border post at Khokrapar and, deemed to be an Indian, was "forcibly removed" into Indian territory. However, at the Indian checkpost he was not recognized as an Indian. He was arrested by the border police for entry without a travel permit, forced to serve a prison sentence, and was deported back to Pakistan in 1951 on the grounds that he was a Pakistani.

If lives can unfold, they can also unravel. Faced with dispossession, Ghulam Ali applied to the courts to be recognized as a Pakistani citizen, but was declared an Indian national in 1956. He then bought himself a Pakistani passport in order to cross the border and return to his familial home in Lucknow. There he applied for Indian citizenship, but despite appeals by his brother, the provincial government of Uttar Pradesh ordered him to leave the country in 1957. When he was deported by an Indian police escort to the Wagah border crossing, the Pakistani officials there in turn arrested him again and, considering him an Indian national, placed him in the "Hindu camp" at Lahore.

Ghulam Ali, barbed wire on either side of him, is that quintessentially Mantoesque figure: like Toba Tek Singh in Saadat Hasan Manto's best-known Urdu short story of Partition's "madness," he invokes all the aporias of belonging in a cartography of nation-states. Where, indeed, is India? Where is Pakistan? Who is an Indian? Who is a Pakistani?

Perhaps the sheer magnitude of the catastrophic experiences of Partition in 1947 is enough to justify this study. Marked by genocidal violence, forced conversions, abductions and rapes in large parts of north India, as well as an unprecedented displacement of people, Partition has been called "a holocaust" of a tragedy.[2] And yet, by placing the events of 1947 at only the beginning of what I argue was *a long Partition*, this book asks us to stretch our very understanding of "Partition violence" to include the bureaucratic violence of drawing political boundaries and nationalizing identities that became, in some lives, interminable.

I came across Ghulam Ali's story in a government file which I requested because I had been "tracking," in ethnographic fashion,[3] Urdu-speaking north Indian Muslim families as they became divided between Delhi, India, and Karachi, Pakistan, in the years following 1947. Divided families are at the heart of this book, for it is through them, their oral histories in two cities, that I was forced into the archive; it was what E. Valentine Daniel calls "the drone of silence" in interviews, caught between "not-being-able-to-speak" and "ought-not-to-speak,"[4] that drove me to read Urdu newspapers of the time, and tucked away, seemingly indifferent government records of both states.

Moving between memory and record, I recover here a remarkable history of how, in the midst of incomprehensible violence, two postcolonial states comprehended, intervened, *and shaped* the colossal displacements of Partition. It was through the making of refugees as a governmental category, through refugee rehabilitation as a tool of planning, that new nations and the borders between them were made, and people, including families, were divided. The highly surveillanced western Indo-Pak border, one of the most difficult for citizens of the region to cross to this day, was not a consequence of the Kashmir conflict, as security studies gurus may suggest, but rather was formed through a series of attempts to resolve the fundamental uncertainty of the political Partition itself—where did, where could, "Muslims" like Ghulam Ali belong.

The *Muslims* I speak of here does not refer to a people constituted by shared beliefs or religious practices, for certainly Muslims in South Asia are linguistically and culturally very diverse. Instead it refers to a constructed category of community and political mobilization that emerged under colonial conditions,[5] and which was to become substantially transformed through the years of the long Partition. There are many contested histories of how the idea of Muslims as a separate political community came to be mobilized as part of the Pakistan movement; how the neologism *Pakistan,* evocatively coined by a Punjabi Muslim student at Cambridge University in 1933 amid numerous "fabulous place-making" exercises, led to the actual "moth-eaten Pakistan" in 1947.[6] It is not my purpose here to add to these studies to understand why Partition happened,[7] but rather to clarify, with a focus on north Indian Muslim families, the postcolonial burden of this political partition.

When the All India Muslim League invoked "Pakistan," it did so on behalf of a nation of "Muslims," even though many Muslims did not support the Pakistan movement, and yet others would be simply left out of a state drawn from regions where Muslims formed an enumerated majority. Furthermore, those who did support the Pakistan movement included Muslims of regions like Delhi and Uttar Pradesh who could not be part of its territorial claims. As David Gilmartin points out, the "two-nation theory," the basis for the Muslim League's Pakistan demand, was "a fundamentally non-territorial vision of nationality," and "for most Muslims the meaning of Pakistan did not hinge primarily on its association with a specific territory."[8]

However, as the Muslim League and the Indian National Congress agreed to the denouement of partition and transfer of power to two territorially distinct postcolonial states, nation as community had to be transformed into nation as citizens of two states. This task came with questions and attendant ambiguities for both emerging states. Where did Hindus and Sikhs belong who resided in the territory now Pakistan? Did they belong to an Indian nation or could they become citizens of Pakistan? And where did Muslims belong who resided in the territory now India? Could they be citizens of India and yet part of an imagined Pakistani nation?

It is at this point that historiography of the subcontinent blurs into a mapped silence as "1947" becomes a threshold. Most histories of the region as a whole end at this "moment of arrival,"[9] as nationalism achieves its celebrated goal of statehood, or thereafter sever into studies of distinct nation-states, as if in this "moment of rupture"[10] "India," "Pakistan," and their borders simply emerge fully formed. This book sits at this threshold, and sutures severed histories to bring together disparate "facts" of genocidal violence and mass displacement, refugee rehabilitation and resettlement, controlling movement of people and the making of citizenship, to show how they were mutually constituted parts of a single history. These "facts," if recovered in archives on any one side of the divide, would have capitulated to a marginal history on the borders of nation. Instead, my cross-border research elucidates the centrality of the dialogic between two states as they marked national difference in the midst of historic chaos.

Michel-Rolph Trouillot's comment that "[h]istory is messy for the people who must live it"[11] is important to foreground, not only for ordinary people caught in the chaos of their times. The mass of ideas of what Partition meant do not fold neatly into our paradigm of sovereign nation-states. From the "hostage theory," which proposed that the Indian state could "safeguard" Hindus and Sikhs in Pakistan by the hostage treatment of Muslims in India,[12] or the Congress leader Sardar Patel's insistence that citizenship in India be conceived so that Hindus and Sikhs in Pakistan were not aliens to it,[13] or the Bengali Muslim League leader H. S. Suhrawardy's address to the Constituent Assembly of Pakistan, where he argued that continuing to live in India did not conflict with his being a member of Pakistan's legislature[14]—the record is littered with ideas in which relationships between citizen and state, nation and territory are nebulous, even for leaders of the time. Thus the years following 1947 are extraordinarily important, for in a whirlwind of people on the move they reveal how these relationships had to be crafted, and at what human cost.

Delhi and Karachi became the two capitals of the post-independence states, and although the two cities were dramatically different before independence, it is Partition itself that binds them together. According to the colonial census of 1941, Delhi had a Muslim minority population of 33.22 percent, while Karachi had a Hindu population of 47.6 percent,[15] and although the enumerative power of the colonial census is unmistakable, it does not capture the enormous cultural significance these religious communities had for the two cities.

Delhi has been described as an "Indo-Islamic city" since it was the seat of power for Delhi sultanates and various Mughal rulers, including Shah Jehan, the builder who left his monumental mark on the geography of the city.[16] When Sayyid Ahmad Khan, the nineteenth-century reformer, sought to uplift *ashraf* Muslims around the time of the Revolt of 1857, he wrote an architectural-cum-genealogical history of Delhi as a Muslim city par excellence.[17] As the city became the colonial capital at the beginning of the twentieth century, many important modern institutions for Islamic learning, for Urdu language, and for pro-Congress and pro–Muslim League nationalism among Muslims all came to be centered here.[18]

In September 1947 genocidal violence from the Punjab spread to the capital city, and most of the city's Muslims were forced to leave their homes and take refuge in camps and wherever they could. By the time the 1951 census was taken 3.3 lakh Muslims of the city had left on the trains to Pakistan, and almost twice the number of Hindu and Sikh refugees had arrived from the Punjab.[19]

Most of the Muslim refugees of Delhi and north India arrived in the city of Karachi. In comparison to Delhi, Karachi had been a small, sleepy port city that served the Sind hinterland, and was largely tied to Bombay and the Malabar coast for its mercantile links. However, as Sind's provincial capital, its highly educated Sindhi Amils and other Hindu communities were essential parts of Sindhi culture and literature, and the region's proud Sufi traditions.[20] As the city's status underwent a dramatic change, from the periphery of British India to being declared the federal capital of the Pakistani state, almost its entire Hindu population had left the city by the census of 1951, despite comparatively little violence in the city, and the city's population as a whole had tripled with the arrival of Muslim refugees from north India.[21]

The complete demographic transformations of entire cities and their urban cultures as a result of Partition's massive displacements are now being accounted for in the growing scholarly attention to Partition's memories.[22] Yet these resettled geographies conceal the completely unsettled character of the first days and years of flight, and the ways in which the combined interventions of the two states shaped them.

Transfer of power took place from colonial rule to national rule in what was a crisis, a state of emergency. Both postcolonial states were formed from a divided albeit unchanged colonial structure of governance and had to restage the modern state on behalf of the nation. Thus their response to this crisis was crucial to establish legitimacy.[23] Both states responded almost immediately by setting up parallel Emergency Committees of the Cabinet to bring "law and order" in murder-cleaved Punjab and Delhi, as well as the Ministries of Relief and Rehabilitation to "manage" the well-being of the millions displaced. It is here that the figure of the "refugee" emerges to carry the scripted and rescripted labor of postcolonial governmentality.

Some 12 million people were displaced in the divided Punjab alone, and some 20 million in the subcontinent as a whole, making it one of the largest displacements of people in the twentieth century, comparable only to the nearly contemporaneous displacements produced by the Second World War in Europe.[24] The comparison with Europe is significant, since the rather well-documented social history of "refugee rehabilitation" there has been considered formative in the later drafting of international refugee laws and the establishment of international organizations for the management of refugees. From the European experience, it has been argued, the refugee emerged as an identifiable social and legal category that could then be studied in the subsequent burgeoning fields of "refugee studies" and "migration studies."[25] The subcontinent's experience of displacements, of the making of refugees, has largely gone unexamined not only because of its peripheral location to the postwar international order, but also because in the region's nation-bound historiographies these refugees have been presumed to have seamlessly folded into two new nations; although two sets of refugees were produced, Hindu and Sikh refugees were displaced to become Indians, while Muslim refugees became Pakistanis.[26] But this was by no means a straightforward process; it was a debated, contested, and fraught historical process of negotiation between two states, in which ultimately there was no consensus on the national status of the "Muslim refugee."

This history of a long Partition unsettles this national closure given to Partition's displacements, by recovering the contingency in which people left their homes in Delhi and Karachi, as well as their numerous attempts to return to them in the ensuing years. Therefore it is with purpose that I use the word *displacement* and not *migration*, to describe the momentous movements of people at this time. The word *migration* came to imply both a movement with the intention of permanent relocation as well as a voluntary exodus, and acquired bureaucratic and juridical meaning in attempts to control, legislate, and ultimately fix these displacements—to produce, with some force, bounded citizens of two nation-states.

In Delhi, for instance, Muslim refugees emerged in the capital in crisis and boarded trains to Pakistan, not necessarily to "migrate" but primarily in search of refuge. In the city's unraveling geography, the Indian state's interventions in the violence were exceedingly important. As Muslim homes became occupied by Hindu and Sikh refugees from the Punjab, the perception that the rehabilitation of "non-Muslim refugees" in need of housing and shelter was pitted against that of "Muslim refugees" profoundly shaped the Muslim exodus.

Path-breaking writings on programs to recover women abducted in the Punjab violence have shown how the two states "fixed" nationality onto religious community with the Indian state attempting to recover and rehabilitate Hindu and Sikh women and the Pakistani state attempting to recover and rehabilitate Muslim women. These writings show how women themselves resisted this national inscription, and many wanted to remain a part of their abductors' families.[27] *But the Punjab was an exception with far-reaching effects.* In the case of Punjab, both the Indian and Pakistani states agreed to a complete "transfer of populations" on the basis of religious community, but there was no such agreement on the rest of the Indian subcontinent. This resulted in the Pakistani state's vehement opposition to the Muslim exodus from Delhi, even as it was unable to deter it, for it argued that Delhi's Muslim refugees were Indians and should be rehabilitated by the Indian state.

In parallel fashion, in Karachi, Hindu houses became a similar source of contention as the Pakistani state tried to house its government there and manage the rehabilitation of Muslim refugees pouring in from Delhi and other parts of north India. Here, despite attempts by M. A. Jinnah, a Karachiite by birth, and Sindhi Muslim politicians to retain this important religious community, the Sind Congress strenuously tried to persuade the Indian state to include Sind's Hindus in its planned evacuation and rehabilitation schemes originally designed for the Punjab. With riots in the city in January 1948, the Indian state eventually formally agreed to include "our people," Sind's Hindu refugees, in its planning for rehabilitation. In turn, the Pakistani state not only was ambiguous about Muslim refugees arriving from outside Punjab, but also formulated "muhajirs" as a governmental category to classify Muslim refugees such that it left open an imagined *muhajir* return to India.

This fact that, in the Indian subcontinent, the figure of the refugee was marked by religious community, and that these people were considered as forming two distinct and opposed sets of refugees, had enormous implications for the entire rubric of refugee rehabilitation and its relationship to the making of the Indo-Pak divide. On the one hand, there were "Muslim refugees" and "Hindu and Sikh refugees," who were also referred to as "non-Muslim refugees."* This differentiation is also evident in Urdu newspapers where the word *panaghirs* or *muhajirs* was used for Muslim refugees, and *sharanatis* for Hindu and Sikh refugees.

On the other hand, both postcolonial states conceived refugee rehabilitation not as a religious duty, but rather as a universal and rational program for the development of the nation as a whole.[28] Bhaskar Rao's *The Story of Rehabilitation* (1967) is a testimony of the new Indian state's epic efforts to rehabilitate refugees as part of a larger vision of national development. In an Indian Constituent Assembly debate on rehabilitation efforts of the government on November 29, 1947, for instance, the need for "planning" and a "scientific" approach to rehabilitation found wide

* Throughout this book "Muslim refugees" and "Hindu and Sikh refugees" or "non-Muslim refugees" should be read in quotation marks as constructed categories that shaped and were shaped by this history.

consensus.[29] Nehru argued before the Assembly that "the refugees . . . have to be looked after and they must be made proper citizens of India." A parallel paradigm for rehabilitation is evident in the *West Pakistan Gazetteer* of 1959, which announced that "the Government of Pakistan from the very outset realized the importance of development . . . The schemes for the rehabilitation of refugees are difficult to separate from the general development plan for Pakistan."[30] In keeping with this view, refugee rehabilitation figured prominently in the first Five-Year Plans of both states.[31] This universal framing of refugee rehabilitation projected a universal figure of the refugee as its central subject, who, through the discursive and institutional regimes of rehabilitation, was to be made into a citizen of the nation.

How was the marked refugee on the ground reconciled with the universal refugee of planning? In the initial conditions of emergency and relief work, the differentiated categories of "Muslim refugees" and "non-Muslim refugees" is evident. However, as institutions of rehabilitation became established on firmer footing in government, these categories of the marked refugee were self-consciously replaced in the universal language of legislations and policy as "displaced persons" and "evacuees." While the shift in categories was by no means consistent, in all Indian refugee rehabilitation programs and legislations the "displaced person" included specifically those displaced from their homes in Pakistan[32] and therefore encompassed only "non-Muslim refugees." In turn, the term "evacuees" in Indian legislation referred to those displaced from their homes in India and therefore differentially encompassed "Muslim refugees." The exact reverse was true of the Pakistani definitions of those categories. Thus when the universal figure of the refugee was invoked as "our people," it only referred to those encompassed in policy and legislation as "displaced persons."

The category of "evacuees" was particularly important because it suggested that this was a group that was departing, or had departed, and their homes, lands, and businesses came to be classified as "evacuee property" which was to be used to rehabilitate "displaced persons." In this economic equation, it became important that those considered "evacuees" did indeed leave, although the term "migration" used to describe their contingent departure was laden with ambiguities. In important respects the classification of evacuee included much more than refugees, for a certain amount of uncertainty accompanied who was leaving their homes and why. Indeed, in some economic calculations, all religious minorities were assumed to be "evacuees," and with the creation of the supplementary classification of "intending evacuee" in evacuee property legislations on both sides, the wide-ranging effects of these legislations could include entire religious communities. The institution of the Custodian of Evacuee Property can be squarely placed in a comparative history of the mid-twentieth century, particularly given its chilling parallels with the Israeli equivalent, which makes evident its silenced effects in "emptying" the land and creating significant internal dispossession.

The logic and rationale of planned refugee rehabilitation as critical to economic development provided both states with almost complete political justification for treating these two sets of refugees, initially within their own territories, differentially. Economic rationalization provided the logic for the agreed "transfer of populations" in the Punjab and became central to the notion that Muslim refugees from elsewhere in India could not be accommodated, that they were an economic liability, for both the Pakistani and the Indian states.

Economic and scientific rationality of planning for the nation not only provided the bureaucratic, legal, and technological functions of the state with legitimacy, but also, as Partha Chatterjee has argued, "provided the political process a rhetoric for conducting its political debates."[33] Thus, while the Indian National Congress claimed a secular platform to represent an all-inclusive "Indian nation," and a significant number of Muslims were part of the Congress, the postcolonial Indian state was able to push out and dispossess Muslims with substantial political legitimacy as it bounded a new nation for the well-being of "our people." In the case of Pakistan, which was claimed ideologically to "safeguard" the interests of all Muslims of the Indian subcontinent, including those who would remain outside its territory, excluding Muslim refugees from India was also a significant ideological compromise of its very premise. Although the Pakistani state classified Muslim refugees as *muhajirs* to invoke the Prophet Muhammad's historic flight from Mecca to Medina, refugee rehabilitation was not undertaken as a religious duty. Despite ideological differences with the Indian state, the Pakistani state shared with it the paradigm and logic of the developmental state. As a result of this logic, from its inception the Pakistani state argued that it could simply not accommodate all the Muslim refugees that might want to come to Pakistan from India, and economic rationalization provided it with a legitimate need to draft limits to its nation. The technologies of permits and passports were therefore not mere documents that led to Ghulam Ali's arrests and incarcerations by both states, but were ostensibly neutral and bureaucratic modes for producing limits to the ideological nation.

Histories of technologies to control the movement of people in Europe and North America have shown how they were fundamentally tied to the making of citizenship through the marking of "insiders" and "outsiders."[34] However, these technologies to regulate movement emerged in divided South Asia to control ongoing displacements of a long Partition, and to fundamentally resolve disputes over where Muslim refugees belonged. Thus drafting limits to new nations was not as simple as fixing citizenship onto religious difference, since not all Muslims could become Pakistanis, and some Muslims wanted to remain in or return to their homes in India. Thus marking "insiders" and "outsiders," always an ambiguous process, became nearly impossible without any representable limit with which to construct this national difference. Thus one could argue that the highly surveillanced and particularly unique forms that the Indo-Pak border took were an outcome of its function as both an international border and an "internal border,"[35] marking citizens from aliens but also producing questions of loyalty and legitimacy as it marked suspect/disloyal citizens from putatively natural ones.

In an essay evocatively titled "Can a Muslim Be an Indian?" Gyanendra Pandey recovered the angry debates that emerged in India in the aftermath of 1947 on Muslim loyalty and belonging. This book historically situates these debates on loyalty and citizenship through not just the discursive, but also their institutional sites on two sides of the emerging border, to make visible the power of modern states to limit and produce bounded nations and the margins within them.[36]

The first part of this book, chapters 1 and 2, unfolds histories of violence and displacements in Delhi and Karachi around 1947, recovering the conditions of contingency in which people left their homes, and the role of the two states in the making of the dual figure of the refugee. The second part, chapters 3 and 4, examines the emergence of permit regulations in 1948 and transformations in evacuee property legislations respectively, as they shaped displacements both across and within new borders. The permit system was instituted by the Indian government to stem the return of Muslim refugees back to their homes, and led to the formulation of citizenship provisions centered on a definition of "migration," while evacuee property legislations on both sides changed the definition of the "evacuee" to create massive displacements and internal dispossession. Both institutions and their effects are part of the region's histories, histories which have been silenced into margins by being deemed insignificant and through conscious erasures. These chapters thus unfold the emerging shapes of two nation-states from these very margins.

The third part of the book, chapters 5 and 6, examines the shift from permits to passports in 1952, a technology to mark distinct national identities and give closure to Partition's ongoing displacements. The shift to passports was introduced by the Pakistani government to stem the continued "illegal" flow of Muslim refugees into Pakistan and thus produced considerable debate on the legitimacy of making Muslims in India into "foreigners" in Pakistan. On the other hand, the contingencies in which the passport emerged meant that classifications of nationhood produced numerous "undefined" and stateless people such as Ghulam Ali who became caught in the limin of new national borders. I trek through an array of political debates, bureaucratic paper trails, and court cases on permits, evacuee property, and passports that went on through the 1950s, some into the 1960s (while some national identity and evacuee property cases continue to this day), to account for this long Partition.

In "India" and "Pakistan" we live in the shadows of this long Partition, and it is by placing its history alongside other histories of a twentieth century, marked by all the violence of making modern, "ethnically cleansed" national identities, that we can interrogate the postcolonial world that we are forced to inhabit, and from which meanings of culture and identity continue to be contested.

WRITING ON THE BORDER

Many histories of the making of national borders have been centered on geographic borderlands, tracking the ways in which a mesh of relationships and ethnic diversity came to be displaced and disciplined by institutions of the state.[37] This history is not about a geographic borderland, and a considerable distance separates the cities of Delhi and Karachi. Instead the border it traces is one which cut through ordinary middle-class households like Mirza Salim's, captured in an exceptional 1973 film,

Garam Hawa. This process of border-making—the hot wind or *garam hawa* of a long Partition—swept through the inner world of familial ties, transforming both those who left and those who remained in their ancestral homes, and displacing old ways of belonging for everyone.

Narrated from the perspective of Mirza Salim in a joint family household in Agra, the film rests upon Salim's ultimate refusal to leave for Pakistan, even as the departure of his loved ones wrecks devastation on the emotional ties within the family, and results in the loss of his familial home and shoe-making business. It is the story of a divided family in the making, and records, in the undertow of its narration, the emergence of permit restrictions, so that when the fiancé of Salim's daughter returns from Pakistan to marry his beloved cousin, he is arrested and deported. The evacuee property laws result in dispossession without their ever leaving home, and the film shows the emergence of the "Muslim" as a figure of suspicion in independent India. Even though *Garam Hawa* tells us only a partial story of the Indian Muslim experience of Partition and almost nothing about the Pakistani experience of Salim's brothers and sisters, it comes as close as is possible within a national frame to represent the Muslim predicament, and the emotional, material, and political dispossession of Muslims who remained in India in the 1950s—a dispossession that I contend was produced by both the Indian and the Pakistani states.

In an interview, the director, M. S. Sathyu, said the aim of the film was to expose "the games these politicians play" and the "suffering it had caused."[38] But while the film does show the unraveling world of a Muslim household, and their suffering is eloquently portrayed, it does not really help us understand the political "games" that shaped this long Partition. How did politicians, many with high ideals and vision, who had fought for freedom and nation, make decisions that caused such dispossession and suffering? Was it inevitable in the logic of Partition itself? Or does history bear the task of putting the very process of making modern nation-states to trial and scrutiny?

Between 1998 and 2000 I traveled back and forth between Delhi and Karachi to do "historical fieldwork"[39] in familial households like Mirza Salim's. Since I belong to a divided family, I grew up with Partition in ways that have unavoidably shaped this historical fieldwork; it shaped my entry into the worlds of other divided families, and placed me in an emotional and political landscape which may have constrained me to "listen" to and struggle with that "drone of silence" that kept surfacing in my interviews.

My tape recorder often brought together family members, as an elder would align stories, many heard before, into an affectionate, sometimes proud, history of the family itself. But, as Dipesh Chakrabarty has pointed out, "memory is a complex phenomenon that reaches out far beyond what normally constitutes an historian's archive."[40] The first narrations, tracking genealogies, childhoods, and other lost worlds were usually enormously powerful in drawing together kin networks, friendships, and a sense of embedded place, so that by the time we got to Partition and the falling apart of remembered worlds, there was always unbearable grief, exhaustion, and speechlessness. Yet these first narrations were also less consciously framed, as memories poured forth with many surprises to form a telling of family histories without the ordering of nation.

However, when I returned months later, with stories from the other side, to ask specific questions to understand unsettled fragments of their earlier narrations, the answers usually became more self-conscious and cautious, shaped not so much by the telling of the past as by the exigencies of the present. This present continues to be shadowed by Indo-Pak hostilities as well as internal margins where Indian Muslims on one side, and *muhajirs* (particularly since the rise of the Muhajir Qaumi Movement) on the other side, have been subjected to violence and suspicion for their cross-border ties.[41] Thus any public narration that conceded relations on the other side, let alone deeply felt affections for them, has been seen as a compromise of loyalty to the nation. The cumulative sense of danger associated with posting letters, making phone calls, and traveling to visit family on the other side, including police reporting and border-crossing harassment, meant that of the numerous members of divided families whom I met, most refused formal interviews, and those who did agree requested that their identities be protected.[42]

These silences have been etched by loss and nation in ways that are not simple to undo. With the two states having been to war, and to the brink of war, more times than I can account for here, historians like Mushirul Hasan have turned to literature (and here one can include *Garam Hawa*, based on the writer Ismet Chugtai's short story with the script written by the poet and writer Kaifi Azmi), to provide alternative narratives of Partition to "defeat the urge to lay blame which keeps animosity alive."[43]

This is partly why historians have eschewed the traditional historian's archive for examining what happened at Partition. Although the reflexive turn in history and postcolonial theory have made silences a productive analytical site for investigations against the grain of nation, my investigations required me to look for the very record that I had to read against. What were the "institutional inscriptions"[44] of government, law, and leaders that had shaped these silences?

This necessarily involved looking for records on both sides of the Indo-Pak divide, for no matter how differently Partition may be invoked on the two sides, it is a shared history of the region for which one simply cannot understand "the whole range of significance of the occurrences to which [sources] testify" on one side alone.[45] Making two nations out of a landscape meant the reordering of people and places on a catastrophic scale, and required the play of both states. The extraordinary parallel of state institutions, carved out of a shared colonial legacy, in and of itself called for a converging of histories.

However, the difficulty of a transnational study extended beyond simply that of crossing tense political boundaries. The very differences in the location of history within the two nation-states made looking for records on both sides an uneven process. The writing of history has been an important critical activity to the making of nation in modern India, in striking contrast to Pakistan. On the one hand, Delhi has maintained a continuity of status as it shifted from being the capital of colonial to independent India, and its institutions of archives are well-maintained and vibrant centers for historical research. I read Delhi's Urdu newspaper, *Al-Jamiat*, published by the pro-Congress Jamiat-e-Ulema-e-Hind, in a national library, and declassified central and local government records in established national archives. Although photocopying documents in Urdu, a marginalized language in contemporary India, posed problems with staff unable to read page numbers and dates in Urdu, and fragments and erasures of documents left uncertain traces, institutional structures of historical production conditioned those margins.

On the other hand, Karachi's status kept shifting, from periphery to capital, to periphery again, with Islamabad becoming the new capital of Pakistan in the early 1960s. Some records kept moving with each change of status, so that parallel institutions like the National Archives and the Sind Archives are relatively new institutions and ambiguous and largely uncatalogued repositories of records. I read the *Jang* newspaper in the newspaper offices itself, for although the daily moved from Delhi to Karachi in 1947 and began largely as a *muhajir* newspaper, it has become, with Urdu as the declared national language of the state, the largest press conglomerate. On the other hand, other newspapers like *Anjam*, which also made this journey from Delhi to Karachi but is no longer extant, were practically impossible to recover. The official records that I did read were mostly from the small rooms of a documentation center inside a high-security government building in Islamabad where the brigadier giving security clearances considered history of little consequence.

In Karachi, looking for a record of the city's past was a scavenger hunt of sorts through a myriad of local government institutions, the absences as telling as the wholesale replacement of curriculum history with compulsory, geopolitical Pakistan Studies. Even in Karachi University's library, as the Freedom Archives were being recast into Pakistan Studies, a librarian suggested that going to India was my best chance of reading any records of Karachi's past! Thus improvisation substantially conditions and in some sense marginalizes all history writing in Pakistan.[46]

And yet it was through crossing the national boundaries of archives that the nation's categorical order in a patchwork of bureaucratic files became denaturalized. If Partition marked being "Muslim," or "Hindu" and "Sikh," in particular and violent ways, then moving between memory and record on both sides of the Indo-Pak divide required a repeated interrogation of how these markings were transformed and folded into this national order. This history then is self-consciously marked by a sense of discovery and surprise, for it brings to analysis that "underside" of nationalized memories that eschews and glosses over the remarkable contestations of ordinary people who moved against the flow of Partition's narrated migrations and maintained ties against the boundaries of hostile nation-states. Before the political trajectory of Partition settles into a common sense about the region's landscape, and maps our memories entirely into nation-states, let us recover the margins that have shaped them and the roads that were not taken.

The Making of Refugees, 1947

1. *Muslim Exodus from Delhi*

Survivors carry history on themselves . . .[1]

Some of the most indelible images of Partition are those of the historic train and foot convoys, the old and the young huddled together, carrying few if any belongings, hoping to reach their destinations in safety. But this sheer fact of terror and mass displacement alone did not create the figure of the refugee. When people left their homes, when their "familiar *way-of-being* in the world"[2] was disrupted by violence, fear, or uncertainty, it was not necessarily with the prospect of permanent displacement. The making of refugees was not "a onetime set of events bounded in time and space,"[3] but was instead profoundly shaped over time by the two postcolonial states as they struggled to classify, enumerate, and manage these displacements.

I want to open up the contingent conditions in which people left their homes as old social geographies unraveled, the uncertainty in which they were displaced, for it was in the hubbub of on-the-ground realities that the bureaucratic record began to give shape to the notion that there were two distinct sets of refugees, Hindu and Sikh refugees on the one hand and Muslim refugees on the other, and that the rehabilitation of one required the exodus of the other. In both Delhi and Karachi, at the center of this official record was a concern with houses and the housing of refugees. This official concern and its effects shaped the first flights for safety and contested urban geographies.

Delhi's transition from capital of British India to the capital of independent India at midnight of August 14–15, 1947, is well remembered from the ramparts of Shah Jehan's Red Fort, where Jawaharlal Nehru famously inaugurated "the old to the new," the achievement of statehood as the expression of "the soul of the nation."[4] Rafi bhai remembered going with his grandfather, a "freedom fighter" in the Indian National Congress, to the inaugural celebrations, and his narration captures another transformation of the city:

RAFI BHAI: *Aur jab Hindustan azad hua to un ko invitation bhi āya ke Lal Qille par Hindustan ka jo jhunḍa lehraya jaye ga Pandit Nehru ke hathon, to us ko witness karne ke liye āp bhi āye. Ye mujhe yād hai ke main aur mere baṛe bhai ko le kar meṛe dada jo the. . . . Lal Qille hum log pohnche. . . . Wahan to ādmion ka samandar tha. Us men hum dada se alag ho gaye. To unhon ne mehsoos kiya ke hum log reh gaye hai. To mujhe zabardastī ghaseeṭa gaya sau logon ke upar se, aur us ke ba'd hum ne socha ke ye program hum nahin attend kar sakenge. Aur darwaza bhi band ho gaya tha Lal Qilae ka. To nīche se hum ne us ko witness kiya.*

AUTHOR: *Kiya ye āp ke bachpan ka baṛa wāqe'a tha?*

RAFI BHAI: *Hanh. Samjhe, 1947 mein . . . ujaṛ gaya . . . sāre chale gaye.*

RAFI BHAI: And when Hindustan became free, then he too got an invitation to the Red Fort where the flag of Hindustan was going to be flown at the hands of Pandit Nehru; to witness this you please come too. I remember that my grandfather took me and my older brother with him to the Red Fort. . . . There was an ocean of people. In this we became separated from my grandfather. He realized that we had gotten left behind. And then I was forcefully dragged over a hundred people, and after this we thought that we would not be able to attend this program. And the doors too of the Red Fort had closed. So then we witnessed it from below.

AUTHOR: Was this a big occasion for your childhood?
RAFI BHAI: Yes. Understand, in 1947 [this place] became desolate . . . everyone left.

When I asked Rafi bhai if this was an important event in his childhood, I had meant the independence celebrations, but the midnight of freedom, witnessed from below, was entirely eclipsed in his memory by the departure of his loved ones, the desolation of mass exodus, as more than 3.3 lakh Muslims, more than a quarter of the city's population, left the city in the ensuing months.

On the heels of independence, by early September 1947 Delhi experienced the kind of horrific violence that had already engulfed large parts of Punjab. It was believed that Hindu and Sikh refugees pouring in from West Punjab were responsible for the violence in the city in which Muslims became the primary target. Some 20,000 Muslims were killed, and one observer noted that "the dead lay rotting in the streets, because there was no one to collect and bury them. The hospitals are choked with dying and wounded, and in imminent danger of attack because of the presence of Moslem staff and Moslem patients."[5] The "new" Indian state responded to this strife in the heart of the nation by setting up, on September 6, an Emergency Committee of the Cabinet along the lines of a war council, and a Ministry of Relief and Rehabilitation for the care of refugees.[6] What role did these institutions play in the shaping of the Muslim exodus? Why did Muslim refugees of Delhi leave for Pakistan despite Gandhi's pleas that these too were "our people," despite the religious neutrality of the new Indian state?

REMEMBERED TERROR

The difficulty of representing violence in academic writing has received a great deal of attention in recent years, from anthropologists in particular but also from those grappling with the events that took place at Partition.[7] One of the difficulties has involved the ways in which certain kinds of violence enter the official record and thus inform history, making invisible the role of the state as well as the use of violence by the state. This is particularly true of what has come to be called "Partition violence," or the "communal violence at Partition," where the focus has largely been on the violence between Hindus and Sikhs versus the Muslims. Although it has been remarked that individuals working for the state (such as the police or government servants) became "communal" in the violence, the modern state as a totality has appeared "transcendental"[8] and therefore a rational arbitrator in the irrational and disruptive violence of the "communalized" body politic.[9]

For instance, in his fortnightly report to the Home Ministry, the chief commissioner of Delhi, Sahibzada Khurshid, described "the communal upheaval" in the city as "an orgy of murder, loot, and arson," and held Hindu and Sikh refugees who had been streaming in since the end of August as responsible for it. "The main cause of the riots," he noted, "was the influx of 1.5 lakhs of refugees from West Punjab who brought harrowing tales of loot, rape, and arson." He argued that "[t]hey naturally gained the sympathy of their co-religionists in Delhi," and that this ignited retaliatory violence against the Muslims of the city.[10] This analysis of the violence in September 1947 in Delhi can be found in the minutes of the Emergency Committee of the Cabinet. Maulana Abul Kalam Azad, who was a member of the Emergency Committee, noted in his autobiography that the "murderous upheaval" in Delhi began with "news of murders in the Punjab . . . followed by the trickle of refugees," and was a "gruesome application" of the hostage theory, whereby Muslims of Delhi were murdered in retaliation for the violence in the Punjab.[11] Furthermore, this kind of account of Delhi's Partition violence can also be read in as general a text as Percival Spear's *A History of India,* where Spear noted that the "tide of refugees [from the Punjab] caused an explosion of communal strife in Delhi in early September."[12]

This narrative of horrific violence—recorded in reports while officials were still "busy dealing with the communal upheaval" (therefore of substantive impact in policy-making), and then sedimented into history writing (and therefore of significance in the making of public memory)—provides a causal explanation for the departure of Delhi's Muslims which, by laying the blame on Hindu and Sikh refugees from the Punjab, makes the violence comprehensible, if not in some sense legitimate. So, for instance, V. N. Datta, in his study of Punjabi refugees' contribution to the growth of Delhi, could go on to explain it as the "blind rage" of the "dispossessed."[13]

Instead I would like to take two excerpts from my interviews with Muslim survivors of this violence in Delhi and interrogate the context of the Muslim exodus, and in particular the role of both states in it. The first is from an interview with Aziz saheb, who continues to live in a *mohalla* in the walled city:

AZIZ SAHEB: *Taqseem ke to bahut baṛe jhagaṛe the. Isne to musalmanon ko nonasi kar diyā. Karol Bagh sārā tabah kar diyā. Paharganj sārā tabah kar diyā. Main special police officer tha. Sabzi Mandi sārā bairā gaṛap kar diyā.*

AUTHOR: *Āp duty par the is waqt?*

AZIZ SAHEB: *Hanh. Sāra Dilli dekha. Chhoṛde, main is ka zikr nahin karnā chāhta. Main apna dimāg kharab nahin karnā chāhtā.*

DAUGHTER-IN-LAW: *Log yād nahin karna chāhte. Itne taklīf-deh hālāt the. Zehn men bhī nahin lānā chāhte.*

AZIZ SAHEB: *Main ne itna muqabala kiyā hai, kuch puchhe nahin . . .*

[Silence.]

AZIZ SAHEB: 47 *men to ādmi ā'e. Woh to qabza kar rahe the. Musalmanon ko nikal rahe the na. Makānon par qabza kar rahe the na.*

AUTHOR: *Kon ādmi?*

AZIZ SAHEB: *Jo Hindu migrated the. Ise ā-ke jagah chahiye thī. Un ki wajah se to jhagra hua hai. Bhai! Woh wahan se apna makān chhoṛ kar ā'e the! Musalman ne Pakistan ke nām par alag hukumat le li thi! To un ko yahan rehne ka koi haq nahin! To un ke hisāb se jab un ko nikāl diyā'e ga'e, un ke ghar se . . .*

[Turns away towards the wall.]

Hamare dukān ke andar chāndnī thī. De diyā tamam logon ko sārā sāmān. ek bhi cheez nahin rahi. Koi cheez bhi. Bahut baṛī dukān thī hamari jis ki chāndnī, sab kuchh. . . . bahut . . . chhoṛ dej'e!. . . . Mere samne, chaṛ baṛas ka aur chaṛ ṭukṛe. Yād āti hai. Nafrat hai mujhe in choron se . . .

AZIZ SAHEB: At the time of Partition there was big fighting. They destroyed the Muslims—Karol Bagh was completely destroyed. Paharganj was completely destroyed. I was a special police officer. Sabzi Mandi was completely destroyed.

AUTHOR: Were you on duty at this time?

AZIZ SAHEB: Yes. I saw all of Delhi. Just leave it! I don't want to talk about it. I don't want to disturb my mind.

DAUGHTER-IN-LAW: People don't want to remember. Those times were so painful. They don't even want to bring it to the mind.

AZIZ SAHEB: I had to face so many confrontations, don't ask!

[Silence.]

AZIZ SAHEB: In '47 people came. They were seizing [houses], pushing out the Muslims from their houses. They were then occupying.

AUTHOR: What people?

AZIZ SAHEB: The Hindus who had migrated. They came and wanted places. Because of them there was the fighting. Bhai! They had left their houses there and had come! Muslims had taken over a separate state there in the name of Pakistan! So they had no right to live here. So according to them since they had been pushed out of their homes . . .

[Turns away towards the wall.]

Our shop had silver. We gave it away to all the people, all the goods. Not one thing remained. It was a big silver shop, ours . . . everything . . . just leave it! . . . . In front of me, a four-year-old cut into four pieces. I remember! I hate those thieves!

The second excerpt is from my interview with Salim saheb, also a resident of old Delhi. He recalled the September violence as follows:

SALIM SAHEB: *Dilli men bhī bahut khun kharaba huā. Ye to 'alāqa mehfuz reh gaya. Lekin Paharganj, Karolbagh, New Delhi, Lodhi Gardens, ye tamām . . . bahut se musalman the. Woh hum ne ānkh se dekha hai. Sabzi Mandi ke, Paharganj ke, Jama Masjid men ākar ṭhere the. Jama Masjid se phir Purana Qille gaye. Be-sar-o-sāmān! Aur chhe chhe bachchain! Sab ne panah lī thī. Bahut buṛa waqt tha. Bahut hi buṛa waqt tha. Hum chhoṭe the. Hamari umar taqseem ke waqt bāra sāl ki thī. Hum apne walid ke sath, baṛon ke sath, Jama Masjid khana taqseem karne jaya karte the. Ab khandani aurtain, khandani laṛkiyan, bahut achhī achhī . . . hath milā kar khati thī.*

ATTIA: *Ye bāt to mere dada bhī batate hai.*

SALIM SAHEB: *Purane Qille men bhī esa hua. Purane Qille men dal diyā. August barish ka mahina tha. Barishain ho rahi thi. Ganddgī thī. Wahan se train ban kar jaya karti thī . . . Pakistan chale gaye.*

SALIM SAHEB: In Delhi also there was a lot of bloodshed. This area was safe [Pahari Imli] but Pahar Ganj, Karol Bagh, New Delhi, Lodhi Gardens, all this . . . there were many Muslims. I have seen it with my own eyes. Those from Sabzi Mandi and Pahar Ganj came and stayed at Jama Masjid. Then from Jama Masjid they went to Purana Qila. Without any belongings whatsoever! And six six [i.e., many] children! All took refuge. They were bad times. They were really bad times. I was small. At the time of Partition my age was twelve years old. I used to go with my father, with the elders, to distribute food at the Jama Masjid. Now women from respected families, girls from respected families, very good [families], used to join their hands together and eat from it.

ATTIA: Yes, my grandfather also used to tell us this.

SALIM SAHEB: In Purana Qila also it was the same. They dumped them in Purana Qila. August was the month of rains. It was raining. It was filthy. From there trains would form and go . . . they left for Pakistan.

Aziz saheb was one of approximately 2,000 civilians who were appointed special police officers on a temporary basis by the Delhi administration, and along with the Madras troops were responsible for bringing the violence "under control." This was because the police force became partisan in the violence, and over 75 percent of the Muslims in the police force, roughly 1,600 men, deserted and took refuge in Purana Qila along with other Muslims of the city.[14] In Salim saheb's case, his father was a well-known "freedom fighter" of old Delhi who helped organize care for the refugees who had collected at Jama Masjid, and it was alongside him, as the son of a respected elder, that he experienced the events that followed Partition.

Both men remembered the terrible violence as witnesses (I saw all of Delhi / I have seen it with my own eyes), but in some respects they witnessed different aspects of the violence. Aziz saheb was an adult at the time, and as a special police officer participated in the actual fighting (he had to face many confrontations). This was a past that still disturbed his mind, and he could barely talk about it. The only way he could express the total moral collapse of his familiar world was through the image of a four-year-old cut into four pieces, violence in excess of murder on a body beyond culpability. In interviews with other survivors of the Delhi violence, this sense of unspeakable violence was repeated through the sign of the child. Anis apa, for example, told me of a boy who had been brought to them at Jamia who would not speak since he had seen the murder of his family, including that of an unweaned baby: " . . . *ek bachcha laya gaya tha. Woh bolta nahin tha . . . kaise ek ek ādmi ko khatam kiyā gayā. Yahan tak ke sheerkhwan bachche ko bhi neze par liyā gayā . . . bachcha itna khofzada ho gaya tha ke woh bolta nahin tha* [a child was brought, who wouldn't speak . . . how each person was finished off, that even an unweaned baby was knifed . . . the child was so terrorized that he wouldn't speak]."

In subsequent interviews, when I tried to ask Aziz saheb more about his role as a special police officer, he told me point-blank to talk to him about other things. Some memories could not be brought to speech for such was the terror of those times, the unspeakable nature of this violence.[15] In Aziz saheb's account, the terror produced by this unspeakable violence was complicit with Muslims of Delhi being pushed out of their homes by "the people who came." *Makān*, houses were at the center of this violence, and here I will examine how the Indian state responded to this aspect of the violence, the occupation of houses in a cycle of forced dispossession.

Salim saheb was still a young boy at this time, and mostly saw Muslim families after they had fled their homes and taken refuge, after they had been dispossessed and were reduced to eating out of their bare hands. It was then from the Muslim camps, and Purana Qila in particular, he recalled, that Muslims left on the trains to Pakistan. The camps were an important intermediary site, under the purview of the state, from where most of the displaced left for Pakistan, and I interrogate this site to understand the decision of thousands to leave after the initial loss of their homes.

The role of the Pakistani state is equally important to understanding the contingent nature of this exodus. As Aziz saheb pointed out, Muslim dispossession was constituted in part by the feeling that because of Pakistan, they, the Muslims, had lost their right to live "here." The agreements between the Indian and Pakistani states on the Punjab displacements threw into sharp relief the disagreements over the Delhi exodus. In a sense, it is here in the debates on the "transfer of populations" that the long Partition begins to unfold.

OCCUPATION OF HOUSES

According to Aziz saheb, the forcible occupation of Muslim homes was a significant part of the violence Delhi experienced in September 1947. Sahibzada Khurshid, the chief commissioner of Delhi, noted that "[a]rson was carried out on a fairly big scale for the first two or three days and only came to a stop when Muslim houses were occupied by Hindus."[16] The Emergency Committee also noted that occupations of Muslim homes were taking place on a large scale.[17] Tai Yong Tan and Gyanesh Kudaisya quote a contemporary observer who estimated that almost 44,000 Muslim houses were occupied in old Delhi alone.[18]

These occupations created a predicament for the new Indian state that would have lasting significance. It was imperative for the Emergency Committee to act "effectively" in this "state of emergency" in the heart of the capital, for it was central to establishing the legitimacy of the new national government that it appear to stand outside the fractures within the body of the putative nation. Thus, the violence, as perceived to be caused by the displaced from the Punjab, had to be brought under control, since this violence, including occupations, was creating another set of displaced people. In the case of areas that were directly affected by "murder and arson," such as Karol Bagh, Paharganj, and Sabzi Mandi, survivors had already fled from their homes to emerging "Muslim camps." However, people from areas not directly affected by violence were also moving to the camps.

Although it was suggested in the Emergency Committee that many of those moving were Muslim Leaguers, or were incited to move by Muslim League propaganda, this did not account for the entire and ongoing exodus to the camps. Zakir Husain, the vice-chancellor of the pro-Congress Jamia Millia Islamia, reported with some distress to the Emergency Committee that he "couldn't understand why these people should have moved, when there had been no incidents in some of the predominantly Muslim areas of Delhi city to impel their movement." It was his feeling that government officials were advising Muslims to move to the camps for their own safety. Safety was of central concern in those terrifying times and people looked to the state to provide it. In addition, groups of Muslims were making direct appeals to members of the Emergency Committee for police protection and guarantees of safety, so that they could stay on in their homes.[19] As a result the Emergency Committee was confronted with difficult questions. What measures should be taken to stop Muslims from leaving their homes, or should "mass evacuation" be carried out? Could the government take responsibility for telling people to stay in their homes and guarantee protection if they did?[20]

Although attempts were made to divert trains from Punjab away from Delhi in order to reduce the number of refugees coming to Delhi,[21] still, according to the 1951 Census of India, 323,320 "non-Muslim refugees" arrived in just the months between August and October 1947.[22] Thus taking care of these displaced people was also important to establishing the legitimacy of the state. It is no coincidence that the Ministry of Relief and Rehabilitation was set up at the same time as the Emergency Committee, with K.C. Neogy as its first minister. The Emergency Committee was already under pressure from refugees from the Punjab to officially give them "evacuated" Muslim houses for purposes of rehabilitation.[23] This made the question of how to respond to these massive occupations all the more difficult. Should the state attempt to enforce the rule of law and attempt to reverse these occupations? How should the state provide shelter for the refugees from the Punjab? What should be done with the city's Muslims who had taken refuge in the burgeoning camps?

The Indian state intervened with two measures in response to the occupation of Muslim houses. First, the evacuee property legislation, which had been formulated for East and West Punjab with Indo-Pak agreement, was extended to Delhi, and accordingly a custodian was appointed for the city to look after "abandoned" properties in trust, until such time that the displaced could return to them. I discuss at length the changing role of the Custodian of Evacuee Property later in the book. However, in its initial phase, the evacuee property legislation protected the rights of the "evacuee" and declared occupations as "illegal." In principle it was meant to enable the return of the displaced, in this case "Muslim refugees," to their homes.

However, at the same time the custodian was permitted to temporarily allocate, or "allot," the "abandoned" Muslim houses it took into its custody to Hindu and Sikh refugees from the Punjab, as a way of providing immediate housing for this first set of displaced people. Given that forcible occupations had already taken place, of the 10,200 Muslim houses taken into this official custody almost all were already occupied, making official allotments redundant. In addition, such occupations had taken place on both sides of the divided Punjab and a large number of angry and destitute Hindu and Sikh refugees were still without shelter. Thus the Indian government adopted the policy that no (non-Muslim) refugee would be evicted for illegal occupation without being provided with alternative accommodation.[24] In effect, Muslims who had taken shelter in camps could not return to their homes if they had been occupied, even after the riots and murders had stopped.

The second intervention remapped the city for Muslims into "mixed areas" and "Muslim areas." Since it was felt that "Muslims no longer feel safe in mixed localities," it was decided that "they should be rehabilitated in predominantly Muslim areas."[25] This led to the creation of what came to be called "Muslim zones." Certain largely Muslim *mohallas* (such as Pahari Imli, Pul Bangash, Phatak Habash Khan, and Sadar Bazar) were cordoned off, and "abandoned" houses there were to be kept empty by police intervention, so that either Muslims could return to them or other Muslims could be moved there and provided safety.[26]

Thus Muslims from "mixed areas" were offered safety by the state if they moved to these "Muslim zones," which were meant to be "safe areas." Sardar Diwan Singh, the editor of *Risalat,* wrote in his account of those days in Delhi about the move to Muslim zones:

> Muslims from mixed areas were asked to move to the Muslim zones. The constable stood at the street corner and they had five minutes to gather their belongings and go. Many thought this was only a matter of a few days and that they would return when the public had calmed down. . . . [Th]e owner of the *Risalat*'s building, Anwar saheb, left his house in [my] care and he did not even put a lock on any of the doors. Next to him his *khala* with her daughter and son-in-law lived and they too left their keys with me. And next to them was an old Muslim man. He said to me, "Sardar saheb, I am a poor man, please look after my house too, so no one loots it." So in this street I was the caretaker of these three houses.[27]

The editor went on to recount how those houses in his care were broken into and occupied by refugees, and how his former neighbors did not or were unable to return. However, the account suggests how the move to

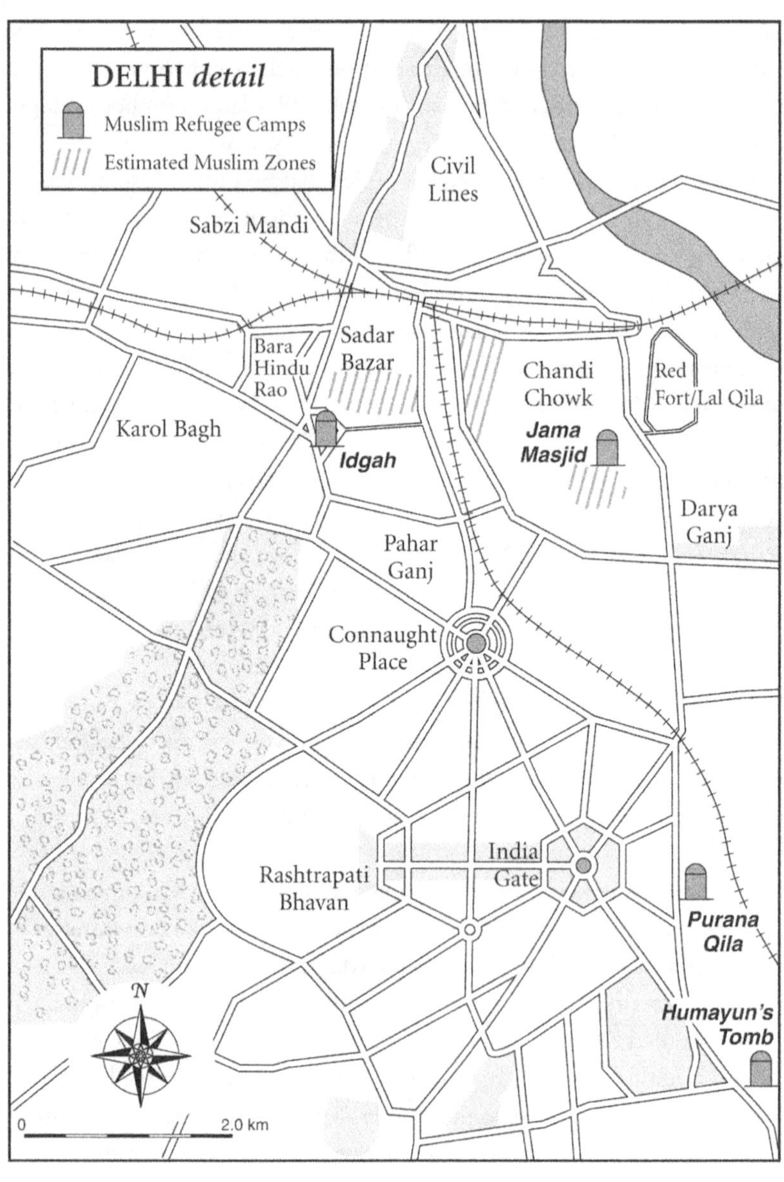

DELHI *detail*
Muslim Refugee Camps
Estimated Muslim Zones
Civil Lines
Sabzi Mandi
Sadar Bazar
Bara Hindu Rao
Chandi Chowk
Red Fort/Lal Qila
Karol Bagh
Idgah
Jama Masjid
Darya Ganj
Pahar Ganj
Connaught Place
India Gate
Rashtrapati Bhavan
Purana Qila
Humayun's Tomb
N
0
2.0 km

"safety areas" was presumed to be of a temporary nature, and that although they, Singh's Muslim neighbors, left their homes, they left all their belongings in them. I emphasize this here because this fact of Muslim "belonging" came to be written out in official discourse on "rehabilitation."

Aziz saheb had used the verb *qabza karnā* to state the fact of occupations, a verb which carries in its meaning the use of force; "to seize" is probably the closer English translation. Furthermore, the word *evacuate* means to move out of a place of danger to a place of safety. Thus one could say that most Muslims of Delhi were forced out or evacuated from their homes. But in discussions that ensued these homes came to be described first as "abandoned" and then as "vacant" and "empty houses," which could then be used for rehabilitation. The violence that accompanied this process of "emptying" was thereby erased.

These "Muslim zones" came under a great deal of criticism in the Constituent Assembly, since some felt that providing shelter for homeless "non-Muslim refugees" should be the government's first priority.[28] In a long debate that followed K.C. Neogy's presentation on November 29, 1947, to the Constituent Assembly on "Relief and Rehabilitation" efforts of the government, it was argued that "refugees" (referring to Hindu and Sikh refugees from the Punjab) had a "right to live in these portions of the country" and that "they must be made proper citizens of India." When it was argued that "empty houses" should be made available for the rehabilitation of shelterless "refugees," it was clear that housing Hindu and Sikh refugees was seen as central to the task of rehabilitation, and that the process of rehabilitation was to make refugees into citizens of the state.[29] The status of Muslim refugees in the city, on the other hand, was less certain.

Jawaharlal Nehru defended the policy of Muslim zones by insisting that despite the acute housing problem for "refugees," Muslims "should not be pushed out."[30] In a later debate Nehru explained what he meant by "pushing out." When Hindu and Sikh refugees occupied houses, he argued, "there was a tendency on the part of the Muslim residents of the other houses, next door, to leave their houses because they felt they were being pushed out. There was a tendency to push out the Muslim residents of the neighboring houses." Nehru further argued that there were still Muslim residents of Delhi in camps—this as late as February 1948—and that he hoped they would return to their houses in the city.[31]

The pressure on "empty houses" in Muslim zones is particularly evident in the Delhi Deputy Commissioner M. S. Randhawa's reports of late

1947. "Muslim zones" came to be seen as the primary focus for the establishment of "law and order" as well as the vast housing problem that faced the city's displaced people. Even after much of the rioting had stopped, these occupations remained a part of the violence in the city. There were repeated "rumors" of outbreaks of violence, which Randhawa interpreted as a "war of nerves" to push out Muslims from their homes. He noted that "[t]he main cause of the trouble which started on 23rd November 1947 was a scramble for empty houses." When stabbings and sporadic looting of Muslim shops took place, he noted that the "main source of the trouble [wa]s the housing and shopping problem" created by the large number of refugees present in Delhi.[32]

Randhawa argued that the "forcible possession of some vacant houses" was an outcome of "refugees who are without shelter [and] wander about from street to street in search of accommodation." Their "miserable plight" and "great hardship" tempted them to "invade empty Muslim houses," and the fact that "they have no hesitation in going to jail" made his task of policing these Muslim zones all the more difficult.[33]

Randhawa thus argued that "the general feeling among the public [wa]s that refugees should be permitted to occupy these houses and shops as is being done in Pakistan." The "empty houses" were the main source of Hindu and Sikh refugee discontent, and therefore key to the process of rehabilitation. As a result, he suggested allotting these "empty houses" to policemen, government servants, and other "suitable non-Muslim refugees" who would, he argued, not push out the localities' Muslim residents.[34]

That Muslims, excluded from "public" opinion, saw the "empty houses" differently is evident in complaints to the chief commissioner of Delhi, and petitions to Congress leaders. For example, Maulana Habibur Rehman of the Central Muslim Relief Committee wrote:

> In Sadar Bazar Muslims have been constantly made to make rooms for the refugees by all sorts of tactics, and of late, endeavors were being made to evict them from Qasabpura and . . . clear the locality of Muslims. In pursuance of this plan last night it is alleged that an offensive was organized and led by some special police officers. . . . Throughout the night he was out to hunt out Muslims from their dwellings, cause women and children to be out in the open, harass and terrorize them, and make them extremely panicky. The display of police force and

> his high-handedness had certainly the effect of demoralizing Muslims and make them to leave the place at the earliest.[35]

Policemen, as Maulana Rehman saw it, were not neutral agents of the state, but directly involved in Muslim displacement. Muslim zones, rather than serving as a refuge for Muslims, became part of a contested and fearful urban geography, in which institutions of the state were complicit in unsettling Muslims. Randhawa noted that an outcome of this contested geography was a "tendency among the Muslims, particularly of the lower-middle-class shopkeepers and laborers . . . to sell off their belongings and go to Pakistan. I have seen in the Muslim areas like Pul Bangash, Bara Hindu Rao, Sadar Bazar, and Jama Masjid that the Muslims spread their household belongings on pavements for sale."[36]

Thus the experience of becoming a Muslim refugee was not just shaped by murderous violence in the city. The violent seizures of their homes by other refugees as they were forced into Muslim camps, as well as the continuing disputes over housing as they were forced into Muslim zones, produced a sense of a partisan state unable to protect them and unwilling to rehabilitate them.

This sense of exclusion from the Indian state's immediate rehabilitation efforts is most poignantly expressed in a letter by Abdul Ghafoor to *Babu* Rajendra Prasad, the first president of independent India. Ghafoor of Matia Mahal, Delhi, narrated his credentials as a "freedom fighter," as a man who had gone to jail nine times in the fight against the British, and who had opposed the Muslim League. His home and that of his family members had been looted, burned down, and occupied, and his wife had been sent to a Muslim camp and from there on to Pakistan. He complained that "*un kī ābadī par kachchī koṛī bhī kharch karnā Indian Union men guna hai* [to spend even a raw cent on their rehabilitation is a sin in the Indian Union]." As a result, for "*bad-qismat* [ill-fated]" Congress Muslims, he concluded that "*in ke liye na Hind men jagah hai na Pakistan men ṭhikānā* [there is no space for them in India, nor a resting place in Pakistan]."[37] Displaced from his home and separated from his wife, Ghafoor's anguish and plea to the state highlights what an extraordinarily difficult decision going, or not going, to Pakistan was for those who had opposed its creation. However, as we shall see in the Muslim camps, even for those without Ghafoor's political commitments the decision to board the trains in search of refuge was both a fearful and contingent one.

MUSLIM CAMPS/PURANA QILA

Muslims in the city sought shelter in all sorts of places, initially with relatives and friends in areas perceived to be "safer," and then places like the Jama Masjid, houses of Muslim Cabinet ministers such as Azad and Rafi Ahmad Kidwai, the Idgah, Humayun's Tomb, and the Purana Qila.[38] These places of refuge emerged spontaneously as large numbers of people congregated, but then some of them came to be organized as "camps." While at Jama Masjid and Idgah relief work was carried out by Muslim volunteers[39] such as Salim saheb's father, Purana Qila and Humayun's Tomb were taken over and managed by the Indian government.

I want to focus here on Purana Qila, for it became the largest "Muslim camp" and an intermediary site where the Indian state intervened, and from there almost all those who took refuge left on the trains for Pakistan. However, as train derailments and organized attacks on trains were leading to massacres across the Punjab, regular trains from Purana Qila to Lahore did not start running until early October.[40] (There were, however, some special trains that departed earlier.) In addition, people continued to move from their homes to camps, such that the Purana Qila camp remained in use until early 1948.

The camp at Purana Qila emerged as some 12,000 government employees who had "opted" to work for Pakistan and their families (who had initially congregated at the Transfer Office of the Pakistan government) were moved there by the Pakistani High Commission, until travel arrangements could be made for their departure to Pakistan. As word spread, other Muslims seeking refuge, with or without intentions to go to Pakistan, also came to Purana Qila, and within days over 50,000 Muslims of Delhi had taken refuge there. With almost no resources in the Qila (there was only one tap for water outside its main entrance), the Pakistan High Commission then requested the Indian government to take over the running of the camp. On September 15, the Indian government took over the camp, though a Muslim guard was retained at the request of the High Commission.[41]

Although a considerable amount of writing exists on refugee camps, Liisa Malkki's suggestion that the refugee camp needs to be understood as not just a place of refuge but rather as a "device of power" is quite significant. In the case of postwar Europe, for instance, the management of refugees did not emerge out of humanitarian considerations alone but was considered a military problem, such that it was the Displaced Persons Branch of the Supreme Headquarters Allied Expeditionary Force that undertook this task, and hundreds of work and concentration camps in Germany were transformed into refugee camps. Since then, Malkki argues, the refugee camp is meant to create supervisable spaces so that administrative and bureaucratic processes can intervene in categorizing, quarantining, and controlling its "inmates."[42]

Although camps like Purana Qila emerged spontaneously and in chaotic conditions, they were also subjected to modern disciplinary imperatives. After Zakir Husain visited Purana Qila at Nehru's request, he reported to the Emergency Committee that "these places could not properly be called camps but rather areas in which humanity was dumped."[43] Anis Kidwai, who worked as a volunteer with refugees, was also overwhelmed by the abject conditions inside Purana Qila, and described it in her memoir as a mass of "disorganized tents and heaps of tin roofs."[44] Yet once the Indian government took over the running of the camp, it is interesting to note the paradigmatic fashion by which organizing the camp involved establishing the post of a "camp commandant" and installing loudspeakers to facilitate control, even prior to providing additional access to water.[45]

The Emergency Committee minutes are quite informative on the concerns of the state in the management of such a camp, although it is uncertain how much of what is recorded here was actually implemented or was implementable in those circumstances. For example, in the search for a cadre of volunteers to help run the camps it was suggested that the Muslim policemen who had deserted to the camp be given back their uniforms. Although this plan was opposed, a consideration of policing skills as an asset was not incidental, for orders were passed to search all refugees entering the camp, and repeated attempts were made to control movement into and out of the camp, such that at one point permits were instated. This control was considered both justified and for the inmates' own welfare, first because of the violent conditions in the city, and then because of an outbreak of cholera in the camp.[46]

It is also evident from the minutes of the Emergency Committee that Muslim refugees in Purana Qila resented these attempts to discipline them, for officials repeatedly commented on their "uncooperative" nature. Gyanendra Pandey has argued that conditions in the Muslim camps were much worse than those in the Hindu camps because of inadequate relief supplies.[47] Yet it was the "uncooperative" nature of the Muslim refugees that was considered a major obstacle in improving the conditions of the camp, as one official noted that "[t]he attitude of the refugees in the Purana Qila continues to be generally hostile to the non-Muslims and this makes it extremely difficult for the camp commandant to improve conditions in the camp." However, it was not only hostility to non-Muslims that was deemed to be the source of the problem, but in addition "[o]ne of the main difficulties was that many of the refugees did not obey the camp commandant or their own leaders."[48]

As studies of contemporary refugees have shown, it is the breakdown of trust which is culturally constituted in a society that forces a person to become a refugee in the first place, and this distrust is only heightened in the hierarchical disciplinary spaces of a refugee camp.[49] From the perspective of Delhi's Muslims, the state had failed to protect them in their homes, the Muslim policemen of Delhi were also in the camp, the sanitary conditions of the camp were so poor that a number of people had died of cholera, and the camp was rife with rumors of what was going on in the city. Thus it is not surprising that the Muslims of Purana Qila were hostile to the camp managers—representatives of the Indian state on whom they were now dependent for their survival. In addition, the camp had brought together Muslims from many different social backgrounds and political orientations, and, as Salim saheb had recalled, stripped many of them of their "respectability." E. Valentine Daniel and John Knudsen describe this as "a state of hyperinformation" in which it becomes very difficult to give meaning to experiences,[50] and it was in this "state of hyperinformation" that Muslims of the camp were then being asked to decide whether they wanted to stay in Delhi or go to Pakistan.

To "arrange census" was perceived by the Emergency Committee as a task of high priority in the management of the Muslim camp. Given the camp's origin, as a refuge of Pakistani government personnel, there were a large number of people in the camp who had decided to leave for Pakistan and were merely awaiting train facilities to do so. Their bags and beddings were decisively packed, so to speak. However, from the start it was suggested that "those in Purana Qila be separated into two lots," those wanting to go to Pakistan and "those who wished to stay." K. C. Neogy, to whom the task of the "census" fell, pointed out the difficulties of categorizing the Muslim refugees but conjectured that "about 90 percent" of the lakh of Muslim inhabitants of Delhi who had gone into refugee camps "seem[ed] to want to leave for Pakistan." The task of the census came up repeatedly for discussion in the Emergency Committee, which suggests that determining the intentions of the "inmates" was not a simple matter. Yet the "general feeling" in the Emergency Committee was that there was "reason to believe that 90 percent wish to go out" or "would want to go to Pakistan." Given that in fact most of the Muslims in Purana Qila did leave for Pakistan, it would seem that the estimates of the Emergency Committee were accurate. However, one report to the Emergency Committee noted that "[e]xact figures for the latter two categories [go to Pakistan or back to city] are extremely difficult—as large numbers have not as yet finally made up their minds."[51]

In this context of "hyperinformation," there were some extremely important efforts to reassure and retain the Muslims of the city. Gandhi's arrival in Delhi in October is widely regarded as the most important intervention in halting the murders and occupations. Sumit Sarkar describes it as the "Mahatama's finest hour,"[52] as a frail but determined Gandhi began to visit Muslim *mohallas* in an effort to restoring the morale of the Muslims.[53] Qamar apa, in my interview with her, recalled hearing about Gandhi's visit to Maulana Ahmad Salim, of the Jamiat-e-Ulema-e-Hind, which she considered of the most importance in her family's decision to remain in Delhi.

Salim saheb, on the other hand, recalled Maulana Azad's *khutba* at the Jama Masjid on October 24, 1947:

> *Maulana Azad ne ākhir dam tak ek ek ādmi ko rokne ki koshish ki. Aur Maulana Azad ki ek tarikhi taqreer hai Jama Masjid pe. Bahut tarikhi taqreer . . . to un kī taqreer se bahut logon ke bandhe hua'e bistar, kehte hai, bandhe hua'e bistar khul gaye . . . Us waqt mohalle men bahs ho rahi thī ke ja'e ya nah ja'e. Main ne batāya na ke Maulana Azad ki taqreer se hazāron bistar khul gaye.*

> Maulana Azad till the very end tried to stop each and every person. And there is a historic speech by Maulana Azad at Jama Masjid. A very historic speech . . . for as a result of his speech many people's packed beddings opened, they say, packed beddings opened . . . at the time in our *mohalla* there was a debate about whether to go or not go. As I said, as a result of Maulana Azad's speech thousands of beddings opened.

Azad, in his historic *khutba,* had argued to the city's Muslims that "this escape that you have given the sacred name of *hijrat*" was a hasty decision, made in fear. He asked them to let these difficult times pass, and said they could always leave later if they felt they wanted to.[54] The impact of the *khutba* went beyond those who were actually present to hear it, for word of mouth and newspapers spread Azad's "*dardnak cheekh* [cry of anguish]." According to Chief Commissioner Khurshid, Muslim refugees "in Purana Qila returned in thousands to the city with more confidence . . . and this was partly the result of the speech by Hon. Maulana Azad."[55]

On January 12, 1948, Gandhi started his fast. Azad noted that the fast had an "electric effect" and that "not only the city but the whole of India was deeply stirred." One of Gandhi's conditions for breaking his fast, according to Azad, was that all Muslims of Delhi be resettled in their own homes. Azad wrote that he did not think that this was a practical solution since "many of the refugees from West Punjab had occupied the houses which were left vacant by Muslims. If it was a matter of [only] a few hundred, perhaps Gandhiji's wishes could have been carried out."[56]

When G.D. Khosla, appointed to undertake an enquiry into the workings of the Custodian of Evacuee Property in Delhi, went to see Gandhi a few days before his assassination, he recalled the following conversation with Gandhi:

> KHOSLA: The Muslims in the Old Fort [Purana Qila] camp have no wish to stay in this country. They told me when I visited them, that they would like to go to Pakistan as soon as possible. Our own people are without houses or shelter. It breaks my heart to see them suffering like this, exposed to the elements. Tell me Bapuji, what should I do?
>
> GANDHI: When I go there they do not say they want to go to Pakistan. . . . They are also our people. You should bring them back and protect them.[57]

Although Khosla asserted that Gandhi convinced him of his moral task, yet the conversation reflects a widely held perception in different sections of the Indian state that "non-Muslim refugees" were "our own people" who had to be rehabilitated, while "Muslim refugees" had questionable entitlement. Thus despite significant attempts by Gandhi and

Azad to reassure the Muslims of Delhi, this overriding perception had important effects. Wedged between divergent views of whether or not Muslim refugees in camps wanted to go to Pakistan was the question of housing Hindu and Sikh refugees. If Muslim refugees in camps like Purana Qila were to remain as Gandhi wished, what would the Indian state do with their occupied houses, and where would they be rehabilitated? The economic equation that the rehabilitation of Hindu and Sikh refugees was contingent upon a Muslim exodus was perhaps most bluntly articulated by Sardar Patel when he noted in an Emergency Committee meeting "that there was bound to be trouble if as a result of these Muslims not moving out, it proved impossible to accommodate non-Muslim refugees coming in from the West."[58]

This equation had far-reaching effects, as we shall see, when those who boarded trains to Pakistan to escape the abject and uncertain conditions of the camps later wanted to return to their homes. If the loss of their homes and contested geographies of Delhi propelled them to leave, their departure and arrival was equally contested in Pakistan, on the other side of this unsettled and shifting landscape.

ON THE TRANSFER OF POPULATIONS

As Aziz saheb noted, Muslim displacement was accompanied by a feeling of dispossession because of the creation of Pakistan. However, as thousands of Delhi's Muslims boarded special trains to Pakistan, the Pakistani government viewed this exodus with alarm.[59]

To understand its alarm, it is necessary to situate it in the context of the agreed "transfer of populations" in the Punjab. By late August 1947 it became evident that the Boundary Force that had been established by the colonial state to deal with outbreaks of violence in the Punjab was terribly inadequate. The Cabinet of the Pakistani government complained bitterly to its Indian counterpart that the Boundary Force had become partisan, and was spectator to or abetting in the violence instead of controlling it.[60] One of the Pakistani Cabinet's concerns was that the Boundary Force consisted of only 20 percent Muslims, and even fewer officers, and that this disproportion had failed to deter a "slaughter of Muslims in large numbers."[61] The loss of confidence in the Boundary Force had taken place on both sides, and thus it was agreed that the problem of controlling the violence and providing safe passage to the "evacuating populations" had to be handled differently. As a result, by August 28 the Boundary Force was replaced by the joint Military Evacuation Organization (MEO).[62] The MEO coordinated now-divided military units so that Pakistan army units escorted Muslim caravans and trains while Indian army units escorted Hindu and Sikh caravans and trains.

The establishment of the MEO brought with it a critical question. What should the official position be regarding the "evacuating populations"? Should they be regarded as refugees, who would return to their homes once the violence was brought to a halt, or was there to be an interstate agreement regarding "the wholesale transfer of population"? The Pakistani Cabinet was concerned, for a "refugee problem" premised on refugee return back to their original homes was "possible to handle," but a transfer of population on religious lines in the Punjab meant the momentous exchange of 12 million people.

In the Cabinet discussions on how to manage the Punjab displacements, an agreement to a "transfer of population" was seen as having two possibly grave implications, and which did indeed have enduring consequences in the ensuing years. An exchange of populations within the Punjab was considered possible because it was believed that since the Muslim population of East Punjab was roughly equal to the non-Muslim population of West Punjab and since the property of the latter was more than that of the former, there would be "no real difficulties in the way of absorbing the entire Muslim population of East Punjab in place of the non-Muslim population of West Punjab."[63] Calculations of property, the homes, businesses, and lands of those departing for safety were exceedingly important to this assessment of the Punjab situation.

However, first there were concerns that if questions of compensation on the basis of property arose, the Pakistani state might have to pay more than it would receive, and this could place a serious strain on its fragile economy. It was argued in the Cabinet that "the Sikhs had demanded the partition of Punjab on the basis of property holdings for the simple reason that they had extensive and valuable holdings in the West Punjab," and that this was bound to become an issue.[64]

Second, it was feared that if an exchange of populations was agreed to in principle in the Punjab, "there was likelihood of trouble breaking out in other parts of the subcontinent with a view to forcing Muslims in the Indian Dominion to move to Pakistan. If that happened we would find ourselves with inadequate land and other resources to support the influx."[65] The Punjab could set a dangerous precedent for the rest of the subcontinent. Given that Muslims in the rest of India, some 42 million, formed a population larger than the entire population of West Pakistan at the time, economic rationality eschewed such a forced migration.

However, in the divided Punjab millions of people were already on the move, and the two governments had to respond to this mass movement. Thus, despite these important reservations, the establishment of the MEO led to an acceptance of a "transfer of populations" in divided Punjab, "to give a sense of security" to ravaged communities on both sides.[66] A statement of the Indian government's position of such a transfer across divided Punjab was made in the legislature by Neogy on November 18, 1947. He stated that although the Indian government's policy was "to discourage mass migration from one province to another," Punjab was to be an exception. In the rest of the subcontinent migrations were not to be on a planned basis, but a matter of individual choice. This exceptional character of movements across divided Punjab needs to be emphasized, for the agreed and "planned evacuations" by the two governments formed the context of those displacements.[67] In contrast, movements of people from other parts of the subcontinent have different negotiated histories.

Delhi fell outside the rubric of Punjab's agreed transfers. Therefore, when violence engulfed Delhi in early September, it became a subject of intense discussion in the parallel Pakistani government's Emergency Committee of the Cabinet.[68] On September 15, 1947, Mohammad Ali Jinnah reported on his discussions with Delhi's Muslim leaders. He argued that Delhi's Muslims had now two courses open to them—one, to demand from the Indian government that they "give the minorities there a fair deal" or, two, "to start a civil war." The possibility of migrating to Pakistan, of seeking refuge or a home there, was not even considered as an option. When it was clear that Muslims were leaving their homes and going to refugee camps in large numbers, a suggestion was made in a meeting of the Pakistani Emergency Committee that in order to stop further abandonment of Delhi by Muslims, Liaqat Ali Khan as prime minister should go there to talk to the refugees and "advise them to stay on and make them understand that they were now nationals of India and should look to the Indian government for protection." This then became the Pakistani position on the matter, that "the Muslims who are forced to leave their homes in India are Indian nationals and so long as they are in India it is the duty of the Indian government to feed and protect them as much as their other citizens."[69]

Although the Pakistani government had accepted the total evacuation of Muslims of East Punjab, it considered it an imperative to deter migrations from elsewhere in India. Despite abject conditions of Muslims in Delhi, the fear of a forced Muslim exodus from the rest of India was so great that as large numbers of Muslims boarded trains in Delhi, the Pakistani government objected to the Indian government's position of allowing "those who wished to leave" to do so. It argued that the Indian government was not giving sufficient assurances to the Muslims there, as "the attitude . . . taken by high officials of the Indian government [was] that Muslims had no future in Delhi and their safety could not be guaranteed if they insisted on staying on in Delhi."[70] However, despite these objections, deterring this exodus was ideologically more complicated.

At the inter-dominion conference on October 5, 1947, at Lahore, the Muslim exodus from Delhi became an important point of contention. The Pakistani government insisted that only those in Purana Qila who had opted to work for the Pakistan government should be allowed to board the special trains to Pakistan, for it had not agreed to the movement of any refugees from Delhi or from Uttar Pradesh (UP). Liaqat Ali Khan took particular exception to what he described as the "dumping" of Muslims across the Pakistan border, and emphasized that the MEO agreement extended to only "members of the minority community" of East and West Punjab, the Punjab States, and the North West Frontier Province.[71]

The Indian government publicized Liaqat's position at the conference, that the government of Pakistan would not accept Muslim refugees from areas other than East Punjab—that "even Muslims who have worked for establishing Pakistan, even if they want to go, their doors are closed."[72] In opposition to the Pakistani policy, the Indian government announced that it was willing to accept "non-Muslim refugees" from both Baluchistan and Sindh, which were also outside the MEO agreement.[73]

This of course challenged the legitimacy of the Pakistani state as a proclaimed Muslim homeland and led to a "clarifying" rejoinder by Liaqat in a press conference on October 9. He claimed that he had only opposed the suggestion of the Indian government that "the Muslim populations of Delhi and UP's western districts be exchanged." The point of contention was that slippery line between "wishing to leave" and feeling "pushed out." Liaqat stated:

> I was told that all the Muslims of Delhi and UP want to come to Pakistan, and Pakistan should facilitate them. This is when I made it very clear that while Pakistan is willing to provide refuge to Muslims, it does not want that Muslims from regions other than East Punjab leave their *watan* and property and come to Pakistan. I placed emphasis that it is the duty of the Government of India to protect these Muslims and they should fulfill their promises. If the Government of India had fulfilled its duty properly then there would be no question of Muslims of Delhi and UP moving. The Partition of the country was done on the principle that minorities would remain in their regions and the governments would provide protection to all its citizens, and give them equal rights.[74]

It was a difficult position to straddle for the Pakistani state, to argue that it was a refuge for all Muslims, and discourage Muslim displacement at the same time. The principle that "minorities would remain in their regions" and be equal citizens of those states was already unsettled by the intervention of the two states in the Punjab violence. Although people were displaced in terror, the agreed transfer of populations in divided Punjab precluded the possibility of their eventual return to their homes, precluded the possibility of rebuilding new lives in old communities. It meant that Hindu and Sikh refugees of West Punjab were not to be regarded as "minorities" and citizens of the Pakistani state, but instead were to be rehabilitated by the Indian state in order to become Indian citizens.

The transfer of populations in the Punjab indeed set in motion an unraveling precedent. How were Muslim refugees from the Punjab to be differentiated from Muslim refugees from elsewhere? Which Muslim refugees were to be regarded as subjects of the Pakistani state, and which Muslim refugees were to be rehabilitated by the Indian state?

Delhi's Muslims left their city in the midst of this ambiguity and interstate disagreement over their initial flight, and this would later lead to questions about their national status and eventual belonging. As they arrived in Karachi, they faced a small, multireligious city in the throes of a different housing crisis, drawing out unresolved questions about the place of religious minorities in this shifting spatial order. If Punjab had unsettled a status quo, then what was the new status of the large Hindu communities in Sind?

2. *Hindu Exodus from Karachi*

For a long time now,
We have stood
On the rooftops of stories
Believing this city is ours.[1]

As refugees from Purana Qila and other "Muslim refugee camps" in Delhi boarded trains to Pakistan, most of them made their way to Karachi, Pakistan's new capital in the province of Sind. In Pakistan, Muslim refugees came to be officially called "*muhajirs*."[2] Although the specific Urdu word for refugees is *panaghir* (the seeker of *panah* or refuge), the word *muhajir*, which means both migrant and refugee, invoked the migration of Prophet Muhammad and his followers from Mecca to Medina in A.D. 622. Naming Muslim refugees who came to Pakistan *muhajirs* has been interpreted as an attempt to ideologically reinforce Muslim League's broad claim that Pakistan would be a home for Muslims, imbue a sense of religious significance to the hardships of displacement, and inspire religious duty among local Muslim inhabitants to receive the displaced. However, it is important to note that the *hijra* of A.D. 622 was an obligatory migration that *had to be* undertaken by all of Muhammad's followers as a matter of faith, and that the Pakistani state adopted this symbolic name despite the fact that mass migration, as we have seen, was actively discouraged by it.[3]

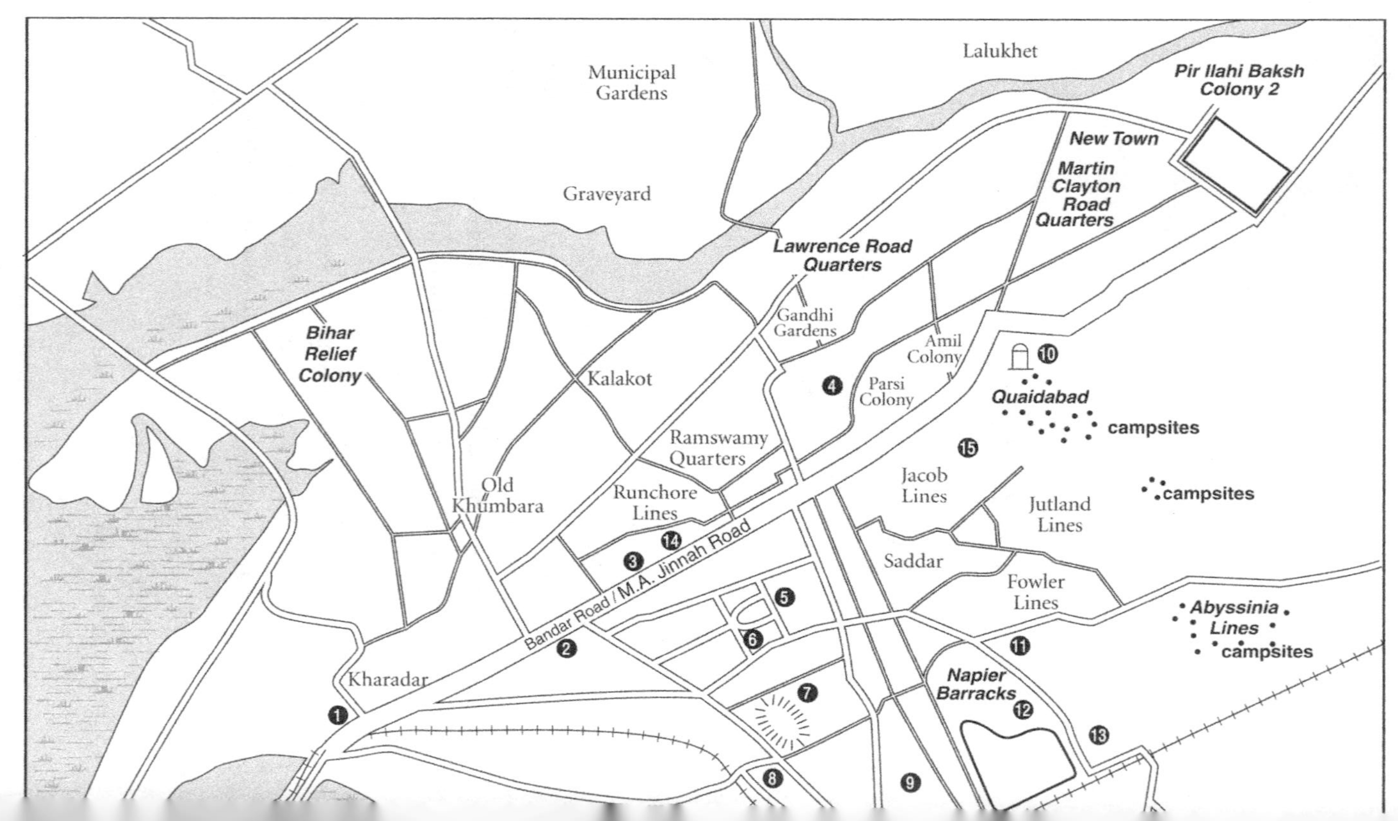
Lalukhet
Pir Ilahi Baksh Colony 2
Municipal Gardens
Graveyard
New Town
Martin Clayton Road Quarters
Lawrence Road Quarters
Gandhi Gardens
Amil Colony
Parsi Colony
Bihar Relief Colony
Kalakot
Quaidabad
campsites
Ramswamy Quarters
Jacob Lines
campsites
Old Khumbara
Runchore Lines
Jutland Lines
Saddar
Bandar Road / M.A. Jinnah Road
Fowler Lines
Abyssinia Lines
campsites
Kharadar
Napier Barracks
1
2
3
4
5
6
7
8
9
10
11
12
13
14
15

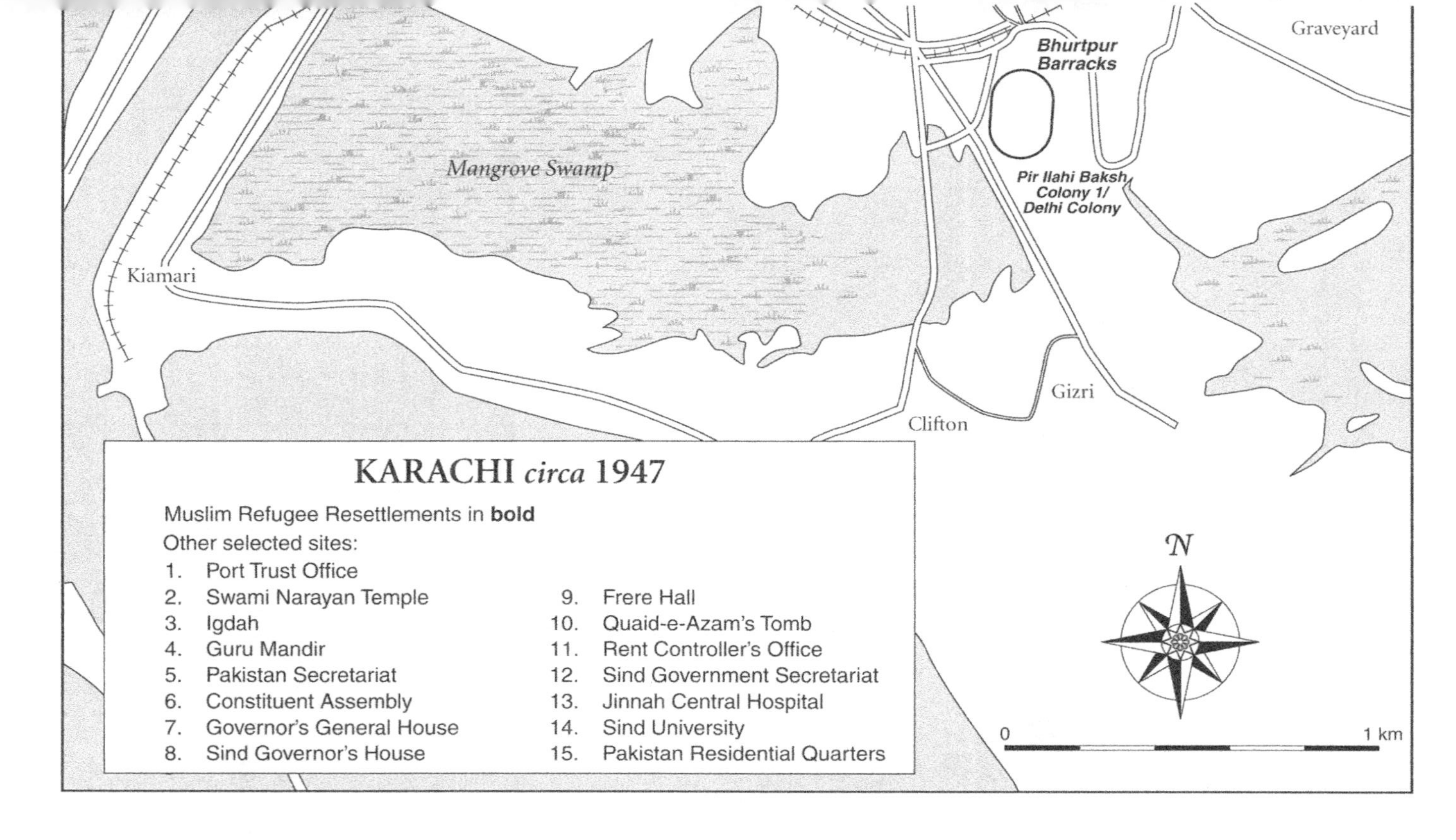
Graveyard
Bhurtpur Barracks
Mangrove Swamp
Pir Ilahi Baksh Colony 1/ Delhi Colony
Kiamari
Gizri
Clifton
KARACHI circa 1947
Muslim Refugee Resettlements in **bold**
Other selected sites:
1. Port Trust Office
2. Swami Narayan Temple
3. Igdah
4. Guru Mandir
5. Pakistan Secretariat
6. Constituent Assembly
7. Governor's General House
8. Sind Governor's House
9. Frere Hall
10. Quaid-e-Azam's Tomb
11. Rent Controller's Office
12. Sind Government Secretariat
13. Jinnah Central Hospital
14. Sind University
15. Pakistan Residential Quarters
N
0
1 km

As a governmental category, "*muhajirs*" figured prominently in the 1951 Census, which enumerated Urdu-speaking *muhajirs* in particular as a majority in the city of Karachi.[4] The census defined *muhajir* as a person who had moved into Pakistan "as the result of or fear of disturbances connected with Partition, no matter from where, when *or for how long a stay they have come*" (emphasis added).[5] This definition was consciously adopted to leave open the notion that while some *muhajirs*, such as those of Punjab, were to remain permanently in Pakistan, other *muhajirs* from the rest of India might return to their homes in India. Thus in many respects *muhajir* was not conceived as a fixed or stable refugee category to be folded into citizens of the new nation, unlike the discursive figure of the "refugee" in India.

However, Sind was a region that was particularly characterized for its "communal harmony," and in the days leading up to Partition, Sind's governor, Francis Mudie, described it as a place which "[c]haractistically . . . carries on almost as if nothing had happened or was going to happen," and that he "[didn't] expect many real Sindhi [Hindus] to leave the Province."[6] In keeping with Mudie's view, Karachi did not experience the scale of violence that had ensued in Punjab and Delhi. Yet soon after Partition, the Hindu population began to leave Karachi, so that in the decade between 1941 and 1951 almost the entire Hindu population had left the city. By the time "the most notable communal incident" took place on January 6, 1948, Hindus and Sikhs were already leaving the city and the province in large numbers. In fact, the "incident" took place as Sikhs from various parts of Sind arrived in Karachi to leave by ship for India, and were taken in open horse carriages to a *gurdwara* in the city. Reportedly, Muslim refugees surrounded the *gurdwara* and attacked it, and this led to rioting in the city which was brought "under control" when the army was deployed.[7]

The postindependence governor of Sind, Ghulam Husain Hidayatullah, attributed the departure of Sindhi Hindus to the incoming Muslim refugees, and argued that "[t]he Sindhi Hindu, a shrewd businessman, does not want any upheaval and the Sindhi Muslim is also free from communal hatred. It is the refugees who have brought heat and passion into the placid life of this province." Although he recognized that "Muslim refugees" had to be "welcomed," he regarded the "refugee problem" as "the gravest problem" facing the province in "the maintenance of law and order in Sind."[8]

I focus in this chapter on the Hindu exodus from Karachi because this part of the region's history has been largely treated as unremarkable and therefore unworthy of reflection in most writings on Pakistan. Although recent accounts of the history of the city have noted that as a result of Partition "[t]he most significant change was demographic," they do not examine why the Hindu and Sikh population left the city. They carry essays which narrate how Parsi, Hindu, Muslim, British, and Goan Christian individuals contributed to the city's pre-Partition growth and glory, but by neglecting to examine the context of the departure of the city's important religious minority, they make it seem that it was "natural" for them to have left what was claimed as a Muslim homeland.[9] Sara Ansari, a historian of Sind, in an essay which examines the impact of Partition on Sind, focuses on Sindhi mixed feelings on the arrival of *muhajirs*, but not on reasons for the exodus that was concomitant.[10] However, I argue here that the departure of Hindus and Sikhs from Karachi was not merely incidental but rather central to understanding the very tensions of Partition's ambiguous new nations. Could Hindus and Sikhs become citizens of Pakistan without belonging to a "Muslim nation"? Or were they considered Indian citizens from the start? As in Delhi, the combined interventions of the two postcolonial states shaped this uncertain flow of refugees, while Hindu houses became a source of contention in the shifting geographies of cities and nation. Ultimately, the Hindu exodus had effects well beyond Karachi, as further displacement of the region's minorities challenged the very equation of where north Indian Muslims could belong, if not in Pakistan.

THE PUSH AND PULL OF DISPLACEMENT

"Mahatma Gandhi and the Congress leaders should be informed that Hindus of Sind cannot live in honor there and therefore the Indian Dominion Government should take up the task of evacuating, relief and rehabilitation," Choithram P. Gidwani, the president of the Sind Provincial Congress Committee, proclaimed to Rajendra Prasad after a meeting of Sindhi Congressmen. Gidwani and other Congress leaders of Sind campaigned vociferously for the Indian government to arrange a planned evacuation of Sind's minorities, along the lines carried out by the MEO in other parts of West Pakistan, but the problem they faced was that "due to peace [in the province], the Government of India [wa]s not assisting them."[11]

Because of the campaign by Sind's Congressmen for the planned evacuation of Sind's minorities, many of Pakistan's leaders and bureaucrats believed that the exodus of the economically significant Hindus of Sind was being orchestrated by Congress leaders to sabotage the very existence of Pakistan. For instance, it was believed that "harijans" were being encouraged to leave so that the sanitation of Karachi, Hyderabad, and Sukkur would be impaired, resulting in "epidemic and pestilence." More seriously, the departure of Hindu merchants, bankers, and other businesses would disrupt the economic life of Karachi and Sind, and this would destabilize the nascent state.[12] In keeping with such a view, Syed Hashim Reza, the first post-independence administrator of Karachi, wrote in his autobiography that soon after Partition, Acharya Kripalani, the president of the All India Congress Committee (AICC), who was from Sind, visited the province and advised Hindus and Sikhs to leave Sind as quickly as possible. Arguing that as no "communal disturbances" had taken place in Sind for centuries, Reza suggested that Kripalani was not so concerned for the safety of the minorities but wanted to destroy the economic structure of the province.[13] Sind police records also claim "on good authority that though Kripalani openly advised Hindus not to migrate, he secretly favored migration and asked Hindus to leave Sind as early as possible."[14] Later, in a Constituent Assembly debate, Hashim Gazder of Sind also took this view when he claimed that Sindhi Hindus "were quite happy here in Sind; there were no murders, no dacoities; there were no loots of any kind." Instead, he held that Sind's minorities were not "pushed out" but rather "they were pulled out according to a planned programme by the Congress leaders" and Kripalani, who came "with the ostensible purpose of telling people not to go from Sind . . . wherever he went he told them to get out of Sind."[15]

Despite this view held by Pakistani officials, large numbers of Hindus and Sikhs had already begun to leave Sind even prior to Kripalani's visit in late September 1947. Ansari, for instance, notes that by mid-September some fifty thousand "non-Muslims" had registered with local Congress organizations for aid in leaving Sind.[16] Although the first departures were largely of Gujeratis, Marathis, and other non-Sindhi Hindus, as anticipated by Mudie,[17] the advice of Kripalani, Gidwani, and other leaders cannot alone account for the mass exodus.

Despite the celebration of Sind's pre-Partition "communal harmony," Mudie's *Fortnightly Reports* suggest that there had been a growing political rift between the provincial Muslim League and the Congress. On a number of provincial issues the Sind Muslim League's stance was seen as a foreboding of Muslim dominance, whereby economically significant Hindus of the province would be marginalized.

For one, when the Sind Assembly opened on February 17, 1947, with a Muslim League majority, the house broke with the region's tradition by adopting both the speaker and the deputy speaker from the League, when the practice had been to select a deputy speaker from the opposition.[18] Further, by March 1947 at least two divisive issues faced the house—the Sind University Bill and the Sind Landholders Mortgage Bill. Even after the separation of Sind from the Bombay Presidency, students in the region had to go to Bombay University to give their matriculation exams, and therefore there had been a long-standing political consensus that Sind needed its own university. However, a Sind University Bill which provided for a Muslim majority on the various university bodies was passed by the Muslim League–dominated Assembly, even though the Congress members vehemently opposed it. The Education Ministry justified this legislation on the basis that Muslims were severely underrepresented in education and government in Sind.[19] But with Partition imminent, the "controversy," widely covered by the press, did little to reassure the province's Hindus, for even after lengthy negotiations only token conciliatory resolutions were passed: to set up a Board of Studies for Hindu Culture, as well as an advisory panel to represent minority interests. Similarly, the Sind Landholders Mortgage Bill was seen as giving Muslim zamindars leverage over Hindu banias by allowing a zamindar to give oral evidence at variance with a sale deed. The Congress's opposition to the passing of this bill was such that an appeal was made to the viceroy in Delhi to withhold his assent to it.[20]

Both these bills were included in a polemical brochure produced by the Sind Congress, "Why the exodus from Sind?"[21] It argued that Hindus were leaving Sind "because in actual fact, the Muslim League government of Sind were *even before Pakistan was established*, deliberately and more or less systematically pursuing with neck-break speed a policy of ruthless suppression of the Hindus of Sind" (emphasis added). The brochure foregrounds the seeds of distrust in regional politics, now being rehearsed amid the anxieties of Partition. At its core was the very uncertainty of what was to be the nature of the Pakistani state, whether, claimed on behalf of Muslims, it could eschew the question of religious identity in the making of its citizens.

Jinnah's often-quoted speech of August 11, 1947—"in course of time, Hindus would cease to be Hindus and Muslims would cease to be Muslims . . . in the political sense as citizens of the State"—is usually offered as evidence of a promise of equal citizenship for all in the Pakistani state. In his autobiography, Reza recalls accompanying Jinnah to the Swami Narayan temple in the heart of Karachi, where "non-Muslim refugees" from different parts of Sind were awaiting their departure by ship to India. Jinnah, according to Reza, made every effort to reassure the province's Hindus, but they said "that while they had full trust in him, it could not be said about the petty officials who had communal bias."[22] Ayub Khuhro, the premier of Sind, and other Sindhi leaders also attempted to retain Sind's minorities, for they also feared a loss of cultural identity with the Hindu exodus. However, when after the riots of January 6, 1948, Khuhro toured Sind with Sri Prakasa, the Indian high commissioner, to urge the Sindhi Hindus to not leave their homes, a *Hindustan Times* reporter observed that "Hindus stopped their car every few miles and urged for arrangements for early evacuation."[23]

Furthermore, the Sind government attempted to use force to stem this exodus by passing the Sind Maintenance of Public Safety Ordinance on September 21, 1947. Given that the majority of Sind government servants were Hindu, their departure meant in the initial stage that many offices could function for only part of their working hours; half the civil and criminal courts were closed, and some banks and businesses were able to operate for only a few hours a day. In addition, it was feared that the departure of Hindu banias would lead to a breakdown in the rural credit system. Thus the ordinance not only gave the government wide powers for policing the province, but also allowed for the "control of essential services" so that those people performing services deemed "essential to the life of the community" were prohibited from leaving.[24] The coercive ordinance only exacerbated fears of mistreatment by the new state, and led to an increase in the exodus.

The Indian state's official position on displacements outside of Punjab was, broadly, that minorities should remain where they were, and in the case of Sind, it was "not to encourage the evacuation of non-Muslims from Sind," although the Indian High Commission in Karachi would give travel assistance to those who wished to depart.[25] It has been argued that in the case of Sind, the Indian high commissioner gave free ship tickets to those who wanted to leave, and thus encouraged migration, although at the time the High Commission denied this.[26]

However, when the high commissioner protested against the Public Safety Ordinance, he not only argued "that persons who desire permanently to go to India and to seek a home there should be afforded every facility to do so." Importantly he also stated that although "who is to be deemed a citizen of Pakistan and who is a citizen of India" was still indeterminate at this stage, "those who wish to go away permanently from Pakistan and to live in India, have chosen to be the citizens of India."[27] Sardar Patel had given an assurance prior to Partition that "whatever the definition [of Indian citizenship] may be, you can be assured that the Hindus and Sikhs of Pakistan cannot be considered as aliens in India."[28] In Patel's view, all Hindus and Sikhs who resided in Pakistan were a natural part of an Indian nation, and this underpinned the Indian state's position on non-Muslim refugees.

When "serious communal rioting" broke out in Karachi on January 6, 1948, Bhaskar H. Rao, official recorder of the Indian government's *Story of Rehabilitation*, described it as an "orgy of looting and arson" in which the Congress office in Karachi was also attacked.[29] It marked the formal change of the Indian government policy on Sind, and a Director General of Evacuation was appointed on January 14, 1948, to formally assist the evacuation of "non-Muslims who wished to migrate from Sind to India."[30] It was at this point that Sind's "non-Muslim refugees" became officially incorporated as "displaced persons" under the rubric of rehabilitation in Indian legislations to follow.

The Indian government's response to Sind's Hindus specifically, and to Hindus and Sikhs in Pakistan more generally, offered a resolution to where these communities might belong. They could migrate to the territory of India and become Indian citizens, and this remained the case even as restrictions on movement and citizenship laws began to be formulated over the following years. This Indian position dramatically set apart and heightened the question of Muslim belonging, as both the Indian and the Pakistani governments handled Muslim refugees with considerable ambiguity.

STATES OF EMERGENCY

Although "peaceful" conditions in Karachi were widely remarked upon, it was a relative and contingent "peace," for a state of emergency encompassed most of the subcontinent as stories of violence in Punjab and Delhi circulated through newspapers and by word of mouth. Its discursive effect can be read in two words that appear in all the official reports in Sind—"panic" and "fear." It was thus "a state of uncertainty, bordering on panic" and "the fear complex" that was used to explain the departure of the province's Hindus. Rumors that Hindus would be slaughtered in place of goats and sheep on Id-ul-Zuha day, or that their drinking water would be poisoned or that their properties would be confiscated, entered police records as if they were outrageous and therefore imaginary or fictive fears that were spreading unnecessary panic.[31] But as writings on rumors in moments of social crisis suggest, the "contagion" and meaning of rumors was constituted by the wider context.[32]

Wild rumors operated alongside extremely partisan accounts of the Punjab violence, the growing visible presence of Muslim refugees on the streets, and a reported increase in stabbings and robberies. Police reports list a string of crimes—a Sikh bookbinder's shop set on fire in Saddar, a crockery shop robbed in Joria Bazar, a temple desecrated, and so on.[33] These facts at another time may not have been as alarming to the city's Hindus, but in this context they served to heighten existing anxieties. The Pakistani state attempted to respond with alacrity, and Jinnah was particularly keen that "law and order" in Karachi be given the highest priority. Thus in early September, curfew was imposed in the city as a preventive measure, and then whenever there appeared to be "trouble."

However, curfew alone could not provide the necessary reassurance to the city's Hindu residents. The "trespass of Hindu houses by Moslem refugees"[34] became one of the most common crimes, and probably contributed the most to a sense of a changing social order in which the place of Hindu residents of the city became uncertain. A Sindhi Muslim newspaper described how the arrival of Muslim refugees had resulted in Hindus feeling like "a stranger or a foreigner in his own land of birth." The author noted that "unauthorized forcible occupation of houses and seizures of property" were taking place. He gave an instance when a government servant in Karachi had gone for a walk with his wife after locking the house, but on his return found that it was occupied by Muslim refugees who would not vacate the premises. He also noted that, in Ramaswami quarters, houses of poor people were broken into and quietly occupied in the absence of the occupants.[35]

Gidwani similarly complained to Liaqat about this "lawlessness," as he noted that when "the inmates [of houses] go out on work and duty, the locks are broken open, the belongings pilfered or thrown out and the flats occupied with impunity. When the occupants return and ask for their belongings only they are violently threatened and made to run away."[36] Thus in letters to Kripalani and other Congress leaders, Sindhi Hindus noted with trepidation that "Punjabis," referring to Muslim refugees, had moved into Hindu buildings, making it "very difficult to live."[37]

As police reports began to classify "trouble from the refugee" another letter requested Congress's help in leaving because "ladies cannot move out on the roads being always under the fear of too many Punjabi Muslims moving on the roads."[38] Although an apparently trivial concern, it articulated the uncertainty and fear that was generated by the arrival of "Muslim refugees." Thus many Hindu men who were employed in Karachi or had ancestral homes and businesses here, began to send their wives and children, and other members of their families, to India, while they remained in the city.

However, "Muslim refugees" were not the only source of anxiety. Another account highlighted the role of the Pakistani state in requisitioning and allotting houses in which people were still living. It noted that "although in several cases stay orders have been issued, considerable excitement has been created among Hindus at the notices served on them. It may be noted that only Hindus have been served with such notices." I discuss in the next section the measures taken by the Pakistani state to house the new government in the city. The same account argued that the government "interprets that any house or bungalow with two or three persons constitutes an abandoned property." It stated that it was "true that several persons have sent part of their family outside, but on that ground to drive out the remaining members of the family in the streets looks extremely unreasonable." In addition, it noted that representatives of the Hindu Cooperative Housing Societies had been called by Minister Pir Ilahi Bux, who asked them to give the government four or five bungalows from each society by making "certain adjustments" such as "voluntarily housing two families in one house."[39] This process of "making room" for the new state, albeit a piece-meal process, led to the expression that "Sindhis [were] squeezed out of Sind."[40]

Other letters to the AICC and Kripalani also record similar fears of discrimination in the new state in urging the Indian state for help to leave. One writer argued that "violence in Punjab" coupled with "new Ordinances from the Government [for housing], their Communal Policy in service, education, business" were some of the reasons for leaving Sind. The Piece Goods Merchants Association wrote to Kripalani for assistance in relocating to Bombay, for they felt that "Muslim outsiders" were receiving facilities from the state over the "legitimate rights and interests of the Hindu merchants."[41]

However, not everyone wrote for help to leave. Some wrote seeking reassurances to stay, and their letters suggest that the decision to leave for many was a contingent one. One Shamdas wrote movingly from Sehwan, "well known from Kalander Lal Shabaz whose shrine and fair is famous throughout the world." He worried that if "at any time situation at Karachi and Hyderabad go worse and my relations might migrate . . . what will be the fate of mine and of my valuable property on which my large family of twelve members is depending?" A Mr. Malkani wrote to Nehru that "Sind is today in the grip of a tidal wave of panic and migration which none but you or Bapu [Gandhi] can stop. You alone can allay this panic and reduce the resulting emigration."[42]

A large number of letters were from the employees of Karachi Port Trust, as they had initially believed that they would have the possibility of "opting" to work for India or Pakistan.[43] When they found out that they were not included in this scheme, they wrote individual letters of appeal for help. One Mr. Thadani of the Port Trust made his case to Kripalani as follows:

> I find that many Hindus are leaving Sind. It may be taken for granted that nothing untoward incident may happen in Sind as both Pakistan and Sind governments have taken strong measures to protect minorities but as many have left and many more are thinking of leaving it may appear awkward for the remaining Hindus to remain in Sind. . . . I think all who remain will be without their kith and kins. It will therefore be advisable if one leaves early "sooner the better."[44]

However, the president of the Sarva Hindu Sind Panchayat wrote to Kripalani to ask for the Sind Congress to be dissolved so that his party could instead represent Hindu interests in the Sind legislature, and provide leadership to those who were considering staying but were uncertain. He optimistically "calculated that 70 percent of Sind Hindus will not leave and if things grow better—as it is hoped—a large number of evacuees will return back."[45]

The Panchayat president's analysis foregrounds the contingent nature of many people's decisions to leave their homes, as well as their hope to return if conditions allowed it. It is with this ambivalence that displacements in Sind began, with many people leaving their ancestral homes as a temporary or uncertain decision. However, the shift in the Indian government's official policy toward Sind's Hindus with the establishment of the Director General of Evacuations, and growing disputes over Hindu houses and lands in the effort to house Muslim refugees, slowly congealed the flow of people.

KARACHI'S HOUSING CRISIS

One letter to the Urdu newspaper, *Jang*, argued that there were three groups of displaced persons that the term *muhajir* encompassed in reference to those who had arrived in Karachi and were in need of housing. First, there were Muslim government employees from all over India who had "opted" to work for the Pakistan government and were looking for housing for their families. Second, there were *sarmayadar muhajirs*, those migrants with *sarmaya* or capital who could afford to buy houses for themselves. And finally, there were the *tabah-o-barbad muhajirs* who had lost everything and were destitute.[46]

Prior to Partition, Karachi had been a small provincial center, albeit Jinnah's birthplace, and was declared the new capital when it was offered by the Sind Muslim League.[47] Because the city had to house a federal government and all its personnel, largely coming in from the "outside," in Karachi, and unlike Delhi, a housing crisis was already anticipated, albeit not of the proportions that ensued. Even though government employees were asked not to bring their families with them, Mudie anticipated having to find accommodation for about 20,000 people in one month, an extravagant number given Karachi's size.[48]

The Sindh government vacated a number of its premises for the federal government and several military barracks were converted to house government employees. Despite these measures, for the first years the government of Pakistan operated "out of packing crates, hutments, tents,"[49] and many government employees remained without housing.

Reza recalled with sentiment in his memoir that the "Central Government had to start from scratch with all sorts of make-shift arrangements. Assistant Secretaries and Superintendents had to work in open verandahs. Thorns were used instead of pins, stools and benches were used instead of chairs and no one complained, such was the joy of working for one's own Government and people."[50] Such felicitous recollections of Karachi's beginnings as Pakistan's capital are common in recent writings on Karachi.[51] Amina apa, who initially lived in a room in Martin Quarters, a converted barrack, recalled how seven of her adult brothers and sisters had to live with their elder brother, a government employee, and his wife and children: "*Ek hī nalka tha, aur subha men lambi line lagti thī . . . magar there were no complaints, woh mahol hī esa tha* [there was only one tap, and in the morning a long line would form . . . but there were no complaints, those conditions were such]."

However, these conditions were not felicitous for everyone, or borne with such forbearance by everyone in the city. In order to house the government, legislations were passed to control building materials and requisition housing, which, as I noted earlier, affected the Hindu residents of the city differently. For instance, Mudie saw his housing task as that of displacing the city's Hindu population when he remarked that "[t]he Pakistan Government want to bring 4000 clerks, in addition to officers. To turn 4000 clerks, mostly Hindu, with their wives and "family members" out of their houses in Karachi and to put in their places 4000 Muslims, mostly from the Punjab and the UP, in one month, is administratively impossible except under war conditions."[52]

However, when government servants began arriving from the terrible conditions of Purana Qila and other Muslim camps, they came to Karachi with their whole families. As a result there was not even sufficient housing for officers, and the Estates Office in charge of housing government servants in general was inundated with more requests than it could fulfill. One "grief-stricken and poor" government clerk wrote a newspaper story that described his suffering after he arrived at Karachi's train station:

> I spent the night on the platform there only, and then the next morning reported to work. At the same time I put in a request for a quarter, and then returned to my family on the platform, to find that my family had been removed from the station and put on the street. This was the harshness of the railway officials. Then we

> remained at the station as my wife had fever and we were worried. I wrote clearly in my request that my wife and children are sick because they have spent the last three months in extreme hardship.[53]

He went on to narrate the ill-treatment he received at the Estates Office, and concluded that "*itna tabah-o-barbad ho-ne ke ba"d abhi kuch kami reh gaī thī jo yahan puri ho rahi hai* [after being devastated so much if there was anything left it is being completed here]."

There were Muslim League supporters and educated and wealthier Muslims, the *sarmayadars*, who had chosen to move to Pakistan or establish second homes here, and in anticipation of Partition had bought houses in the city. Mudie noted that "[t]he leading Muslim Advocate in Lucknow told me recently that he was to retire in a year and settle down in Karachi, and one of the largest Muslim *taluqdars* in Oudh bought a house here about two months ago. Even the Nawab of Bhopal is trying to buy land near Karachi on which to build a house."[54] These *muhajirs* were able to buy properties from departing Hindu families, and this set them apart.

But by early September, Hidayatullah noted that "destitute refugees" were arriving in Karachi at the rate of 400 daily.[55] By mid-September, 27,000 refugees were reported to have come to Sind, and a week later their numbers had doubled.[56] It was these Muslim refugees who were considered to be the "refugee problem"[57] since the increase in incidents of violence in the city was associated with them, and they were received with some hostility by the Sind government. Initially there were no arrangements for organizing them into camps, and they quickly became a visible presence in the city as footpaths filled up.[58] By the time some camps were set up many more refugees had arrived, and housing refugees became a critical issue.

The housing crisis put the Pakistani state in a predicament similar to that of the Indian state with Delhi. On the one hand the Pakistani state was attempting to reassure Sind's Hindus to remain in their homes but on the other there were thousands of shelterless Muslim refugees. However, in response to the housing crisis, the government passed the Sind Economic Rehabilitation Bill for taking over "abandoned" properties and allotting them to Muslim refugees. This task of taking over and allotting "abandoned" houses to *muhajirs* fell to the Rent Controller's Office. A Custodian of Evacuee Property was not set up in Karachi until 1948, for unlike the Punjab and Delhi there had been no instant "mass abandonment" due to violence. This also made the Rent Controller's task an extremely difficult one, for although Hindus were leaving, it was unclear if a house was "abandoned" or not if the owner left without declaring his intentions. As I argued earlier, in those conditions most people were uncertain of the future and their decisions to leave were largely tentative, contingent. So many had locked their homes and gone but, with the hope of returning once conditions improved. Furthermore, in many cases part of a family remained in Karachi while another left for India. So although Hindus were leaving, their houses were not "empty." At the same time "abandoned houses" were being demanded by angry Muslim refugees who claimed an entitlement to the new nation-state.

The first large group of Muslim refugees arrived from Delhi. The Urdu newspaper *Jang*, which had also moved from Delhi to Karachi, initially catered to Delhi's Muslim refugees, carrying announcements of those who had arrived and were looking for their relatives, lists of missing people, and detailed stories of what was going on in Delhi. Hakims, tailors, restaurants, and a number of other businesses used *Jang* to announce their new addresses in Karachi, as well as to invite job applications from cooks and tailors specifically from Delhi. This was also where *muhajir* grievances were registered, and it is here that the struggles over housing are most evident.

Muhajir anger was two-fold—on the one hand it was directed against the Pakistani state and in particular the Sind government, and on the other it was directed against Hindus of the city. The ambiguous reception of the Sind government toward *muhajirs* led to complaints of ill-treatment and "un-islamic behaviour"[59] for not receiving them with the hospitality that they had expected of *ansārs,* following the example of the people of Medina who received Mohammad and his *muhajirs* in A.D. 622. The cartoons in *Jang* are graphic expressions of this sense of being duped or deceived into believing that they would be welcomed in Pakistan, which would be a haven for them (see figures 2.1 and 2.2). As one *Jang* editorial remarked, "the heaven that [they] had imagined and come to, it is completely different from that."[60]

The perception that the government did not care about their well-being was most pronounced when a Muhajir Committee, set up by the government of Sind, resigned on the grounds that they were unable to do their job of housing *muhajirs*. *Jang* argued that although the committee had presented its problems to the chief minister of Sind, they were met with indifference. In addition, the Rent Controller's Office became the focus of a great deal of dissatisfaction, since some felt it had become corrupt in the face of a demand for houses that exceeded supply. There

FIGURE 2.1 "What sycophancy (*khushamad*) to win our hearts / How eyes turned away after obtaining what was wanted," *Jang*, January 1, 1948. Right image, a Sindhi says to a Delhi/UP Muslim, before Partition was obtained, "Please come, the memory of Muhajireen-e-Medina will come alive." Left image, after Partition was obtained: "Sind is only for Sindhis. You get out!"

At bottom: Maulana Shabbir Ahmad Usmani has said that before the establishment of Pakistan, Muslims were told that the new government would protect 10 crore Muslims, but now the ill-fated Muslims are being told that in Pakistan there is no space for them.

were charges that only "those who bribe get a house," and that in return for payoffs several allotment orders were being issued for a single house. Thus *Jang* argued that "poor *muhajirs* who get an allotment order do not get a house because several allotment notices are issued because of the high amount of corruption."[61]

Because the Rent Controller's Office was the only means to officially obtain houses for those who could not afford to buy them, *muhajirs* gathered there every day in large numbers. It is not surprising that it became the site of many altercations. On one occasion, *Jang* reported that a refugee entered the Rent Controller's Office to tell him

FIGURE 2.2 "Here work is done by donkeys," *Jang*, December 9, 1947. The pickets read as follows: "BSc. London, Dr. of Lit. (Germany), B.A. Aligarh, Poet/Writer, Artist, B.A. (Oxon) Bar-at-Law, B.A. LLB, etc." The message is that in Pakistan's capital, donkeys are employed, but educated people are lying around and no one is even taking the work of a donkey cart driver from them.

his complaints, and the rent controller slapped and pushed him out of his office. This immediately fed into a general perception of insult and ill-treatment of *muhajirs* in the new state, and a threatening crowd gathered and started chanting anti–rent controller slogans. A frightened rent controller, it was reported, sneaked out through a back door and the office was closed. *Jang* sympathized with the *muhajir* predicament when it remarked that "on the one hand non-Muslims are asking twice thrice the price for their houses and goods, and on the other hand people who have to go to the Rent Controller's Office have to face so much harassment."[62]

Thus government attempts to convince Sindhi Hindus to stay in the province were criticized by *muhajirs* as "the Hindu-appeasing policy" of

FIGURE 2.3 "We left Delhi but they haven't left us," *Jang*, December 26, 1947. Right to left, counterclockwise: 1) In Delhi, Hindu army fires at a Muslim. 2) In Delhi, Hindu police beat a Muslim with a stick. 3) In Delhi, a Muslim is evicted from his house. 4) After coming to Pakistan, a Hindu landlord says "Get out or I'll call the police." 5) In offices, Hindu employees place obstacles. A Muslim controller says, "It's only twelve o'clock. How will work get done like this?" The Hindu replies, "We only work for ourselves." 6) Now Muslims have to understand [illegible] if they are in Pakistan or not.

the government, and Hindus became the focus of both anger and suspicion. While many *muhajirs*, including those from Delhi, were survivors of considerable violence, the resentment of ill-treatment elsewhere became directed against Hindus in Sind. A cartoon titled "We left Delhi but they have not left us" illustrates this sentiment (see figure 2.3). There was indignation that Hindus were evacuating safely to India while Muslim refugees were being "plundered" in India. "Sind's Hindus are so lucky," one article remarked, "that although the rest of the country is on fire Sindh is safe . . . and they are able to sell their ten-year-old and small houses for double, triple the price."[63] In addition, Hindu loyalty to Pakistan was questioned, as described in the cartoon which declared that their hearts were still in India (see figure 2.4). Sinister intentions were attributed to

FIGURE 2.4 "Come and give a helping hand," *Jang*, March 23, 1948. The car being pushed is marked "Pakistan." The man says to the "Hindu" standing aside, "Wearing our clothes is not enough. Your heart is still in India. Come and give a helping hand." Note: Quaid-e-Azam has told Parliament members from East Bengal in answer to a question that they have to help run the government.

the city's Hindus as claims were made by *Jang* that "for the third time attempts have been made to poison the water tank of government quarters at Jacob Lines and Jat Lines." (See figure 2.5.) It remarked with bitterness that "yet the Sind government is dreaming of their return."[64]

By questioning their degree of belonging and rendering them suspicious, an equation emerged in *muhajir* opinion whereby Hindus were believed to be leaving (sooner or later) and so their houses were there for the taking. If there were still people living in the houses this was only because they were trying to sell or rent their properties to the *sarmayadar muhajirs*. "Karachi's rich Hindus" (as well as Sind's Muslims, as in figure 2.6) were seen as making a profit out of their plight, in particular through the customary *pagri* system. A *pagri* was a form of "illegal payment" that had developed as a way to circumvent colonial rent restrictions. Landlords demanded a large lump-sum payment in lieu of the low monthly rent, and this also made it very difficult for refugees without means to rent houses in the city.[65]

نئی دیوانگی
WATER TANK
اطلاع ملی ہے کہ جیکب لائن کے پانی کے ٹینک میں زہر ملانے والے گرفتار شدہ ہندو کو
ہندو پولیس افسر نے پاگل قرار دیا ہے۔

FIGURE 2.5 "New Madness," *Jang*, November 19, 1947. "We have received news that the Hindu who tried to poison the Jacob Lines tank was arrested by a Hindu policeman who has deemed him to be mad." In the image he is being taken to the mental asylum instead of the city jail.

This situation, combined with the corruption and inefficiencies of the Rent Controller's Office, was seen as leaving poor *muhajirs* on the streets with no choice but to "break in and occupy houses." Breaking in was still not a resolution to their housing problem, for after forcible occupation, "they go and submit a request for allotment for that house. But if someone has already submitted an application for that house before him, then the house is allotted to the first person, who comes with the police to take possession, and the second *muhajir* is once again on the street." Thus the poor refugees were "roaming with their families from place to place."[66]

Jang editorials were largely sympathetic to these seizures, and explained that:

> In this regard, Hindus have also left, but leaving behind one or two persons in the house. Often *muhajirs* find such people's closed

FIGURE 2.6 "Lo, they are also saying that there is honor and shame / If I knew that I would not have given up my home," *Jang*, December 1, 1947. Right, *muhajir* says: "Thank God! I have reached Pakistan." He receives the reply: "You are welcome, you are our Muslim brother." Left image, *muhajir* says: "I need a house to live in." He receives the reply: "Brother, first arrange the money for the *pagri*."

> houses and they think that they are empty, and therefore they try to occupy/seize it. Hindus complain, make a noise and run away from Sind. Then the government tries to stop them and for this it comes up with such harsh policies.[67]

The "harsh policies" that the government adopted involved reversing these occupations through police intervention. These attempts were represented in *Jang* as denying *muhajirs* of their rightful housing. One letter to *Jang* complained of a "Hindu policeman" in Artillery Maidan who despite "hundreds of empty houses" in the area, prevented those even with permits from the rent controller from occupying the houses there. The writer complained that "without finding out the occupying Muslim's position he speaks in a crude and rough manner and this is unacceptable."[68]

Several proposals were put forward, none of which involved the Rent Controller's Office, to identify houses which were truly "empty." One plan was for the government of Sind to announce that any Hindu leaving Karachi should inform the Refugee Committee that his room would be "empty," and be allowed to leave only on approval from the committee. This way the Refugee Committee could make a list and provide housing to the Muslim refugees.[69] Another article in *Jang* argued that "stopping the fleeing Hindus and finding housing for the *muhajirs*" were connected problems: Hindus were leaving because "*muhajir*een threaten them" in order to get housing. Therefore identifying "empty houses" was imperative. The Muhajir Committee could be given extended powers to find houses and issue orders for occupation. In order to find "empty houses" the ration card should be taken of any Hindu leaving Karachi, and from that their home address could be found out and added to "the list of vacated houses." Furthermore, only fifteen days should be given to Hindus who make "the excuse of temporary departure" and then the house should be considered vacated. Also, the Muhajir Committee should enforce allotments and not allow transfers in order to end competing occupations and *pagri-bazi*.[70]

The Sind government was unlikely to give such powers to a Muhajir Committee, and continued trying to reverse occupations which were increasing with growing numbers of *muhajirs*. In December, a crowd of reportedly over five hundred refugees gathered and attempted to forcefully occupy a building which still had people living in it. The residents fought back the attackers, and the police arrived and removed the *muhajir* intruders. *Jang* focused on the plight of the homeless refugees and described them as screaming and yelling in desperation when they were brutally pulled out by the police.[71] But such occupations, despite their reversals, could only have been terrifying for the residents, as they became threatened on an everyday basis.

The riots of January 6, 1948, were in a sense a continuation of this ongoing violence, and massive looting and seizures of houses were an important part of the riots. The scale and visible nature of the violence dispelled the notional "peace" in Karachi, and sharpened contending political discourses. It became an occasion for local Hindu leaders as well as Sindhi Congressmen in India to emphasize that "Hindus no longer feel safe in Sind," but it also allowed the Sind government to announce that there was no more place for *muhajirs*.[72]

Jang made conciliatory statements that Sind's Hindus should not leave. Since refugees were targets of policing and the refugee camps were searched for arms, *Jang* complained it was unfair to blame *muhajirs* for the violence. As one article argued, "Muslim *muhajirs* saved not just one, but hundreds of Hindu lives," the present restrictions against them were unwarranted, and the searches were particularly harsh. Khuhro was targeted for his statements blaming *muhajirs* for the violence, and led one editorial to state that "the premier of Sind is a friend of the Hindus and does not want to see Hindustan's Muslim *muhajirs* in Sind."[73]

SURPLUS AND QUOTAS

As Sara Ansari has argued, Sindhi Muslim leaders tried to limit the flow of Muslim refugees into the province because they began to fear that the refugees would benefit more than Sind's Muslims from Partition, and that Sind's economic and cultural life would be impaired by the Hindu exodus.[74] As a result, tensions arose between the Sind government and the Pakistan government as to how many Muslim refugees Sind could accommodate as part of rehabilitation efforts. A file on the discussion between the provincial and central government is quite revealing of the science of planning and rehabilitation in the making of a national economy of a modern state.

The Ministry of Refugees and Rehabilitation argued, on the basis of figures provided by the MEO, that West Punjab had received a "surplus" of 12 lakh refugees. The notion of "surplus" was based on numbers of Muslim refugees that had arrived "over and above the non-Muslim population that ha[d] left the province" of West Punjab. It was stated that this "excess" was composed entirely of "agriculturalists" since the "exchange" of "urban non-agriculturalists" had been almost equal.[75] In order to "distribute" this surplus, a conference of district officers was held November 22 and 23, 1947, at Lahore to discuss how many refugees each district could "absorb." "Quotas" were set for each province, and it was agreed by the bureaucrats present that Sind should "absorb" 5 lakh of this "excess." Their planning was informed by "A Note on Statistics of the Refugees and Evacuees Problem," a set of tables and charts prepared by Professor M. Hasan at the Secretary of the Board of Economic Inquiry of West Punjab.[76]

This quantifying of people into classifiable populations that could be neatly represented in calculations of planning is not in itself remarkable. James C. Scott has argued how aspirations of "legibility" have been central to a bureaucratic and scientific control of "reality" and this is borne out here.[77] A statistical notion of "surplus" and "quotas" was extracted from the terror and confusion of people's lives, to make "refugees" manageable in a national economy. However, these calculations had far-reaching power in constructing a political common sense about how many Muslim refugees the Pakistani state could accommodate. In this equation, the Pakistani state was a finite territorial entity which could only accommodate as many people as equaled those "non-Muslim refugees" who were leaving. The notion of surplus or excess was predicated on assumptions about how many people a piece of land could support, assumptions which more contemporary debates on "overpopulation" and "population control" have since brought into question.[78]

Furthermore, Professor Hasan based his "absorption figures" for Sind on the numbers of "non-Muslim evacuees *who must have left the Province of Sind by now*." According to Hasan, Sind had 7.81 lakh non-Muslim "agriculturalists or rural non-agriculturalists," and "as *most of these must have left Sind*" (both emphases added), he argued that the province could accept 5 lakh Muslim refugees in their place. However, he himself noted that his calculations faced the "limitation that all non-Muslims will not be evacuating from Sind." Here the term "evacuee" no longer meant a person leaving to take temporary refuge, but rather presumed a permanent departure, and an entire religious community was being regarded as "evacuee" to make "space" in a new nation regarded as both territorially and corporeally contained.

When Sind's political leaders refused to accept their "quotas" of refugees and contended that Sind could instead accept only 1.5 lakh refugees, the quibble over numbers was not, as Scott argues, merely planning gone wrong, because on-the-ground realities had not been sufficiently accounted for. "Planning" by the new state had to grapple with an emerging politics of entitlement to the nation. It is important to note here that in the discussions that ensued there was no argument on the calculated numbers of departing "non-Muslims," or on the question of their possible return to their homes.

Ayub Khuhro, in a letter to Jinnah, argued that Hasan's figures were incorrect on a number of accounts. Khuhro stated that there were 14 lakh Hindus in Sind but most of these were living in urban areas and 2.5 lakh in Karachi alone. However, he argued that 4 lakh Muslims had already "replaced the outgoing urban Hindus since the 15th of August 1947," and in other towns of Sind the population had also doubled. Furthermore, people were still coming in by rail from Rajputana and by ship to Karachi, and there was "no means of stopping or controlling this influx." Thus Khuhro pointed out that Muslim refugees coming in from outside divided Punjab were not being included in the official resettlement calculus, but were a reality in Sind.

Khuhro argued importantly that in rural areas, the center of contention, "the Hindus were no doubt owners of land but it was the Muslim who actually tilled the soil," and the Sindhi Muslim peasants should have first rights to the land. Thus according to Khuhro, this left only lands abandoned by Sikhs in Sind, an area which could support 10,000 families, that is, a total of 50,000 people. In addition, Sind's [Muslim] zamindars might perhaps be persuaded to employ another 10,000 families. By this means he considered it possible to resettle not more than 1 lakh refugees.[79]

Khuhro's resistance to the central government's rehabilitation figures was based on claims of entitlement for Sind's Muslims to the new economy of the nation. But his calculations of how many Muslim refugees could be accommodated on Sind's lands drew upon the same assumptions as that of the central government—that the land could support only the number of "evacuees" who were leaving. This conception, of people on land in an economy of the modern state, filtered into political debates on how many Muslim refugees from India a finite territory could accommodate, and thus there was a perceived legitimate need to draft limits to the proclaimed nation.

UNMAKING THE "MUSLIM NATION"

If Professor Hasan's statistics provided a mathematical clarity for the shaping of bureaucratic policy, there were also numerous claims on the idea of the Muslim nation which now had to contend with these calculations of the modern state. In both *Jang* and *Al-Jamiat*, in Karachi and Delhi, editorials and articles debated the ambiguous status of Muslims who remained in India in the midst of massive, ongoing displacements. They attempted to reconcile ideas of a Muslim nation with shifting realities of two nation-states, and had divergent views on the ongoing Hindu exodus from the city.

As Muslim refugees in Karachi confronted substantial ambivalence from the Sind government, which wanted to restrict their numbers, an important narrative of "*muhajir qurbani*" or "sacrifice" began to take shape as a trope to claim inclusion in the emerging nation-state. This trope made claims to extraordinary entitlement to Pakistan by arguing that *muhajirs*, or north Indian Muslims, had been at the forefront of the Pakistan movement, and had made the greatest *qurbani* for it by leaving their homes in India. For instance, one *Jang* editorial argued:

> *Pak sarzameen Karachi men ek taraf Hind se muhajireen ārahe hain. In men ziyāda tar log hain jo Pakistan ka 'alam baland karne aur Pakistan hasil karne men sab se ziyada qurbanian di hain.*
>
> *Muhajirs* are coming from India to the pure land of Karachi. Most of these people made the most sacrifices for raising the flag of Pakistan and for obtaining Pakistan.

This trope would gain increasing prominence in the ensuing years as a way of arguing against growing restrictions by the Pakistani state on the coming of Muslim refugees from India. It was also fundamentally tied to the argument that Muslims in India could not be legitimately excluded from a Pakistani nation-state, for they were a part of a Muslim nation that the very idea of Pakistan was meant to "safeguard."

In the introduction I referred to H.S. Suhrawardy's extraordinary address to the first Constituent Assembly of Pakistan, in which he argued that there was no contradiction in continuing to live in India and being a member of Pakistan's legislature. The core of his address centered on Pakistan's responsibility to Muslims that remained in India:

> At the time when we were divided, it was not said as I have heard it said by the Satraps of Pakistan that Muslims of the Indian Union were warned that you will be in the hopeless minority, that you may be exterminated, that you may have to suffer all kinds of difficulties, that you may be enchained, enslaved and that the Muslims of the Indian Union then said that it did not matter if that was going to be their lot so long as a large number of their brethren living in the majority Provinces were able to have an administration of their own. . . . Sir, that is only one side of the story. The other side of the story was that you told the Muslims of the Indian Union at the same time that the division of India would solve the communal problem; that that would be the greatest safeguard for the minorities within Pakistan and the greatest safeguard for the minorities within the Indian Union. You have forgotten that aspect of it. . . . Your corners are closed to the Muslims of the Indian Union. You have said that they may not come here and perhaps, Sir, from the point of view of Pakistan that is the best policy, because if the Muslims of the Indian Union have to leave those shores and are decimated on the way, say, out of three crores even one and a half crores find their way struggling into Pakistan, Pakistan will be overwhelmed. It is perhaps true that you have no other alternative but to say that. I do not want you, Sir, to fight for me . . . I want you to give a fair deal to the minorities in Pakistan.[80]

His address grappled with the claim of the Pakistan movement that "the division of India would solve the communal problem." But how was the reality of a Pakistani state to serve as a "safeguard" for the Muslim minorities in India? Although critical of attempts to keep out Muslim refugees, he believed that the state would be "overwhelmed" if large numbers of Muslim refugees came to Pakistan, and argued that there was "no other alternative" but to give "a fair deal to minorities in Pakistan" as a way to protect Muslim minorities in India.

This was the "hostage theory," and it found repeated expression in the public debates that followed. After the riots of January 6, 1948, a *Jang* editorial appealed to the paper's *muhajir* readers to maintain peace in the city, since riots in Karachi would adversely affect Muslim minorities in India. It argued that:

> *Hindustani musalman Pakistan ke musalmanon se kuch nahin chahtā. Woh sirf us se tadabur aur sabr ki bheek mangtā raha hai. Hame chahye ke hum un apne bhaion ko jin ki qurbanion se hame dolat-e-āzadi naseeb huī hai un ki zindagiyon ko khatre men nahin ḍale.*

> Hindustan's Muslims don't ask anything of Pakistan's Muslims. They only beg of them forbearance and patience. We should not put the lives of our brothers, whose sacrifices have given us this treasure of freedom, in danger.[81]

This logic of the "hostage theory" tied the treatment of Muslim minorities in India to the treatment meted out to Hindus in Pakistan. Muslim refugees in Karachi had to be "patient" with Hindus in the city, for aggression on their part could put their "brothers" who remained in India in jeopardy. This formulation made Muslims in Pakistan responsible for the well-being of Hindustan's Muslims, and for Muslim refugees/*muhajirs* this link had meaning not only through an abstract imaginary of a Muslim nation, but through real ties of family and friends. However, to make an argument for Pakistan's duty toward Muslims in India, the diversity of Muslims who remained in India was harnessed to the cause of Pakistan. For instance, one *Jang* editorial wrote that "those poor [Muslims in India], their only fault is that they are Muslims and have spent their whole life at the forefront in the support of Muslim League."[82]

It is striking, then, that in Delhi's *Al-Jamiat*, an Urdu newspaper of the pro-Congress Jamiat-e-Ulema-e-Hind, Pakistan was also held responsible for collective Muslim well-being through the treatment of its hostage religious minorities:

> In Pakistan, extreme concern is being shown for 4 crore Indian Muslims, but Pakistan better open its ears and listen that by upsetting their non-Muslim people they are doing no service to us. All roads to our aid are closed, except one—the [good] treatment of their non-Muslims.[83]

This is one of the reasons why the Hindu exodus from Karachi became so significant, for the near-total departure of non-Muslims from West Pakistan unsettled the workability of this tenuous hostage theory. Thus it became important, according to opinions in *Al-Jamiat,* that conditions be created in Pakistan for Hindus who had left *to return back* to their homes. It was argued that this refugee return was the "human and religious duty" of the Pakistan government. *Al-Jamiat* campaigned vociferously for reversing displacements and for the return of refugees to their homes. For instance, it promoted the "Phir Basao Conference" led by Lala Bhim Singh for the return of Hindus and Sikhs to their ancestral homes in West Punjab.

An announcement in *Al-Jamiat* (see figure 2.7) is particularly poignant in making this point. It appealed to Delhi's Muslims to write letters to Liaqat Ali Khan, who was to visit Delhi, to not only bring back Sind's Hindus, but also cancel the agreement on the transfer of populations in divided Punjab. It argued that this, the return of a substantial religious minority in West Pakistan, was the only possibility for Muslims in India to "live in peace."[84] It is noteworthy that this letter-writing campaign focused on Liaqat Ali Khan, and not the Congress leadership of independent India.

However, in *Jang*, in opposition to reversing displacements to uphold a failing hostage theory, there also emerged ideas of a total "exchange of populations." This total "exchange of populations" had been clamored for by a range of different groups, including those who saw it as a logical outcome of Partition and essential for the making of a Hindu nation.[85] Here these ideas were attempts to resolve the perceived dilemma of how to "safeguard" Muslims in India. An article on *tabadala-e-ābadi* (exchange of populations) argued that "[d]ue to Pakistan and Partition, crores of Muslims are now slaves of the Indian government, and crores of Hindu have been freed of the Pakistan government." Therefore, given the departure of minority religious communities from West Pakistan, the "Pakistan government should announce that all the Muslims in India should be brought over here." However this exchange was proposed only across the western border, since religious minorities in East and West Bengal were perceived as "balanced."

وزیر اعظم پاکستان کو خط بھیجئے

۱۰ جون کو وزیر اعظم پاکستان دہلی آ رہے ہیں۔ اگر آپ امن و اطمینان کی زندگی چاہتے ہیں تو
نام حسب ذیل مضمون کا خط بھیجئے۔

محترم وزیر اعظم پاکستان! السلام مسنون
پاکستان سے جو غیر مسلم ترک وطن پر مجبور ہوئے ہیں ان کو اطمینان دلا کر واپس
پاکستان میں آباد ہونے کا موقعہ دیجئے ان کے مال اور جان کی حفاظت کا ذمہ لیجئے۔
مشرقی پنجاب اور مغربی پنجاب کے متعلق تبادلہ آبادی کا جو معاہدہ ہوا ہے اس کو
منسوخ کرائیے۔ انڈین یونین کے ساڑھے چار کروڑ مسلمانوں کا یہ متفقہ مطالبہ
ہے۔ اگر آپ نے ہندوستانی مسلمانوں کا یہ متفقہ مطالبہ پورا کر دیا تو ہم آپ کو
یقین دلاتے ہیں کہ دونوں ملک امن و سلامتی اور خوش حالی کا گہوارہ بن جائیں گے

خط کا پتہ یہ ہو گا
مسٹر لیاقت علی خاں وزیر اعظم پاکستان گورنمنٹ ہاؤس نئی دہلی

FIGURE 2.7 "Write a letter to the prime minister of Pakistan," *Al-Jamiat*, June 14, 1948: "The Pakistani prime minister is coming to Delhi. If you want to live in peace then write this letter. 'Dear Prime Minister: The non-Muslims who have been forced to become evacuees from Pakistan should be reassured and brought back to Pakistan and given a chance to resettle, and responsibility should be taken to protect their property and lives. The agreement on the transfer of populations between East and West Punjab should be cancelled. Indian Union's four and a half crore Muslims are making this proposition. If the Indian Muslims' proposition is accepted, believe us, both countries will live in peace and prosperity.'"

Importantly, this notion that the chief constraint against all Muslims coming from India to Pakistan lay in the latter's territorial limits (an equation of how many people a land's resources could support) was resolved by making such an exchange conditional upon an expansion of those territorial limits through mutual negotiation with India. This idea of a total exchange of populations on the basis of religious community, and conditioned on more land, reappeared, as we shall see, with greater force in ensuing years.[86]

The belief that Muslims who remained in India were brothers who needed to be saved (*apne bichare hue bhaion ko bachane ke liye*) was so strong in the *muhajir* press that the predicament that the state could not shoulder "the burden" of unlimited Muslim refugees, whom it was nevertheless obligated to protect, found repeated expression:

> ... now the biggest problem facing both governments is how to protect the minorities in both places. We cannot accept that Pakistan rejoin the Indian Union and are opposed to it ... at the same time we cannot leave the [Muslim] minorities unprotected ... [A]t the present time Pakistan cannot take the burden of India's Muslims, if they should migrate and come to Pakistan ... so how should these innocent Muslims be saved, who because they fought and struggled so hard for Pakistan, are now in this unenviable predicament.[87]

Others suggested an intergovernmental mechanism like the Minority Board, but it was believed that such a board could only be effective if a significant number of Hindus remained in Pakistan. Therefore the refrain—"We must try and keep as many Hindus as possible in Pakistan to protect the Muslim minorities on the other side"—found repeated articulation. One of the recommendations of the Minority Board had been that both the All India Muslim League and the All India Congress should cease to function as unified organizations operating in two states, and be separated in command and direction. One of the reasons for its recommendation was that because the Muslim League was being blamed for the Partition, Muslims in India were being persecuted. But there was opposition to this idea on the grounds that the Muslim League was deemed responsible for all Muslims of the subcontinent, and north Indian Muslims "who were in the forefront of the League's struggle for Pakistan" needed to be strengthened, not abandoned, by Pakistan's Muslim League.[88] Thus this proposal by the Minority Board for improving the condition of Muslim minorities in India was perceived as severing ties between Pakistan's Muslims and India's Muslims, and this was considered unacceptable at the time.

One writer proposed that a stronger Pakistani high commissioner be appointed in India. This high commissioner would take an active role in the protection of Muslim minorities there, go wherever there were "communal problems," and "talk to the Indian government in strong and fearless terms."[89] The writer's proposal was of course unclear about how a Pakistani high commissioner's authority would be constituted, or what would be the national status of the group the high commissioner would be protecting as a representative of the Pakistani state.

In another "solution" to the predicament of Muslims that remained in India, a *Jang* editorial tried to gather support for a proposal put forward by the editor of Patna's *New Life* newspaper. Syed Mohammad Jalil argued that it had become impossible for them, Indian Muslims, to remain as Muslims in India, and that this was ultimately "the failure of Pakistan." His view of the Indian Muslim predicament (or *Jang*'s representation of it) was extremely dire. In his view there were only three "roads" open to Indian Muslims: 1) to migrate to Pakistan, but there was not enough space for them there; 2) to become Hindu, but this was also not deemed acceptable; or 3) to be slowly killed off.

Given this dire landscape, it was with some urgency that Jalil suggested the creation of "Muslim zones" within India where the 4.5 crore Muslim minorities could be protected. He asked *muhajirs* to fight alongside the Muslims in India to appeal to the United Nations to intervene and protect Indian Muslims. He argued that even if the UN refused to take any action, at least their plight would be given the status of an "inter-national" issue. Then pressure could be brought to bear upon the Indian government to make distinct "Muslim zones" within Indian territory where Muslims could live with security.[90] This idea of multiple "Muslim zones" within India was not particularly original, and drew upon previous schemes from the 1930s formulated prior to the Pakistan demand.[91] The Muslim predicament, argued as an "inter-national" problem, carried now all the burden of the creation of Pakistan itself; these zones would be dubbed and attacked as "miniature Pakistans."

Jang took Jalil's appeal to *muhajirs*, to fight on behalf of Muslims in India very seriously, and argued that it was time the *muhajirs* took a leading role in organizing to protect their brothers in India. There was also a sense of bewilderment at the unmaking of an imagined "Muslim nation" with the realization of a Pakistani state, for, as one editorial noted, "at this time Muslims [in India] have no choice but to be patient. But we, Pakistani Muslims, what should we do, what part should we play in this drama? The truth is that we do not, nor does anyone else, have an answer to this question."[92]

It is striking that north Indian Muslims in Karachi and Delhi saw themselves as part of a shared landscape, albeit a shifting and uncertain one. In this context, *Jang* and its readers in Karachi faced a two-pronged struggle as the Pakistani state seemingly faltered in fulfilling its many expectations. M*uhajirs* found they had to fight for inclusion in a Pakistani state that viewed Muslim refugees with ambiguity, and they struggled to make the case for Pakistan's responsibility toward Muslims remaining in India. Political imagination and the realities of displacements could not be easily reconciled, and it was by no means self-evident to most of the displaced how *or where* their lives should unfold.

Moving People, Immovable Property

3. Refugees, Boundaries, Citizens

It's well known that he who returns never left . . .[1]

In the previous chapters I attempted to open up the categorical closure that accompanies Partition's indelible images, of Hindu and Sikh refugees moving to India and Muslim refugees to Pakistan, by examining the contingent and uncertain conditions in which they moved. Yet the power of these images in a national ordering has been such that I was surprised when I discovered that in 1948 the tide turned, and large numbers of north Indian Muslim refugees began to return to their homes in India. This return had enormous significance, for the first restrictions on movement in the region came in the form of an emergency permit system instituted by the Indian government to stem this tide and led to the introduction of citizenship provisions ahead of the constitution itself.

Any claim of "discovery" is built upon some hierarchy of knowledge which structures silences. However, silences are produced not only by what is said, but also by what we think is important to ask. It is at this conjunction of the "unspeakable" and the "unthinkable" that personal experience escapes the significance of history.[2] It was my interview with Rafi bhai in Delhi that led me to investigate the permit system. In the aftermath of the horrific violence in the city, his family of committed Congressites realized that most of their extended kin had left for Pakistan. Thus he recounted how in early 1948 he traveled with his paternal grandfather, his *dada*, and his parents to Pakistan to look for their departed relatives:

RAFI BHAI: *Jab Pakistan gaye 1948 men azizon ko dekhne ke liye, in men se kon bacha kon kis hāl men hai . . . phir hum log Pakistan men to permit ka system shuru ho gaya. Is waqt tak koi system nahin tha. Phir ekdam se ye hua ke permit ho gaya . . . to phir permit le kar āye to yāni ye bahut strange bāt hai ke jo log Pakistan chale gaye the un men se koi ādmi ye kahe. Har log the. Jaise Pakistan ke governor-general jo the, us waqt Ghulam Mohammad woh Aligarh ke paṛhe hue the. Hamare dada ke marasi the usī zamane ke liye aur phir . . . unhon ne bhī kaha aur, aur bhī jannewalle the ke āp ab āgae hai jaye nahin. Yahin rehye. Magar zindagī bhar ek usool par committed rahe. To us ākhri umar ke hisse men jo hai us ko think karnā – yāni Muslim League ke khilāf the ye log aur Congress ke sāth the. To is liye un ne tasleem nahin kiyā. Aur woh Hindustan āgae. To Hindustan men ye tamasha hua ke –ke jo hamarī jāedād thī woh evacuee qarar kardī gaī. . . . Sārā jo case tha woh laṛte rahe akele yahan par . . .*

AUTHOR: *Kiya case?*

RAFI BHAI: *Citizenship ka mā'mlā tha.*

AUTHOR: *Kaise?*

RAFI BHAI: *Pakistan chale gae wahan se āe hai to barhāl inhon ne sabit kar diya ke main jāne se phele tak tankhwa leta raha hun. Yahan men ne resign nahin kiya. Yahan mera lian hai aur bas main chuṭī par gaya tha apne azizon se milne aur mera koi irādā Pakistan men rahne ka nahin tha. Government of India ne phir one of the gazettes of India declared that we are citizens of India.*

RAFI BHAI: When we went to Pakistan in 1948, to see our relatives, of them who had survived, how they were . . . then when we were in Pakistan, then the permit system started. Until then there was no system. There was no system. Then suddenly . . . so we obtained a permit to return. But this was a strange thing that those people who had gone to Pakistan, of them anyone would say this. There were all sorts of people there. Like the governor-general of Pakistan. At this time it was Ghulam Mohammad. He had studied at Aligarh. Our grandfather, *dada,* was his classmate. At this time and then . . . even he said and others who had gone,

"You have come now, don't go. Stay here." But all his life he had one principle to which he had remained committed. So at this, at the last stage of his life, to even think this—I mean he was against the Muslim League, these people, and was with the Congress. So that is why he never acknowledged them. And he came to Hindustan. In Hindustan there was this drama that our properties were declared evacuee . . . all that he did then was fight, alone, the case . . .

AUTHOR: What case?

RAFI BHAI: It was a matter of citizenship.

AUTHOR: How come?

RAFI BHAI: Had gone to Pakistan and come back from there. Anyhow he proved it that I until I left was drawing my pay. Here I have not resigned. Here is my life, and that I had just gone on my vacation to visit my relatives and that I had no intention of staying in Pakistan. The Government of India then in one of the *Gazettes* declared that we are citizens of India.

According to Rafi bhai, his family had gone to Pakistan to visit relatives in concern for their well-being, and therefore their return home should have been unremarkable. Furthermore, in all my other interviews and conversations with divided families no one had mentioned something that could be called a "return movement," and so at first I considered their family's experience an entirely personal one. It was to understand how travel on a permit could lead to a court case about citizenship that initially directed my archival research, for it seemed extraordinary that a mere vacation could have such grave consequences.

In addition, it did not occur to me to ask *why* a permit system had been established, for the regulation of movement seemed an accepted part of statehood, and therefore a *natural* intermediary to a passport system. John Torpey and Radhika Mongia have shown how in Europe and North America this technology of modern statehood came to be instituted within specific debates on nation, territory, and citizenship in the nineteenth and early twentieth century.[3] Yet I took it for granted that in the Indian subcontinent such controls on movement came as fully formed parts of an already established international order.

When I began to look for information about the permit system I found a startling abundance of sources, as if the vast governmental paper trail on "returning Muslim refugees" could hardly be considered a discovery at all. We have seen how the Muslim exodus was shaped by attempts to rehabilitate Hindu and Sikh refugees. This governmental discourse on returning Muslim refugees was similarly also tied to planning for refugee rehabilitation, and provided the logic for the institution of permits to control the movement of refugees.

Rafi bhai pointed out the suddenness with which the permit system came into place, such that many like his family were caught utterly by surprise.[4] Rafi bhai's surprise was not unfounded. The Partition Council, which oversaw the administrative division of British India, had left the question of nationality laws to the two emerging states but had gone so far as to amend British Indian passport rules "so that there should be no restrictions on the movement of persons from one Dominion to another."[5] Thus when the government of India unilaterally announced on July 14, 1948, the introduction of the permit system across its western frontier with Pakistan, and then promulgated the Influx from Pakistan (Control) Ordinance to enforce this control regime by making entering India without a permit a criminal and punishable act[6]—for people of the subcontinent at the time this was not a natural or an inevitable consequence of Partition's new mapping. The Pakistani government put its own permit system into effect by October 15 and promulgated a parallel Pakistan (Control of Entry) Ordinance 1948.[7] Together these measures formed the first set of restrictions on movement of people between the two postcolonial states, and even though they affected movement across the western border only, it was for many the "real" Partition:

> Government of India invented the permit system and Pakistan on its part has put it into effect, and so the real partition has taken place now, making a distance of a few miles so difficult to cross.[8]

From the moment the permit system was announced by the Indian government, right up to the time it was replaced by the passport system in 1952, the hope was repeatedly expressed that it would be brought to an end, and unrestricted movement within the subcontinent restored. Newspapers in Urdu in particular, letters to the editor, articles, and statements by various Muslim leaders articulated this sentiment with fervor, and especially during each inter-dominion conference when the subject of permits came up for discussion. The "real partition" was an emotive issue, and as one letter to *Al-Jamiat* put it, "there should be no permit system, so that after Partition our hearts are not partitioned."[9]

I became aware of the disciplinary effects of the permit system on the expression of emotions when I interviewed Rafi bhai's mother's youngest sister, his *khala*, in Karachi. She remembered their visit to Pakistan in 1948 from the perspective of Rafi bhai's mother. This is how she recalled her sister's coming to Pakistan:

NASEEM APA: *Woh itnī bicharī majbuur thī. Because she could not leave her husband aur father-in-law. Bahut chahā. Shuru men kehtī thī. Aur woh khud un par be-had taras khāte the. Bahut mohabat karte the. Kehte the ke mujhe bahut taras āta hai ke puṛā khandān chala gayā, puṛā ghar chala gayā, puṛā shehr chala gayā. Aur ye akeli reh gaī. Lekin woh kehtī thī ke main in logon ko kaise chhoṛ sakti hun. Main ne batāyā woh āe the lekin yahan ke mahol wagera dekh kar woh wapas chale gae . . . āti thī woh yahan par, jitnī dafa ātī thī to har dafa kehtī thī ke sab ko dekh kar itna achha lagta hai. Dil chahta hai ke yahin ājāuun. Lekin kehne lagī phir sochtī hun ke nahin apna ghar wahī theek hai. . . .*

[Later in the interview]

Hanh, woh ābhi gae the Pakistan lekin dubara chale gae. Kyon ke un logon ne us waqt ye decide kar liya. Halanke un ka nuqsan hua us men. Nuqsan uṭhaya un ne.

NASEEM APA: The poor thing was so constrained. Because she could not leave her husband and father-in-law. She really wanted to [stay in Pakistan]. In the beginning she used to say [this]. And he would himself feel really sorry for her. He really loved her. He used to say that he felt really pity for her that the whole family had gone. The entire house had gone. The entire city had gone. And she has been left entirely alone. But she would say, "How can I leave these people?" I told you, they had come here but looking at the conditions etc. here they went back. That was from the beginning. The condition of the people. She used to come and every time she came she would say how nice it was to see everybody. My heart wishes that I just stay here. But then she said, then I think, no, my home there is all right.

[Later in the interview]

NASEEM APA: Yes. They had come to Pakistan, but they went back again. Because those people at the time decided that. Although they suffered a loss because of that. They had to bear the loss.

Narrated from the perspective of Rafi bhai's mother, the meaning of the "visit" was transformed as it became laden with the loss of family and a conflicted desire for reunion with them. Rafi bhai had earlier explained to me that his mother's special place in their family was due to the fact that his *dada* had lost his wife while still in his youth, but had not remarried. As a result she was the wife of his only son, and as the only "woman of the house" was deeply loved and respected. The departure of her brother and sisters, their entire kin network, due to Partition's displacements was a particularly painful loss for her, but her pain was shared by those who loved her.

However, for Rafi bhai any suggestion that the journey to Pakistan was entwined with longing for the order of the family not to be separated was rendered unspeakable. The permit system restricted the flow of "returning Muslims" by declaring all those who had gone to Pakistan as having migrated, and it was the intention to migrate and not the desire to return that came to determine Indian citizenship for Muslims.

In my second interview with Rafi bhai I specifically asked him to tell me more about their visit to Pakistan and the court case. He was reluctant to discuss it further, and tried to answer my question briefly, as if it had not been of particular significance:

RAFI BHAI: *Dada se hum ne sirf ye sunā ke case ban gaya tha ke āp kaise āgae hai, kiya hai, to phir jate rahe court. Ye mujhe yād hai ke inhon ne yahan [workplace] men jo resgister tha signature karte the, le gae dikhāne ke liye. Ye mujhe yād hai kehte the ke Zakir saheb ne mujh se ye kaha ke main is mā'mle men āp ki madad nahin kar sakta. Is ka ye un ka reaction tha ke main āp se kahonga bhī nahin. Aur ye hukumat agar mujhe tasleem kartī hai as a shehrī, main ne jo kuch bhī kiyā yahan par – tasleem kartī hai warna main aur duniya ke dusre mulk hai main wahan ja kar reh longa. Magar main āp se nahin puchhonga ke shehriyat ke liye. Main apna right māng raha hun main ye to . . . main apne azizon ko dekhne gaya hun, ye mera haq hai ke main apne azizon ko dekhne ja'on. Kon zinda hai kon nahin. Itna baṛa inqilab āya hai. Main āp se nahin kahonga. Aur ye hī hua ke kagazāt pesh kiye gaye honge aur it was proved.*

RAFI BHAI: From our grandfather we only heard that there was a case, that how have you come, what is this, so then he used to go to the court. I remember that he here at [his workplace] had a register where he used to sign. He took that to show. This I remember that he said that Zakir saheb [Zakir Husain] had said that in this matter he would not help. His reaction was that I will not even ask you. And this government, if it does not acknowledge me as a citizen, after all that I have done here, acknowledges me, or else in this world there are many countries, and I can go there and live. But I will not ask you for citizenship. I am asking for my right, I am not . . . I went to see my relatives and this is my right to go and see my relatives. Who is alive and who is not. Such a big revolution/upheaval has taken place. I will not ask you. And this is what happened. He must have presented his papers and it was proved.

Rafi bhai was careful to maintain that their journey to Pakistan was merely a visit of rightful familial concern, and aligned all belonging and affect within the order of the state, to silence that of the family.

This chapter tracks the bureaucratic discourse on "Muslim refugees" in both India and Pakistan, to examine how technology regulating the movement of people was first rationalized and then uniquely designed to specifically control the movement of "Muslims" and "fix" their belonging. It simultaneously reveals the familial worlds of emotive ties, shorn open for bureaucratic discipline and legal adjudication, to foreground the highly contested and gendered character of this attempt at making and unmaking citizens of two nations.

RETURNING MUSLIM REFUGEES

It is significant that most of the returning Muslim refugees were coming from Karachi, Pakistan's new capital, and its province Sind, where, as I discussed in the previous chapter, a severe housing crisis in what had been relatively small urban centers, was coupled with the provincial government's ambiguous reception toward arriving Muslim refugees. Tensions in Karachi reached a peak when the Sind government was seen as particularly targeting *muhajirs* in response to riots in the city on January 6, 1948, leading a *Jang* editorial to state that "the Premier of Sind . . . does not like to see Hindustan's Muslim *muhajirs* in Sind."[10]

Perhaps even more important for turning the tide was Mahatma Gandhi's fast on January 12 to restore peace to Delhi, and bring security to its Muslim population. It had a dramatic effect on Muslim morale and aided attempts to reduce communal tensions in the city.[11] A few weeks later, his shocking murder on January 30 at the hands of Nathu Ram Godse further served to discredit Hindu extremist groups, and it has been suggested that this also increased the confidence of the north Indian Muslim population.[12] As the cartoon in *Jang* suggests (figure 3.1), there was even a feeling that conditions in Delhi had changed such that Muslims would be welcomed back. Thus it is possible to conjecture that in the following month, as letters and news were exchanged between Muslims in Karachi and Delhi, between friends and family, many who had never intended to stay permanently in Pakistan or were disappointed decided to return to their homes.

In official Indian discourse, however, it was their numbers that became particularly important. By mid-March 1948, the Indian High Commission in Pakistan had stated that every day a thousand Muslim refugees were returning to their homes in India. By mid-May, the United Kingdom High Commission in Delhi first quoted local newspapers as saying that 200,000 to 300,000 Muslims had returned, while in a later report to the Commonwealth Relations Office it suggested that 100,000 to 250,000 Muslims had returned, with 40,000 having returned to Delhi alone. In yet another report it quoted local news that 2,000 Muslims were returning every day.[13]

While it is uncertain how these numbers were arrived at, in the absence of any precise mechanisms for counting, the numbers became important enough that from April 3, 1948, the Criminal Investigation Department (CID) of the Delhi Police began quantifying Muslim arrivals and departures in the city in its weekly reports.

Table 3.1 is my tabulation of figures from these reports. According to these statistics, the total number of Muslims arriving in Delhi up to the end of May is 16,350, and if the number leaving (almost 4,450, but otherwise

FIGURE 3.1 "A visit to Chandni Chowk," *Jang*, January 15, 1948. The vendors are shouting "Kebabs, hot kebabs!" The man with the bottle is selling alcohol. Two men at the center are speaking to each other, and one of them says, "Brother, we were better off with Muslims than with these Sikhs."

unremarked) is subtracted, then an increase in the Muslim population of the city amounted to only 11,900—nowhere near the suggested 40,000 people. In drawing attention to the CID enumerations, my purpose is not to invest a truth in them, but rather to argue that these numbers were important not for their precision. They accumulated to give shape and authority to a "problem" that came to be described in local government reports as "the indiscriminate flux of Muslim refugees," "the steady influx of Muslim repatriates," "the inordinate influx of Muslims," or simply "the Muslim influx." The reports conjured an invasive and continuous flow of people that would later provide justification for the drafting of the Influx from Pakistan (Control) Ordinance.[14]

This counting and classification of a Muslim influx began to acquire threatening significance in the bureaucratic record as the return of Muslim refugees folded into a rehabilitation discourse centered on the housing of Hindu and Sikh refugees. During the September 1947 violence

TABLE 3.1 CID Enumeration of Muslim Movements

CID Report for the week ending	*Number of Muslims arriving in Delhi*	*Number of Muslims departing Delhi*
March 27, 1948	2500 (mostly Meos)	
April 3	2000	1100
April 10	2000	630
April 17	2300	400
May 1	2400	500
May 8	2400	500
May 15	1100	400
May 22	650	470
May 29	1000	450
June 5	800	600
June 19	750	375
July10	1350	1700
July 17	1960	750
July 24	200	570
July 31	120	300
August 7	20	450
August 14	235	400
August 21	250	410
August 28	210	500

These figures have been extracted from the Diary of Superintendent of Police, CID Delhi, March 27,1948, DSA, CC 60/47-C, p. 101, and Weekly Reports, CID Delhi, DSA, 68/47-C.

in Delhi, most Muslim homes had come to be occupied by Hindu and Sikh refugees displaced from the Punjab. Thus the CID enumeration of Muslim movement was reported alongside the "indignation" of Hindu and Sikh refugees who had "spent large sums of money to repair Muslim houses" that they had occupied, and now feared "ejectment . . . from vacant Muslim houses without [anyone] providing for them elsewhere." This fear was stated as so great that "[t]he non-Muslim refugees fe[lt] that it would have been better for them to embrace Islam in Pakistan rather than suffer ignominy in India." Delhi's police inspector-general reported that the hostility of the refugees meant that "if Muslims are put back in their houses in these areas they will be safe only as long as police protection is there. As soon as the police picket is withdrawn there is bound to be an attack on the Muslims by the non-Muslim refugees of the locality." The inspector-general's report further suggested that any attempts by the government to "support" Muslims would be interpreted by Hindus and Sikhs as being directed against them. Observers of a police-enforced clearing of a mosque were quoted as saying that "the time was fast approaching when all the locks put on Muslim houses and mosques would be broken open and occupied by Hindus and Sikhs and at that time no Muslim would be allowed to occupy any house in Delhi."[15]

These reports adopted a point of view which not only privileged Hindu and Sikh refugee fears, described repeatedly as the "public mind,"[16] but also positioned Hindu and Sikh interests entirely in opposition to those of Muslims as an undifferentiated category (including Muslims who had remained in Delhi through the violence, as well as those who were now returning). By focusing on the ferocity of anti-Muslim sentiment and "vacant Muslim houses," Muslims were not only left categorically outside the "public," but the violence that had forced them to leave their homes was completely written out.

This is not to say that the Hindu and Sikh refugees were not anxious, or that they did not harbor resentment towards Muslims in general; many of the Hindus and Sikhs had recently survived terrible violence inflicted by other Muslims in the Punjab. But Hindu and Sikh anger was also directed against government officials who they felt were not doing enough to alleviate their plight.[17] However, in the official record, Muslims, instead of being included in government plans for "refugee rehabilitation," became the obstacle to them.

Housing refugees as part of a rehabilitation program served a double function: it incorporated refugees into the new nation and defined the nation's spatial order. In addition to houses that were already occupied, "empty houses" in Muslim zones became another space of contention. "Muslim zones" had been set up in Delhi during the violence of September 1947 to provide "safe areas" for Muslims to move into from camps and other parts of the city. In Deputy Commissioner Randhawa's reports these Muslim zones were from the start perceived as a central impediment to the rehabilitation of Hindu and Sikh refugees since they could not be housed there. The return of Muslim refugees, possibly to these very "empty houses" in declared Muslim zones, further threatened the rehabilitation of Hindu and Sikh refugees. Randhawa began to argue vehemently that the "discontent among the refugee population" was because "refugees are afraid that they will be deprived of the houses which have been already occupied by them and the prospects of their getting empty houses will fade out for good." He insisted that these "empty houses" in Muslim zones were such "a bone of contention" that only if "these empty houses are occupied people's attention will be diverted towards the construction of new houses."[18] Eliminating "Muslim zones" thus became necessary, he argued, for undertaking any further planning for rehabilitation.

Among these official reports, there is one report from Randhawa that is particularly noteworthy both for its content as well as its margins. On June 1, 1948, Randhawa wrote:

> There are rumors that some trouble will take place in the last week of June . . . the return of Muslims in large numbers from Pakistan and the occupation of houses which have been lying vacant seems to be the major cause of these rumors. The refugees were living in the hope that they will be able to get these houses, but with the return of Muslims, these hopes are vanishing. Consequently they want to create panic among Muslims by spreading rumors that some trouble will take place. Creation of *so-called Muslim zones which are nothing but miniature Pakistans* is also resented. Common criticism is that if we are building a secular state then why this compartmentalization and zoning of citizens. (emphasis added)[19]

In the margins of the page, Chief Commissioner Sahibzada Khurshid Ahmed, Randhawa's superior, penciled in his own comments alongside the typed script of his deputy:

> Forward this copy with [illegible] that I generally agree with Muslim influx. D.C. [deputy commissioner] Housing problem has to be tackled with vigor and imagination. Much time has been wasted in pursuing stereotyped plans. Assigned Muslim zones *I hope when D.C. says they are nothing but miniature Pakistans he is not explaining his own views but the views held by unbalanced refugees* . . . [signed, 2/6] (emphasis added)

Sahibzada Khurshid was one of the few senior Muslim officials in the Indian Civil Service (ICS) who opted to work for India, and remained the chief commissioner of Delhi through the post-Partition violence. His marginal voice can perhaps be understood from two different perspectives. In his autobiography, Maulana Azad criticized Khurshid as a weak and ineffectual officer who was afraid to show favor to Muslims and so allowed Randhawa to control affairs and treat Muslims unfairly in the riots.[20] On the other hand, I interviewed Khurshid's niece, Begum Kadiruddin, in Karachi. She was given refuge in Khurshid's home during the September violence even though she was married to the president of Delhi's Muslim League chapter. According to her recollections, her *chacha* was a deeply frustrated man in those days because he felt that his deputy was bypassing him in the Delhi administration and corresponding with and receiving orders directly from Khurshid's superiors. His frustration, she argued, only grew when, at the time of the imposition of the permit system, he was transferred from his position as chief commissioner of Delhi to a less significant position as head of an ICS training facility.[21]

Khurshid's pencil notes can be read as an erasable, shadowy critique of Randhawa's sustained argument against the continuation of "Muslim zones." Khurshid vaguely suggests that the obstinate focus on "empty houses" for purposes of rehabilitation is a "stereotyped plan." He seems generally concerned by the labeling of "Muslim zones" into "miniature Pakistans," but his stated concern is his deputy's point of view. He only implies that the labeling is an "unbalanced" view, by referring to the view of "unbalanced refugees," and appeals to the virtues of a rational and neutral state that stands outside of society's prejudices. Khurshid's inability to directly challenge the making of a bureaucratic discourse which was repeatedly constructing Muslims as a problem of governance reflects not just his peripheral position as a Muslim official in the Indian state, but also the power of this bureaucratic discourse itself.

The sinister implications of calling a collection of Muslim homes "miniature Pakistans" become evident when Randhawa suggests that Muslim return was not just a problem for rehabilitation, but also "a serious menace to law and order."[22] Here he not only means the possibility of renewed communal conflict, but also "fifth columnist" activity[23]:

> My attention has been drawn to the steady influx of Muslim repatriates in Delhi who are returning from West Pakistan in steadily increasing numbers. Out of these there are some who are returning from the land of their dreams genuinely disappointed and may be expected to settle down as loyal citizens. However, there are some among them who are returning without their families and are potential saboteurs

> and fifth columnists. I have been told by a Muslim friend that some of them are actually saying that *the Pakistan Army will celebrate next Idd in the Jama Masjid of Delhi*. Some check is necessary on the activities of such persons.
>
> My suggestion is that all Muslims who are returning from West Pakistan should be placed in a Quarantine Camp for a specified period before they are allowed to mingle with the population of Delhi. When in camp enquiries be made about their antecedents and character and proposed place of stay and address in Delhi be also noted. This will enable the police to keep a check on their activities. Apart from reasons of security, this will also enable us to know the exact number of persons who are returning, their professions and also whether they can be usefully re-absorbed in the urban economy of Delhi.[24]

A *Jang* cartoon from Karachi actually depicts a Muslim refugee from Delhi tearfully longing to celebrate the festival of Eid at Delhi's Jama Masjid (see figure 3.2). In Randhawa's report this very sentiment is rendered suspect, and transformed into an aggressive and invasive intent. Randhawa's perception of a threat draws authenticity from an informant who is a "Muslim friend," and this allows him to place his analysis and policy proposal of Quarantine Camps within the neutral frame of a state concerned for the well being of an abstract nation, rather than a partisan view.

While some returning Muslim refugees could be made into "loyal citizens," others were "potential saboteurs and fifth columnists" who needed to be quarantined and policed. "Mini-Pakistans" was semantically charged with the danger of an invading Pakistan Army, and this notion was voiced in subsequent police and deputy commissioner reports which reiterated that "the influx of a large number of Muslims to this place is due to a deep conspiracy aimed at the establishment of a Muslim rule at this place."[25] The reports also argued that Muslims were returning because they wanted to create communal disturbances in order to prejudice the United Nations Organization (UNO) commission that was to arrive in India to deliberate on claims to Kashmir made by both India and Pakistan.[26] One CID report argued that in addition to influencing the UNO commission, returning Muslims were part of a conspiracy of revenge in which occupied Muslim houses were once again essentially at stake:

FIGURE 3.2 "Eid in Delhi vs. Eid in Pakistan," *Jang*, August 8, 1948. The couplet above the image translates as "Autumn makes me weep with the memory of spring's harvest / How can I enjoy the happiness of Eid for I am in mourning."

> It is understood that some Muslims who had come from Rawalpindi and other places and who had been noticed moving about in the Sabzimandi area clad in Hindu fashion had told the refugees from Rawalpindi and Wazirabad, etc., that they had come to Delhi to create distrubances and avenge the wrongs done to the Muslims of Delhi. According to the Muslim *goondas* [thugs], the Sabzimandi area was formerly predominated over by Muslims but now all their houses had been occupied by Hindus and Sikhs and they would see that all the Muslim houses were evicted of the non-Muslims. . . . Thus, there appears to be a regular conspiracy of the Muslims with the tacit support of the Pakistan Government to create communal flareup in India to prejudice the world opinion against the Indian Union.[27]

With Muslims described as belligerent agents of the Pakistani state, their claims to homes in the city were made transgressive and illegitimate. Thus by the time the permit system was introduced, it was greeted with approval by the administrative apparatus, including Delhi's new chief commissioner, Shankar Prasad, who noted that "it reduces the growing menace of enemy espionage" and "the pressure on population caused by one-way traffic."[28]

"One-way traffic" became the phrase that summarized the rationale for imposition of the permit system. It was based on the argument that both Hindu and Muslim refugees were flowing from Pakistan to India, while there was no such flow of refugees from India to Pakistan. It was to stem this "one-way traffic" that the permit system was required. As we have seen in the previous chapter, the Indian state had embraced the flow of Hindu refugees from Pakistan to India, and therefore it was largely the flow of Muslim refugees that was considered a problem of both economics and loyalty.

The impact of the bureaucratic discourse on national politics is striking. When the "open-door policy for these refugees coming from Pakistan to India" was first discussed in the Constituent Assembly on March 22, 1948, the fear was expressed that they were returning to reclaim their homes with all its consequences for Hindu and Sikh refugees. However, Jawaharlal Nehru reminded the Assembly "of certain pledges that we have given in regard to this matter to Mahatma Gandhi just before his death" and insisted that regardless of the Pakistan government's actions toward minorities, the Indian government would abide by Gandhi's wish to welcome and retain India's Muslim population.[29]

However, in the ensuing months, as the bureaucratic discourse gathered force, the tenor of political debate in the Assembly changed. After the imposition of the permit system, a question was raised in the Constituent Assembly on August 10 as to whether the permit restrictions "violate[d] any of the conditions on the basis of which Mahatma Gandhi broke his fast." Sardar Patel replied that "[c]onditions in Delhi have been normal and peaceful for the last several months and the government presumes that all those who had left Delhi on account of general insecurity prevailing last year in the month of September have already returned. The residue must be taken to be those who left Delhi to settle permanently in Pakistan. Therefore the question of violation of Gandhi's fast does not arise." Patel's statement marked an important political shift which made the permit system a legitimate set of restrictions on Muslim return. A line was drawn: Muslim refugees remaining in Pakistan were declared to be emigrants who could no longer claim a right of belonging in India.

NOAH'S ARK

The large-scale departure of Muslim refugees from Karachi and Sind did raise alarms in Pakistan. The *Jang*, a *muhajir* newspaper, expressed outrage at this return movement. On the one hand, it addressed itself to *muhajirs* to tie them to the Pakistan idea itself. A cartoon, for instance, portrayed them as the rightful pallbearers of Pakistan, symbolized by the mosque, and poignantly asked who would be left to build Pakistan if all the *muhajirs* left Pakistan for Hindustan. (See figure 3.3.)

On the other hand, letters and articles criticized the Pakistani government for failing to provide adequate refuge to the very people who had struggled for it:

FIGURE 3.3 "Alas! this selfish world!" *Jang,* April 9, 1948. Note at the bottom translates as: "If all the *muhajirs* leave then only government officers will be left to build this country."

> From Hyderabad, Sind, and Karachi those going back to Hindustan are a source of real sadness . . . approximately 500 to a thousand are going back every day from Sind. . . . Is this why we made such sacrifices for making a great Islamic country?[30]

> From the Indian Union Muslims came to Pakistan for they had conviction that they would find refuge in Pakistan. . . . But what a sad state of affairs that these very people who came running to Pakistan are today upset with Pakistan, and disappointed they are returning to Hindustan. First we had heard that from Karachi and Sind every day 300 Muslims were returning to Delhi and the Indian Union, but now their number has tripled. Now Hind's deputy high commissioner, Mr. Naganathan, has said that every day 1000 *muhajirs* are returning to the Indian Union. Shame! Shame! O Pakistan you could not give your own brothers refuge. . . .[31]

This image of disheartened and disappointed Muslim refugees returning to their homes added bite to ongoing criticisms of the Pakistani government's relief and rehabilitation efforts (see figures 3.4 and 3.5). The moral pressure this stirred was substantial and led to the announcement of new rehabilitation schemes for Karachi and Sind.[32]

When the Resolution for the Rehabilitation of Refugees was discussed in the Constituent Assembly of Pakistan on May 20, 1948, the return of Muslim refugees became a visibly emotional issue. The rehabilitation of refugees was assumed to be central to their incorporation in the new nation, and the failure of such rehabilitation efforts was believed to have led to refugee departures. The former Sind premier, M.A. Khuhro (who had been in office when the January 6 riot had taken place), in particular received criticism for spreading anti-refugee feeling. This highlighted existing political tensions between the Sindhi politicians and *muhajir* leaders. Some members of the Assembly lamented the plight of Muslim refugees who "after coming over here . . . feel that they can neither live here or go back." One member asked why conditions in Pakistan were so bad that people were returning "to the places from where they had been turned out."

Ghazanfar Ali Khan, the minister for refugees and rehabilitation, responded to these criticisms, on this occasion and when the matter was raised again on May 25 and 26. His statements are particularly significant

FIGURE 3.4 "Once someone leaves this world, help comes too late," *Jang*, April 24, 1948. A *panaghir* craftsman is saying "Pakistan Zindabad!" The snail is carrying a sign which says "Good news! The Rehabilitation Ministry has made a committee for rehabilitation of *panaghir* craftsmen."

FIGURE 3.5 "Indian Death/Pakistani Death," *Jang*, April 2, 1948. The family is labeled "*muhajir*" and the man says, "If one has to die then what Pakistan, what Hindustan!"

because they articulate the Pakistani state's ambiguity toward Muslim refugees from outside divided Punjab. He largely blamed the Indian government for representing the Muslim refugees' return to India as being caused by their ill treatment in Pakistan. His assessment was that those who were returning included primarily the Meos, about whom an intergovernmental agreement had been reached, and others who were returning to their families and relatives in India. These Muslims had sought refuge in Pakistan but had never intended to make Pakistan their home.[33]

Furthermore, he insisted that contrary to Nehru's telegrams about the "one-way traffic" of people between India and Pakistan, thousands of Muslims from India were continuing to come to Pakistan by sea, and thus the "traffic" was not one-way at all. For Khan, this continuing movement of Muslims from India to Pakistan was the real source of the problem. Khan argued that the Indian government was not doing enough "to retain those Muslims who had declared their allegiance to India" and that the Indian government "should not allow them to come here." As far as the Pakistani government was concerned, those Muslims who lived in India should be looked after by the Indian state. Yet the Pakistan movement had been claimed on behalf of *all* Muslims of the subcontinent, and so he added with rhetorical bluster:

> . . . we have no right to close the doors of Pakistan on the refugees who have migrated from India to Pakistan . . . [I]t will be our duty to drag to the roof every flood-stricken person, but so many should not be taken on the roof that it should collapse and all be lost in the floods . . . Pakistan is not only his home, but is the home of all the Musalmans of the world.[34]

We have already seen Liaqat Ali Khan straddle these two competing positions when faced with the initial Muslim exodus from Delhi, and here Ghazanfar Ali Khan follows the same coupling of arguments—Muslims in India should not come to Pakistan, even though Pakistan was at the same time their refuge and homeland and could not close its doors on them. But these two positions were not easy to reconcile politically in the face of continuing Muslim displacement from India. The Indian government's introduction of the permit system, however, offered the Pakistani government a potential bureaucratic solution to its political problem.

Initially the Pakistani government opposed the Indian permit system and stated that "no regulation of traffic in this way was necessary."[35] At the inter-dominion conference in Lahore on July 22, 1948, Pakistan's demand to end the permit system was discussed. The Indian government responded with a proposal for a governmentally controlled "two-way traffic" in which refugees could return to their original homes if they wanted to. One could argue that this was an opportunity of sorts to reverse Partition's displacements, since much of the communal violence that had sparked it had subsided and movements like the Phir Basao Conference suggested the desire of some to return home. But the official record has left only this trace, in which Liaqat Ali Khan declared it "out of the question."[36] Instead, the Pakistani government went so far as to threaten India that if it did not lift its permit restrictions, then it would impose retaliatory restrictions on movement not only in the west, but also in East Pakistan, where Hindu business interests across divided Bengal would be particularly affected.[37]

However, a turning point came in the Pakistani state's position on permits when the central government began discussions with the provincial governments on the implementation of such a retaliatory permit system. The premiers of West Punjab and North West Frontier Province (NWFP) argued that the permit system should be conceived of not just as a retaliatory gesture, but rather as a necessity for purposes of "security."[38] According to the West Punjab premier, there were many Muslims, some Anglo-Indians, and Hindus who were constantly coming into West Punjab from East Punjab and vice versa for espionage, "acting as enemy agents." He cited the case of a Muslim in West Punjab who was found writing a letter to a friend in East Punjab suggesting that the proper time to bomb Lahore was when a large congregation had gathered for Eid prayers at the Badshahi mosque. Given the threat posed by moving people—Muslims and non-Muslims alike—they emphasized the advantages of the permit system for the surveillance of "visitors" and policing of "suspicious characters."

The report of this meeting was influential in determining the Pakistani Cabinet's decision on September 4, 1948, to adopt a permit system parallel to India's; inter-dominion discussions to end the system were abandoned.[39] It was to be introduced immediately for travel from India to West Pakistan, and, after "administrative arrangements," from India to East Pakistan. In a discussion centered around achieving "full security," the permit system was deemed as "a real check against the entry of undesirable elements (Muslim or non-Muslim) into Pakistan" and it was recommended that "an officer who has experience of intelligence work" be posted to the High Commission in Delhi. Thus when the Pakistan (Control of Entry) Ordinance of 1948 was drafted, it was "prepared primarily as an internal security measure" in which Muslims were as suspect as non-Muslims.[40]

However, there was resistance from at least two fronts within the Pakistani government to the imposition of the permit system, and the defense of that system reveals its full intended purposes. The East Bengal government objected to the extension of the permit system to its borders, even though it had agreed to it during the first round of provincial discussions. Its premier argued that the initial agreement had been acceded to primarily to threaten India into withdrawing her permit system, but its actual imposition was considered opposed to "our people's needs."[41]

The inconvenience lay in the particular geography of divided Bengal. The premier argued that people particularly from upcountry would have to come down to Dacca to obtain a permit, and from certain parts of the country, such as Jessore and Khulna, a person had to pass through Indian territory in order to get to Dacca itself. On the other hand, most people who crossed from the West to the East primarily came from Calcutta and would not face the same amount of difficulty. The permit system would be ineffective as a security mechanism, for any strict control of movement of people would in effect isolate a section of "nationals" as well as "national territory" itself.[42]

The Cabinet discussed East Bengal's opposition, and particularly debated the "security" effectiveness of the permit system. Some felt it would "enable better control" of "undesirable characters from India" while others argued that "most of the troublemakers in East Bengal belonged to that place" itself and would not be circumscribed by a permit system. Thus "security" was not a sufficient reason for introducing the permits. This ambivalence of the central government toward Bengal, and its "troublemakers" within, is perhaps indicative of the rift between East and West Pakistan that was to follow later. However, for the time being, an economic rationale overrode "security" in the decision to *not* apply the permit system across the eastern frontier. The Cabinet agreed that thousands of persons living in East Bengal daily crossed over to the West to make their livelihood, and many conducted business both in Calcutta and in East Bengal. Restricting their activities to one dominion could result in economic hardship and the loss of business to East Bengal.

The government of East Bengal was not alone in questioning the necessity of a permit system. Soon after the permit system was introduced in West Pakistan, the Ministry of Foreign Affairs, required to undertake the administration of the permit system in India, began to oppose it as well. The minister of interior wrote to Liaqat Ali Khan about the growing rift between the two ministries over the permit system.[43] Foreign Affairs also believed that the permit system was an ineffective security mechanism given "the extensive land frontiers and the long seacoast of Western Pakistan, which cannot be sealed up, and because the spies and saboteurs have their own specialized methods to gain entry." Foreign Affairs essentially argued that it was impossible for the state to assert complete territorial vigilance, or assert total corporal control.

Muslim refugees were Foreign Affairs' second reason for opposing permits. Although unstated elsewhere in these declassified documents on the permit system, Foreign Affairs believed that a function of the permit system was to keep Muslim refugees out of Pakistan. It argued that rather than the permit system, "other methods of keeping out refugees such as control of the issue of lower-class tickets can be adopted and they are simpler and less objectionable methods." The suggestion of controlling the sale of lower-class tickets for trains and ships is evidence that keeping out poor Muslim refugees, in particular, those who would require rehabilitation, was one of the central purposes of the permit system for Pakistan.

The response of the Ministry of Interior to these charges is equally revealing. It defended the permit system primarily on the grounds that keeping Muslim refugees out of Pakistan was imperative to its economy:

> . . . it is considered that the permit system must be tightened up and enforced strictly as it is eventually bound up with the stability of Pakistan's economy. Pakistan's resources are already overstrained and the government cannot for some time to come afford to take on refugees in any large numbers without *grave risk to the country's economy*. Karachi's problem has particularly become difficult on account of its ever increasing population. Unless immigration is appreciably cut down, the town may soon be threatened with a breakdown of its essential services and an impossible task of refugee rehabilitation. (emphasis added)[44]

The Ministry of Interior argued that the permit system was the most effective means to serve this imperative, and that "[n]one of the alternative methods suggested by the Ministry of Foreign Affairs for keeping out refugees could be even half as useful or feasible as the permit system with all its limitations was." Proof of the permit system's effectiveness lay in the case of the princely state of Hyderabad, in central India, which had a significant Muslim population. The nawab of the princely state had resisted accession to the Indian state, but it was taken over by force by the Indian Army in September 1948. The ministry prided itself on "the permit system [which] was introduced just in time to save Pakistan from what might have been a deluge from the Hyderabad State." It warned that if the permit system was removed then Pakistan may be faced "with a delicate security problem and a more difficult refugee problem entailing far more serious expenditure than any permit system could involve."[45]

This argument between ministries centered on the best technique for restricting numbers of Muslim refugees, but took the economic threat posed by refugees as a given. The calculation that the government could not "afford" more refugees had such rational power that it legitimated the exclusion of Muslim refugees from India. On the one hand, the Indian government drew upon a similar rationality to institute the permit system to control the movement of Muslim refugees from Pakistan back to India, and on the other hand, this provided the Pakistani government with a technological solution outside political debate to control the movement of Muslims from India into Pakistan.

PERMITS QUA CITIZENSHIP

In a letter to Nehru, Dr. Rajendra Prasad expressed alarm at newspaper reports of crowds of Muslims applying for permits to return to India, and calculated that at the rate of 350 permits a day, about 30,000 or 40,000 Muslims could potentially be returning every month. They would demand to "be treated on his return to India as a national of India and in the same way as any other national."[46] Prasad's anxiety reflects the relative inability of the permit system to stem the tide of returning Muslim refugees in its initial phase and anticipates a central question raised by its introduction: who could become Indian citizens?

When the permit system was first introduced, the Indian constitution was still in the making and citizenship laws had not yet been drafted. But as people, like Ghulam Ali, continued to cross the border with or without permits, an array of permit court cases necessitated the introduction of legal citizenship provisions in advance of the constitution itself. The violations of permit regulations thus became the first site for contesting and giving shape to the unresolved questions of citizenship in a partitioned subcontinent.

However, to understand these legal contestations in the making of citizens, the historical conditions and the technological intervention of permits need to be foregrounded. Permits were introduced by the Indian state as an emergency measure, announced and then brought into effect within five days. The permit system thus cut across both a time of uncertainty and a range of disordered familial formations. Even in the midst of violence in Delhi and a large-scale exodus, some male members of families had stayed behind in an attempt to protect homes or businesses, or retain jobs. In other cases, young men in the family had gone to Pakistan in search of business opportunities or employment, leaving behind their wives, children, elderly parents, brothers, and sisters at "home." Many Muslims who had "opted" to work in the new Pakistan government continued to maintain their homes and families in India. In other cases, sections of extended families had gone to Pakistan, while others had remained in India. A couplet by the poet Rais Amrohi, in the *Jang* newspaper, captures one of the many kinds of post-Partition families the permit system intersected and divided.

Begum hai Hind men, to mian Sindh men muqeem
Do no ko hai farāq ka shakwā naseeb se
Kiyā qeher hai keh in ki mullaqat ke liye
Permit hai shart—Woh kaise mille ga raqīb se.[47]

Wife in Hindustan, husband in Sindh
Both have complaints against fate's partition
What severe punishment that in order to meet
Permit they need—how will it be obtained from the gatekeeper

The numerous letters to the editor in *Jang* in Karachi, and *Al-Jamiat* in Delhi, record the confusion and plight that divided families-in-the-making experienced as simple travel between loved ones began to be interpolated by an array of official paperwork and state officials.[48] It forced decisions about where and how a family was going to live. One CID report noted that after the permit system, "local Muslims are thinking of either shifting permanently to Pakistan or of making immediate arrangements for the repatriation of their families now staying in Pakistan."[49]

While permits as a technology for regulation of movement had precedence in both colonial metropoles and colonies, the form in which they were implemented to control the flow of Partition's refugees is perhaps unique. When it came into effect the Indian High Commission in Pakistan began to issue five different kinds of permits. There were permits

1) for temporary visits,
2) for permanent return to India (for Muslims wishing to return permanently to India),
3) for repeated journeys (for businessmen and officials),
4) for transit travel (for traveling across the two halves of Pakistan), and
5) for permanent resettlement (for Hindus who wanted to migrate permanently).[50]

The difference between the "permit for permanent return to India" and the "permit for permanent resettlement" reflected the different treatment by the Indian state of Muslim refugees on the one hand and of Hindu and Sikh refugees on the other. Those in the latter category who wanted to move from Pakistan to India could apply for "permanent resettlement" and were entitled to government's rehabilitation programs, as well as ultimately citizenship in the nation-state. But Muslim refugees who wanted to return to their homes in India had to apply for "permanent return," and this was made exceedingly difficult through bureaucratic process, and entailed receiving permission from the provincial government where the person wanted to return. Thus most Muslims obtained temporary permits to travel back to their homes in India. Between July 19 and August 5, 1948, the Indian High Commission in Karachi reportedly issued 300 temporary permits daily to Muslim refugees.[51]

One man from Sahranpur, UP, explained in his letter to *Al-Jamiat* the near impossibility of getting a permanent permit for Muslim return, and the difficulties of even getting a temporary one:

> When the permit system between India and Pakistan was introduced it created great difficulties and those who have always lived here and even during the violence of 1947 did not leave, they coincidentally went to visit friends and relatives, and suddenly the permit system came in. Many were such that they could not afford airfare and after the announcement there was not even enough time to come by rail. And those who could afford the plane could not come because they couldn't book the seat in time. And there are many among them who could not come temporarily because they didn't have a file for coming temporarily and a permanent permit cannot be obtained. Therefore it is important that the government offer a permanent permit or, even better, end this permit system altogether.[52]

Thus although a permit for permanent return had an official reality and function to prevent large-scale return of Muslim refugees, in practice people who wanted to return home either applied for both a permanent permit and a temporary one, or simply returned home on a temporary permit and once at home discarded the permit paper. On application forms for temporary permits, many even wrote in earnest that the "purpose of their visit" was "Returning Home."[53]

A story in *Jang* on a police raid on a travel agency in Bombay is quite revealing of the ways in which people on the move found ways to circumvent the controls of the permit system. The travel agency bought temporary permits from those who had come from Pakistan but did not want to go back there. The agency then sold these temporary permits to those who wanted to permanently migrate to Pakistan.[54] These attempts to circumvent the permit restrictions were certainly noted by Delhi's chief commissioner, who reported that "[t]he influx of Muslims has decreased with the enforcement of permit system. Many Muslims have, however, arrived with temporary permits and there is a tendency to overstay or to have the temporary permit converted into a permanent one."[55]

The state's anxiety about the ineffectiveness of the permit system in restricting the return of Muslim refugees led to repeated attempts to improve its techniques. This meant that Muslims who were moving were subjected to increasing regimes of control and surveillance. A No Objection Certificate (NOC) was introduced which Muslims, who were living in India and wanted to visit Pakistan, had to first obtain from the police and district magistrate. Before leaving India, they had to establish themselves as belonging to India. Later, those visiting from or going to Pakistan were required to report to the police station on their arrival. Furthermore, "bona fide reasons" for travel to the "other side" had to be proved, through medical certificates from a civil surgeon for visiting a sick relative or guarantee bonds from inviting relatives.[56] Continuing reports of forged and false permits resulted in the introduction of photographs on application forms as well as on permits.[57]

Most significantly, the Influx from Pakistan (Control) Ordinance and the Pakistan (Control of Entry) Ordinance were both amended to make overstaying on a temporary permit a criminal offense[58] punishable by fines, imprisonment, or most decisively, deportation. Thus many who thought they had simply returned home became criminalized, fought court cases, or faced deportations.

The Pakistani government permit regulations mirrored the Indian techniques. However, for Muslims going to West Pakistan on forged or temporary permits, it was easier to "disappear" if they did not want to return to India. Karachi came to be largely dominated by *muhajirs*, who became a significant part of its government apparatus and its civil institutions, and there was a sufficient informal network willing to assist "illegal" arrivals, or relax enforcement of the law. On the other hand, Hindus who remained in West Pakistan or attempted to return to their homes there were less able to evade the permit's disciplinary regimes.[59]

Because of their larger numbers, Muslims returning to India were perhaps most affected. A significant number of people started to be arrested for overstaying temporary permits, but the courts found that the "crime" was not so simple to adjudicate: most of these people claimed a belonging in India, ancestral abodes as well as familial ties. They argued that even if they had gone to Pakistan, they had never planned to make it their home. In the absence of citizenship laws which could adjudicate on the question of their belonging, a number of persons spent up to two years in jail before a judgment was passed. Citizenship provisions (Articles 5–9) were brought into force on November 26, 1949, in advance of the Indian constitution itself,[60] in all probability to deal with these increasing arrests and court cases.

There were two articles in the citizenship provisions which were particularly significant and established key relationships between birth, residence, migration, and citizenship. Article 5 established "domicile" and birth "in the territory of India" as criteria for citizenship. The condition of "domicile" for purposes of adjudication had been passed down through colonial law and derived from English law: it defined the domicile of children below the age of eighteen, considered "minors," as vested in that of the father; the domicile of women was dependent on that of the father until marriage, and then in her marriage was defined as that of the husband.

By making domicile a condition of citizenship, the new Indian citizenship laws (mirrored by the later Pakistani citizenship laws) were not unique in subjecting the citizenship of women to fathers and husbands. Gendered studies of citizenship point out that well into the twentieth century and virtually everywhere in the world wives were subjects of their husbands and could not be autonomous citizens.[61] The requirements of domicile established patrilocal residence as normative for citizenship, with important effects for women and children in this disarray of familial orders. For one, the "wife in Hindustan" of Amrohi's couplet would lose her entitlement by birth to Indian citizenship without ever leaving her home. However, as permits were issued both to individuals and heads of households on behalf of entire families, few permit court cases were about women or children in particular, although that would change as permits came to be replaced by passports—individual documents for individual citizens—in the years to follow.

Returning Muslims could not invoke Article 5 to claim citizenship because of Article 7, which dealt specifically with Partition's displacements. It established that those who had "after the first day of March 1947 migrated from the territory of India to the territory now included in Pakistan" would "not be deemed to be a citizen of India." However, "a person who, after having migrated to the territory now included in Pakistan, has returned to the territory of India under a permit for resettlement or permanent return" would be considered an exception.[62] Most of the court cases for overstaying temporary permits were decided on the basis of Article 7 and raised critical questions of what constituted migration. Could it be a matter of individual choice? Or did the law function to produce historical closure in the making of Partition's new nations?

One of the earliest judgments to be reported from the Allahabad High Court in 1951 was the case of Badruzzaman of district Rae Barelli in UP. His entire family had continued to reside in their village, Bawan Buzrug, when he went to West Pakistan in May 1948, just before the announcement of the permit system. He returned to India on June 22, 1949, on a temporary permit valid for one month. His stated purpose of visit was "second marriage and fetching his family." Subsequently he secured extensions on his permit until October 7. The government argued that it had "evidence" that the "applicant's second wife refused to accompany him to Pakistan" and therefore he had remained in India beyond the permitted period. He had attempted to obtain further extensions, and had tried to get himself registered as a citizen of India. These attempts had been unsuccessful, and as a result he was arrested on October 11, under the Influx from Pakistan (Control) Act, convicted, and sentenced to nine months' rigorous imprisonment. On appeal, his sentence had been reduced to 500 rupees or three months of imprisonment.

Badruzzaman, in opposition to the government, claimed that he did not want to return to Pakistan, and came to India on a temporary permit only because a permanent one was not available. He insisted that he had never given up his Indian nationality and that he was still an Indian citizen. His "evidence" included letters that he had written to his family during his time in Pakistan, expressing his longing to return to his father, and mourning his failed attempts to obtain a permanent permit. The judge did not give much weight to these letters and noted in the judgment that given "the great exodus of Muslim population from Indian territory to Pakistan and of Hindu population from Pakistan to India and the historical events which led to the partition of the country and the establishment of the two dominions—the facts proved would undoubtedly indicate that when the applicant left India in May 1948 he did so in order to settle down in Pakistan and to adopt it as his home country."[63]

The judgment asserted a narrative of Partition and its displacements in which Muslim refugees could only enter history by the fact of leaving. Citizenship was determined by Badruzzaman's departure, which was taken to legally constitute "migration," and *not* by his "ardent desire to return." The judgment declared his claims of belonging through established familial ties as insufficient evidence of belonging to nation.

The much-referenced case of Shabbir Husain is a particularly important one because it questioned the judgment in Badruzzaman's case and debated the very meaning of the word *migration* as defined in the citizenship provisions. Could any journey to Pakistan constitute "migration"?

How significant were the conditions in which a given journey to Pakistan had been undertaken?

Shabbir Husain was a resident of the village Kalyanpur, in district Bijnor of UP, where he had lived since his birth. He went to Lahore in 1948, when the permit system was introduced, and returned to India on a temporary permit that was valid until January 1, 1949, although he had in fact applied for a permit for permanent return. He overstayed his temporary permit and was convicted under the Influx from Pakistan (Control) Ordinance of 1948. He applied to the UP government for permanent return but was denied and an order was passed for his removal and deportation to Pakistan. He was arrested from what he described as his ancestral home on July 21, 1950, and remained confined in Bijnor jail until a judgment was passed in his favor in 1952.

When Shabbir Husain went to Pakistan, he took with him an affidavit, sworn before a magistrate in Bombay, that he was going to Lahore for business and would return to India after disposing of his goods in two months. He obtained this affidavit just prior to his departure from Bombay, as he had been unable to obtain an NOC in Bijnor. When he submitted this affidavit along with his application for permanent return at the Indian High Commission, he was given a temporary permit to return home in lieu of the time needed for verification of his document.

Given Husain's affidavit, and what might seem to be an absolutely clear declaration of intention, the two judges of the high court deliberated over eight pages on the meaning of the word *migration* as used in prior cases, including Badruzzaman's, as well as the *Oxford English Dictionary*. Judge Raghubar Dayal concluded that Article 7 of the constitution defined *migration* as "the intention of shifting his permanent residence from India to Pakistan," a matter of changing "domicile," while Judge P.L. Bhargava argued that migration "has the notion of transference of allegiance from the country of departure to the country of adoption." Thus the mere fact of departure from India did not constitute "migration" and could not be folded into a history of mass exodus. Both judges agreed that Shabbir Husain had no intention of permanent relocation or transfer of allegiance, and was thus released.[64]

The Shabbir Husain case set the precedent that "migration," according to law, had to have the "intention" of permanent relocation, and was different from a mere journey. This led to countless deliberations on the "intentions" of journeys and allowed some persons who were arrested for overstaying their temporary permits to obtain acquittal, avoid deportation, and be eventually deemed "Indian citizens." But interpreting "intention to migrate" was a subjective matter and a range of rulings suggest the arbitrary albeit legal process of determining which Muslims could be citizens and which could not.

Here are two examples of this arbitrariness. Najib Khan claimed to have merely gone to Pakistan to search for his sister's son, but was judged to have migrated to Pakistan, not only because he had returned on a temporary permit but because he had also applied for permanent return. The application for permanent return, instead of affirming his "intentions" to live in India, was interpreted as a confession of migration, for the application was technically only for those who had already migrated to Pakistan.[65] In the case of some residents of Kutch it was customary practice in conditions of famine to move to an area that had now become Pakistan. They, as a result, took no permit with them, and also returned without a permit. When arrested under the influx law they challenged the permit system as infringing on their right to movement guaranteed by the constitution, and claimed their permanent homes in Kutch. The court considered the restrictions of the permit system as "reasonable and in the interest of the public" and they were deemed to have migrated because they went to Pakistan with the purpose of making a living there.[66]

The effects of these permit prosecutions extended beyond those who had gone to Pakistan for a range of reasons and were attempting to return. In some of the cases, the person claimed to have never gone to Pakistan to begin with, and therefore claimed that the permit case against them was unfounded. The case of Izhar Ahmad is one such remarkable one. He was arrested by police on August 20, 1952, under the influx law and was deported the next morning. He claimed that he had never been to Pakistan, but since he had already been deported, his brother, Iqbal Ahmad, applied to the courts for his return. Izhar Ahmad's entire family, his parents and his wife as well as his siblings, were resident in Bhopal. An astonishing array of records were presented to attempt to prove that Izhar Ahmad had never gone to Pakistan. This included school certificates, *nikahnama* or marriage certificate, ration cards, a subscription to a mosque, electoral rolls and voter's list for the Legislative Council and Municipal Board. However, the state claimed that he had gone to Pakistan and returned through the eastern front where there were no regulations on movement, and that it had obtained this information by a "secret method" which could not be disclosed in the interest of the public. This left Izhar Ahmad's family without the possibility of countering the evidence against him to allow his return.[67]

With growing numbers of deportations to enforce the permit system (Ghulam Ali was not an exceptional case), the case of *Ebrahim Vazir Mavat and Others v. the State of Bombay* reached the Supreme Court on the question of whether deportation "oversteps the limits of control and regulation when it provides for the removal of a citizen from his own country." Ebrahim Vazir Mavat had gone to Pakistan in March 1948, before the introduction of the permit system, and had returned a year later on a permanent return permit. However, a few months after his return on the permanent permit he was prosecuted for concealing the fact that he had come to India earlier on a temporary permit. Although two and a half years later the prosecution was withdrawn, he was served with a deportation notice. This case also included Inamullah Khan, who claimed to have never gone to Pakistan. Inamullah Khan, alias Qamar Jamali, was the editor of the weekly *Tarjuman* in Bhopal. He was arrested on November 24, 1952, and taken to the border at Khokrapar for deportation on March 18, 1953. Mavat and Khan, among others, argued that deportation stripped citizens of their rights to contest the state's charges of permit violations, while the government argued that deportation simply placed those who had "illegally" entered in the same place as those who were denied permits for entry to begin with. Although this important Supreme Court judgment ruled that deportation was indeed "an excessive power" that also contravened the constitutional rights of a citizen, the defendants had to first prove that they were indeed citizens.[68] For most this meant continued contestations in court, for permit violations inevitably engaged questions of citizenship.

It is difficult to ascertain how many such cases took place all over India, since only those that reach the high court were reported in law digests. But the sheer number of popular legal guides (such as Mazhar Husain's *The Law Relating to Foreigners in India and the Citizenship Laws of India and Pakistan,* reprinted four times) on such cases that were available in the 1950s and even the 1960s indicates how significant these arrests, deportations, and contestations in court over citizenship were for Muslims who remained, or wanted to remain, in India. The effects of these cases extended beyond those individuals who were directly criminalized and prosecuted. Reported in *Al-Jamiat*[69] and presumably in other Urdu newspapers, and circulated by word of mouth, they communicated the terrifying necessity of aligning lives with bounded national identities as Muslims in India began to be pushed out—literally across borders, and symbolically into margins.

DISCIPLINING GOVERNMENT SERVANTS

Government servants of the colonial state were asked to "opt" for India or Pakistan in the months before Partition, but in recognition of the uncertainties that accompanied Partition a third "provisional" option was also possible. In addition to the numerous "provisional optees" who changed their service selection after Partition, there were thousands of Muslims who "opted" for India but then went to work in Pakistan, and there were over 16,000 Muslim employees who "opted" for Pakistan but then desired to remain in India.[70] The boundary between state and society is a conceptual one which, as Timothy Mitchell has argued, has important effects. However, that conceptual boundary blurs as we look within the state at bureaucratic self-regulation, for the uncertainty in society permeates the functionaries of state.

I would like to focus here on the disciplining of familial ties of government servants after the introduction of the permit system. The fact that government servants had "opted" to work for one state but had members of families residing in the society of the other state became a source of anxiety for both India and Pakistan, a source of "pollution" and danger. Both governments demanded that its Hindu and later Muslim functionaries in the Pakistani case, and Muslim functionaries in the Indian case, "show" that their families were residing with them or face termination of employment.

In the case of the Delhi administration, the chief commissioner's files are an archive of this process of disciplining the state's bureaucracy. Lists of Muslims employed in every institution that came under the Delhi government were drawn up, and they were asked to provide information regarding the whereabouts of their "family." If any of their family was in Pakistan, they were served with notices that if they did not bring them back in one month their employment would be terminated. It was announced that having family in Pakistan "would be prima facie evidence of disloyalty to the Dominion of India."[71]

Family here was defined as the government servant's nuclear or elementary family, made up of those legally constituted as "dependents." Here the focus was on the male civil servant's wife, unmarried daughters, and minor sons.[72] By insisting that they reside with him, the state considered the patrilocal familial order as necessary for a Muslim male to be a "loyal citizen."

The lists drawn up by the various institutions of the Delhi government are spreadsheets of Muslim familial ties and their spatial and affective reconfiguration by Partition. Abdul Hamid, employed with the district and sessions judge, could not locate his family since the disturbances. Umar Baksh at the Malaria Institute of India had one brother as well as his parents in Pakistan. Although the wife and two sons of Umar Daraz, a superintendent of education, were in Pakistan, he argued that he had not been on good terms with them for two years before Partition and did not desire their return. On the other hand, Mohammad Ramzan's wife and one child were with him, but three of his adult sons and their wives were living in Pakistan.

I examine here the responses of Muslims in the Delhi government to the demand to bring back the family, as well as that of their supervisors. I have reproduced an excerpt from one of the many lists in the file (see table 3.2). The lists are brief, but suggestive of how while some Muslim government servants made clear decisions to resign, others attempted to keep their employment by expressing "keenness" to bring back their families, a desire for reunion that was met with a classification of "doubtful." The category of "doubtful" could be read as an intermediary to "disloyal" but captures all the ambivalence of casting long-standing employees, colleagues, and sometimes friends into a field of suspicion, unemployment, and ultimately, dispossession. Only in one case in this entire list is the "keenness" to remain in India rejected outright by the classification of "disloyal." In the other cases, "doubtful" raised skepticism about the explanation but at the same time left the government servant/colleague some room to maneuver, and negotiate with the state in what were still uncertain conditions.

Those who were classified as "doubtful" were required to submit explanations for the absence of their families. These explanations were often lengthy in making the case that while they did wish to remain in India, the particular and extraordinary nature of their familial circumstances prevented them from bringing their families back from Pakistan. For instance, Sahibzada Aziz Ahmad Khan, a sub-registrar, wrote about his nervous

TABLE 3.2 Muslim Civil Servants in the Delhi Administration

Name	*Department*	*Explanation*	*Remarks of Head of Office*
A.A.	Chief Commissioner's Office	Hasn't brought back his family by Dec. 3, 1948	Resigned and relieved of his duties, Jan. 17, 1949.
N.M.	Inspector-General of Police's Office	All but his sons murdered, sons are in camps in Sind. Both are of majority age.	Superintendent of Police (SP) doesn't think he can bring his boys back.
M.T.	Inspector-General of Police's Office	Only son is in service in Pakistan, rest of family is in Delhi.	SP says son is of majority age, no need to bring him.
N.T.	Inspector-General of Police's Office	Family in Pakistan, and on four months' leave prior to retirement.	Doubtful
A.S.	Inspector-General of Police's Office	Traffic policeman keen to get his wife back who is in Lahore with her brother, but she hasn't replied to his letters.	Doubtful
A.G.	Inspector-General of Police's Office	Has two wives, one is here and the other and her children are in Pakistan. Not good relations, does not want to send for her.	SP says that in the circumstances bringing second wife does not arise
A.A.	Inspector-General of Police's Office	On four months' leave. Has submitted medical certificate saying his wife is too ill to be moved.	Doubtful

(continued)

TABLE 3.2 Muslim Civil Servants in the Delhi Administration *(continued)*

Name	*Department*	*Explanation*	*Remarks of Head of Office*
M.K.	Secretary and engineer, Delhi Joint Water and Sewage Board	His two sisters migrated, so mother and younger sister went there to see them and then permits were imposed and younger sister is ill.	Doubtful
R.M.	Deputy Commissioner's Office	Son and daughter left with sister to Pakistan. Requests two months' leave to fetch them	Given leave for twenty days to bring them.
A.T.	CID	Family killed in disturbances. Survivors in Pakistan. Houses looted and not keen to bring back family.	Deputy Superintendent of Police says he will settle in Pakistan.
S.A.	Inspector-General of Police's Office	Says he doesn't have money to send for them now but has opted for service in India. Family left due to communal disturbances without his knowledge. States that he has lost three children in a refugee camp in Pakistan, but he is keen to remain in Indian Dominion.	SP reports that this man does not intend to bring his family to India and considers him to be disloyal and has classified him as "Doubtful."
K.A.	Inspector-General of Police's Office	Wife and children with his brother in Sheikhapura, and doesn't have money to bring them.	SP says that if government gives him money he'll bring them.

sister, fevered daughter, and his own poor health and longing for his family in his request for more time to bring them back:

> Mine is a bit hard case. My wife died leaving two minor children and I have not married since. These children were brought up by my elder sister, who nursed them during their tender years. Naturally both the sister and the children are immensely attached to each other. My sister preferred to remain unmarried and spent all her life giving care and attention on these children. During the last disturbances, cases of fatal stabbing and arson occurred in . . . our *mohalla*. . . . All these news had a very adverse effect on my already nervous and old sister . . . the climax was reached when the news reached us that our eldest brother-in-law who migrated to Pakistan under orders died soon after reaching Lahore, leaving his children stranded. My sister's nerves gave way and she firmly decided to go to Lahore and attend the death ceremonies. She proceeded to Lahore with some of our relatives and took my children with her. Since last two months I am receiving letter from Lahore that my daughter is not keeping well, she occasionally gets temperature. The latest news about her is that she has cough as well. I am much nervous about her health. . . . All these factors have a telling effect on my nerves, as I am very much attached to my children. My health is running down, and I often get slight gout attacks and neuralgic and gastric trouble. I myself badly need them back.[73]

Mubashir Ali, a superintendent in the Ministry of Relief and Rehabilitation, argued that in addition to transportation problems, his father's and wife's illnesses and their destitution prevented their return; he was more concerned for their return than the government was:

> I went to Karachi to bring down my family to Delhi . . . I could not however do so owing to the reason that the Jodhpur Railway had stopped . . . and I could hardly afford to bring my family by means of air transport. As a result I came back to Delhi alone on the 31st of August 1948. Soon after my leaving Karachi the condition of my father who was already sick, became serious and my wife was also taken ill, and as there was nobody else who could look after them during their sickness, my wife was compelled to come down . . . to

> Multan where besides her father she had a number of other relatives who could attend to them. . . . Since they expressed their inability even to move from the bed, I did not consider it worth a while to do anything in this direction [of arranging their return]. I need not here mention the troubles which my family is facing in Multan. Suffice it to say that there being no proper accommodation my aged and sickly father is passing this winter season on the roadside; my two children of school going age are neither having any education nor coaching; and due to the lack of proper medical advice the condition both of my father and wife is going from bad to worse every day. . . .[74]

As these excerpts show, these letters of explanation did not make abstract claims of loyalty to the state by expressing love for the nation. Instead their authors stated their love for their families, their suffering caused by separation, and their desire to be together. These are personal and emotional appeals meant to solicit sympathy for the suffering wrought by Partition's dislocations. These appeals were made to supervisors who probably knew them, and had met them face to face.

These letters were passed on with the supervisor's remarks to the central government, the Ministry of Home Affairs. There a secretary made the final decision to grant, or not grant, extensions on the time to bring back families, and instructed the departments to terminate employment accordingly. Here the decision became impersonal and abstract, and the secretary at Home Affairs issued letters to take "disciplinary action" against those still classified as "doubtful."

However, in the case of a few individuals the correspondence between supervisors and Home Affairs was lengthy, and tracks resistance to the state's attempt to self-discipline. The case of Mirza, a head clerk in Delhi's office of the Chief Medical Officer (CMO), is one such example. He explained that his wife and three children had gone to see her brother in New Delhi when disturbances broke out, and all of them had to take refuge in Purana Qila. From there they left for Pakistan. Although he had since tried to compel them to return to Delhi, his wife's brother refused to let her go because of "the disastrous scenes he had had the chance to see during the disturbances." Mirza's explanation was favorably received by his supervisor, for the latter noted that Mirza had "worked fearlessly through the disturbances," and also had an exceptional service record:

twenty-four years of "loyalty and conscientiousness." The CMO himself added a handwritten note of agreement to this characterization of Mirza.[75] Therefore, even though Home Affairs deemed his explanation "not at all satisfactory,"[76] it was compelled to grant a "relaxation of rules" for him. However, when a year later Mirza's family had still not rejoined him, Home Affairs issued a directive for "proper disciplinary action." After twenty-four years of hardworking "loyalty," Mirza, through the stroke of bureaucratic vigilance, became classified as "disloyal."

Azmatullah, an official receiver at the Small Cause Courts, moved in his own case from being classified as "doubtful" to "disloyal." Azmatullah's explanation for his family's absence was that his home on 4051 Sir Sayed Ahmad Road in Daryaganj had been occupied by a refugee, and he had been forced to live with his sister. Therefore, he had not brought his family back because he did not have a place for them to stay.[77] The Office of the Judge did not consider his argument credible and counterargued that "any number of houses are available for Mohammadans in the localities especially reserved for them."[78] Although the office had waited for him to return to work after the "disturbances" until the end of December, they now found "his conduct doubtful." The judge's office also noted that Azmatullah's adult son had opted to work for the government of Pakistan. Azmatullah was given two weeks to bring his family back.

In July 1949, Azmatullah returned from Pakistan and claimed that he was unable to get a permit for his wife, Ayesha Sultan Begum, although she was ready to return with him. To make his case he made presentations to a number of senior government officials, including Dr. Zakir Husain, who wrote to Shankar Prasad, the chief commissioner of Delhi, on July 6, 1949, to say that Azmatullah "is a good man and genuinely anxious to stay in India."[79] His file contains numerous petitions, including those to the joint secretary at the Ministry of Relief and Rehabilitation to obtain a permanent permit for his wife.[80] As a result of what can only be interpreted as a determined attempt, he obtained an extension on the deadline for the return of his "family." (It appears that only his wife, as "family," was in question here.)

However, as late as 1950, when a CID investigation[81] into his property was initiated by the custodian's office, Azmatullah was moved into the category of the "disloyal." The CID investigation inquired into all his siblings and their whereabouts and revealed that Azmatullah had a brother, a Major Basharatullah, who had opted for the Pakistan Army, although his sisters and brothers-in-law were employed and living in India. It was during the horrific September violence in Delhi that Azmatullah and his mother, wife, and children had left for Pakistan. Although he had returned prior to the permit system, the others had remained in Pakistan. The fact that he had visited Pakistan four times, and spent the September holidays, when civil courts close, in Pakistan was held against him. In addition he was reported as trying to sell his house, which had been declared evacuee property, to its current occupant, and this was interpreted as moving assets with a view to move to Pakistan. (As I discuss in the next chapter, once a property was declared evacuee the ownership became virtual, and selling it was probably one of the few possibilities open to Azmatullah, although there were restrictions on selling as well.)

Finally, an anonymous "Complaint Against the Official Receiver Maulvi Mohammad Azmatullah" described him as "a disloyal subject of Indian Dominion inasmuch as he keeps a Pakistan calendar in his office" and therefore is considered to have "League Leanings." The complaint proved decisive. Home Affairs concluded that he "has been trying to get the best of both worlds for as long as he can," and the time had come for him to be disciplined into a new national order.[82]

In the next chapter I examine the institution of the Custodian of Evacuee Property and its role in producing displacements and internal dispossession. However, here one can only conjecture as to what extent the custodian's inquiry played a role in Azmatullah being declared "disloyal" by the state, and to what extent family formations across this emerging divide, and the ownership of a Pakistani calendar, sealed his fate.

Nonetheless, controlling the movement of specific people in a time of massive displacement set in motion a political process with enormous institutional effects, and made "doubtful" and "disloyal" into critical categories for transforming markers of religious community into citizens of new nation-states.

4. *Economies of Displacement*

[T]he houses that were lost forever continue to live on in us.[1]

The displaced of the Partition, both "Muslim refugees" and "non-Muslim refugees," lost their homes. This loss cannot be underestimated in the making of Partition's new nations. After people took flight they were unable to return to their homes because those houses had come to be occupied by others. The laws that came to govern the leaving and occupation of homes were the evacuee property legislations.

As we have seen, the Custodian of Evacuee Property was initially set up to protect the properties of the displaced, the "evacuees," until such time that they could return to them. Thus it is ironic that the very formulation of evacuee property laws as a cornerstone of rehabilitation programs of both states ended up fixing the two sets of refugees in an oppositional relationship, to make refugee return almost impossible. In India, the Muslim refugees were the "evacuees" while Hindu and Sikh refugees became "displaced persons" who were to be rehabilitated through allotments of "evacuee property." The departure of Muslim "evacuees" thus came to be perceived as necessary to accommodate Hindu and Sikh refugees. In Pakistan, Hindu and Sikh refugees became "evacuees" whose properties the custodian took over, while Muslim refugees or *muhajirs* became "displaced persons" who could apply for the allotment of evacuee property.[2] Thus, as we have seen, the departure of Hindu and Sikh "evacuees" came to be used as the basis for calculating how many Muslim refugees could be accommodated by the Pakistani state.

However, an important effect of evacuee property laws was that the "evacuee" became a refugee category that began to encompass entire religious communities and not just those who had been displaced by violence. This transformation in the character of evacuee property laws was not immediate, but rather a piecemeal process in which the retaliatory logic of the hostage theory legitimated countless amendments by both states "in response" to each other. In this chapter I examine the national economy of this transformation.

To be declared "evacuee" by the nation-state meant having "emptied," or having been forced to "empty," one's home as a space of belonging, of being dispossessed of more than just a familial abode. Rafi bhai had mentioned how his having returned from Pakistan on a permit led to his familial home being declared "evacuee property." Although the courts eventually acknowledged him and his family as Indian citizens, they were unable to regain their familial home. This effect of evacuee property laws, such that people who were considered legally Indian citizens became at the same time "evacuees," made the institution an instrument of internal displacement and dispossession.

The meaning of this dispossession was suggested to me when Rafi bhai, at the end of a long interview, remembered that which was on the verge of being forgotten:

> *Hanh! Ek cheez main bhul gaya batana āp ko! Ke khandān ki history aur makān kaise bana—is sab ka ek scroll hai jo likh kar, ek botal ke undar rakh kar, is makān ka jo darwaza hai is ke nīche dafan hai. Woh to bahut deep ho ga kahī. Main ne puchha tha ke ye kyā hai, to inhon ne kaha ke kabhi historically, kabhi makān ṭoṭa, aur us kī khuddaī hoī, to us waqt ye nikal āye ga. Aur ye makān kin logon ka tha, aur us ka background tha, kiya us par kharcha ā'ya—ye sarī cheezain thī . . .*

[Long pause.]

> *Ye reh ga, ya nahin. Kaisī kaisī tehzibain khatm ho gaī. Haṛappa, Mohenjodaro. Dekhye āp. "Rahe nām Allah ka," ye kehte hai na jab esī kahanian bataī jatī hai.*

> Ah! I have forgotten to tell you one thing! This family's history and how this house was made. There is a scroll for all this, on which it is all written, and then placed inside a bottle, and is buried under the doorway of the house. It must be very deep somewhere. I had asked what is this, and they told me that at some time historically, at some time when the house is finished (destroyed) and then it is excavated, so, at that time this will come out. And who did this house belong to, what was their background, how much it cost—all these things are in it.
>
> [Long pause.]
>
> Will it survive or not? So many cultures have been finished. Harrappa, Mohenjodaro. We shall see. "Allah's name will remain," they say this, don't they, when stories like these are told.

For Rafi bhai, the physical site of this house (*makān*) was tied to his familial history (*khandān ki* history) not just through emotionally laden memories of time spent there. The physical house, the scroll under the threshold, contained a "written" record for posterity, for recovering a particular history in which he located his very belonging. The need to remember and tell me that which was on the verge of being forgotten, whose survival was tenuous, was tied to a loss of this history itself.

As the past has repeatedly been folded into nation, the loss of Rafi bhai's familial home, as a result of it being declared evacuee property, was further heightened by silences in the official record of the institution itself. In India, the evacuee property laws were abrogated in 1954, and although court cases continue to this day, the government record in Delhi was almost entirely destroyed in the 1960s. As a result, the secondary sources that I draw upon here on the Custodian of Evacuee Property are largely from the 1950s. In Karachi, I trekked through the offices of the Surveyor General, the Karachi Municipal Cooperation, the Karachi Development Authority, the Sind Archives, and the Evacuee Property Trust, which today administers only non-Muslim religious buildings under its care. At each of these institutions no one could find any records.

If the sentiment of loss is a product of the modern world's ordering of place and our knowledge of it, then the silence on evacuee property in the economy of nation obliged me to recover its history in the rubble of lost houses.[3] It is from fragments and memory that I put together this "lost" history, of the Muslim experience with the institution of evacuee property in India (from the perspective of "evacuees") as well as of evacuee property in Karachi (from the perspective of "displaced persons"). I track how it "emptied" out religious minorities and pushed them to the margins of nations-in-the-making—with chilling political legitimacy on both sides.

NATIONS, PROPERTIES, MINORITIES

Amid the mayhem in divided Punjab, as large numbers of people fled from their homes and lands and massive looting and occupations followed, the Joint Defense Council decided at its meeting in Lahore on August 29, 1947, to create the office of the "Custodian of Refugee's Property" to protect the properties of the displaced. In that state of emergency, the institution of the custodian was meant to take possession of these properties and "manage" them, until such time that refugees could return to them. Both governments also agreed not to recognize occupations and seizures of property, and this combined intervention was meant to enable the return of the displaced back to their homes and lands.[4]

To this effect, in early September 1947 the East and West Punjab Evacuee Property (Preservation) Ordinances were passed in divided Punjab to empower the position of the custodian, and this legislation was extended a few days later to Delhi when the city was also engulfed by violence. Thus renamed (from "refugee property" to "evacuee property"), the office of the "Custodian of Evacuee Property" emerged, and this institution, contrary to its initial premise of refugee return, made the displacements more or less permanent by making one set of refugees into "evacuees" and another set of refugees into "displaced persons."

What transformed the fundamental nature of this intervention was a dispute between the two states, which Jyoti Bhusan Das Gupta, in her dissertation on Indo-Pak relations in 1958, described as equivalent to the Kashmir dispute because of its belligerent nature.[5] The problem emerged concomitant with the formation of the Military Evacuation Organization (MEO) and the "planned" nature of Punjab's displacements. As I argued in the first chapter, the Pakistani government agreed to a transfer of populations along religious lines in divided Punjab with certain reservations. The considerably larger properties that Hindus and Sikhs would leave behind, it conjectured, would allow it to accommodate the Muslim refugees that were already arriving, but it feared that if a question of compensation arose then it would have to make payments that it could not afford. Yet, accepting the principle of the transfer, the government of West Punjab issued a West Punjab Economic Rehabilitation Ordinance alongside the evacuee property legislation, which simultaneously created the position of rehabilitation commissioner, who was empowered to take possession of abandoned properties, agricultural lands, and businesses and "allot" them to Muslim refugees for a period of one year.[6] By the end of the year, it passed an additional ordinance whereby transfer of evacuee property could only be done with permission from the custodian, thus curtailing individual attempts by "non-Muslim refugees," or now "evacuees," to sell or exchange properties.[7] In response, the Indian evacuee property legislation was altered so that the office of the custodian could also "allot" evacuee property to "displaced persons" and made transfers equally difficult. Also, it decided that those who had occupied houses would not be removed until alternative housing could be found for them. It needs to be emphasized that despite occupations and allotments of evacuee property, a cornerstone of the evacuee property agreement was that the displaced maintained a right in their properties left behind—people who had moved, and their property that had not, remained tied to each other, albeit in what would come to be called "imaginary ownership."[8]

It has been argued that a nation is "a collection of individuals and their properties."[9] However, here not only were individuals and their properties separated, but other individuals had occupied their properties left behind. If the impossibility of the displaced being able to return to their homes had been recognized and the institution of evacuee property declared null and void then the Custodian of Evacuee Property would not have had the far-reaching effects it did. Yet the "evacuee" and evacuee property were retained as a device of rehabilitation, and calculations of the economic value of these properties acquired significance in the intergovernmental dispute that ensued.

The dispute occurred, as feared by the Pakistani government, over the question of compensation.[10] The Indian government wanted evacuee property to be settled between the two governments, since the possibility of refugee return, the unmaking of refugees, was already curtailed by the agreement on the transfer of populations in Punjab and by the emergence of permits. The Indian government claimed that since the evacuee property left behind by non-Muslims was far greater in value than the evacuee property of Muslims in India—a difference it calculated to the sum of 400 crores[11]—the Pakistani government should pay India for it. In addition, the Indian government's rehabilitation scheme involved compensating the now retitled "displaced persons" from a collective "compensation pool" that would include Muslim evacuee property in India and the differential payments Pakistan would make.

This mathematics was of course disadvantageous to the Pakistani government, which argued that it was India's "obsession that much more evacuee property lay within the boundaries of Pakistan" and that this "obsession" was "not based upon any reliable figures . . . but only upon a general feeling."[12] The Pakistani government took the official position that the value of evacuee property on the two sides of divided Punjab and Delhi was more or less equivalent, and that therefore refugees on an individual basis should sell or transfer their properties that they had left behind and obtain whatever they could for their properties on the market.

The most important negotiations on evacuee property took place in January 1949 and resulted in what was called the Karachi Agreement. In the Karachi Agreement, the rights of "evacuees" in their property was reaffirmed and it was agreed that 1) the laws would encompass only "agreed areas"[13] from where mass migration had occurred due to "disturbances"; 2) that the free sale and exchange of urban immovable property would be allowed; and 3) that while the properties could be used temporarily for rehabilitation, with allotments made for up to three years, the custodian would collect rent on those properties and transfer the amount to the other dominion.[14]

However, notes made by Pakistani officials at the negotiations show that the "agreement" was an uneasy one. There were disagreements over not only what regions should be included in "agreed areas" but also over who was to be considered an "evacuee." Pakistan wanted to contain the category of the "evacuee," while the Indian officials wanted to leave it open. Therefore, Pakistani officials at first suggested that evacuee property laws should only apply to government servants, but not otherwise, while the Indian side argued that this distinction was arbitrary. In response, the Pakistani officials suggested a "limit date" to include those who had migrated before September 30, 1948. India opposed this definition, claiming it would be unfair to Hindus and Sikhs who had "migrated" after that date (those leaving Sind, for example). Pakistan's minister of refugees remarked that "India does not seem to have given expression to her real reasons for opposing a 'limiting' date . . . [because] it may be that India is thinking not of Hindu/Sikh evacuees but of Muslims still in the 'agreed areas' in India whose migration to Pakistan they wish to encourage . . . for the imposition of a limiting date for migration would automatically limit the Muslim evacuee property in those areas to whatever has already been abandoned."[15]

Soon after the Karachi Agreement, there were rapid transformations in evacuee property legislation and abusive application on both sides. As a result it came to be described as an "abnormal law" and a "necessary evil"[16] by the time of its repeal by the Indian government in 1954. Failure to collect and transfer rents on the Pakistani side led to an Indian view that the intergovernmental solution was not tenable; Pakistan could not be compelled to pay its part toward the compensation pool. As a result, the Indian state undertook a number of changes in legislation, changes which were mirrored by the Pakistani state.

First, soon after the Karachi Agreement, which allowed for the sale or exchange of evacuee property, the Indian government believed that "as a result of recent evacuee property legislation, a large number of Muslim evacuees from Pakistan [we]re coming to India on temporary permits in order to make arrangements for the disposal of their properties before they are taken over by the custodian." The following circular was sent by the Ministry of Rehabilitation:

> I am to point out that it is extremely essential that Muslims coming to India on temporary visits are *not* allowed to dispose of their properties in India and that any property which is evacuee property under the law, is taken over by the custodian concerned . . . I am to request that every possible care should be taken to ensure that properties belonging to Muslims which fall under the definition of evacuee property are not allowed to go undetected.[17]

Thus the Ministry of Rehabilitation directed district administrations that counterfoils of temporary permits issued by the High Commission in Pakistan, which were usually sent to the superintendents of police, be forwarded to the custodian or deputy custodian of evacuee property for that area, so that he could "trace out the properties of such persons, if any, and to take them over as evacuee property." In keeping with the use of permits for surveillance, a set of questions on evacuee property became part of permit application forms. This included information regarding the applicant's immovable property, details of properties owned in India, the identities of its current residents, and whether it had been declared evacuee or not. In addition, the form asked if any property was owned or allotted in Pakistan, for an affirmative in this regard could lead to a person being declared "evacuee."[18]

Second, the Indian government extended the jurisdiction of the evacuee property laws to the whole of India, with the exception of Bengal. In divided Bengal these laws were very differently executed because of a larger attempt not to disturb the equilibrium between minorities on both sides.[19] The extension of evacuee property laws had implications, for the original legislation in the Punjab and Delhi defined an "evacuee" as "any person displaced from his usual place of habitation." This meant that "a person could be declared evacuee if he left his ordinary place of residence and migrated either to another *mohalla* or another quarter of the same town." This definition carried over into legislations in UP as well as Bombay, and therefore meant that, as A.P. Jain, the minister of rehabilitation later noted, persons who had not migrated to Pakistan or who had not received any allotment of evacuee or abandoned property in Pakistan were also declared as "evacuee." It was only in 1950 that the definition of an "evacuee" was clarified to mean only persons who had migrated to Pakistan.[20]

Third, in the same year, and on the heels of this redefinition of an "evacuee," another category was added to legislation: that of "intending evacuee." The "intending evacuee" was meant to enlarge the compensation pool by encompassing "someone seen as making a preparation for his migration"; a mechanism was thereby created to take control of their property *before* they became "evacuee." A person who had never gone to Pakistan could become an "intending evacuee," and as a consequence his property could not be transferred in any way until the custodian decided whether it was evacuee or not.[21] Although there were conditions attached to who could be declared "intending evacuee," they only added to the capriciousness of the term "evacuee," allowing it to be used to encompass virtually all Muslims who owned property in India, and similarly all Hindus in West Pakistan.

On April 6, 1951, an important debate took place in Pakistan's Constituent Assembly on evacuee property when the Pakistan (Administration of Evacuee Property) Act was amended to add the "intending evacuee" clause to mirror the Indian legislation.[22] The retaliatory logic of the hostage theory entirely legitimated this amendment, even though only about 2 lakh Hindus remained in West Pakistan and the amendment could not possibly add substantially to the value of evacuee property there, but was certain to further discriminate against this remaining community. Dhirendra Nath Dutta pointed out that the clause would leave much to the "imagination of the custodian," and Raj Kumar Chakraverty criticized its retaliatory logic. Seth Sukhdev of Sind noted with great sadness that "very bad times [we]re coming" for it would "push out" the last remaining Hindus that had property in West Pakistan. Yet Dr. I.H. Querishi, the former history professor from Delhi University and now the minister of refugees and rehabilitation, legitimized this amendment in the laws because the Indian state was perceived to be profiting "at the cost of her own Muslim nationals." He responded to the "alarm of minorities" by arguing that if "a certain section of the population is put to a little more inconvenience than the others; on such occasions it is the duty of all loyal citizens of the state to bear those hardships." It is evident in this debate that there were no illusions about the effects of the institution in encompassing entire religious minorities, who were to be "punished" for the treatment Muslims were receiving in India. In other words, evacuee property by this time was no longer about rehabilitation alone, but was being retained and expanded in legislation to function as an internal border-making device, separating minority religious communities by asking them to prove their "loyalty," even if this meant internal dispossession and being "pushed out."

Fourth, the Evacuee Interest (Separation) Act was passed in India in 1951 to take into custody properties whose part-owners were "evacuees," and it provided rules for the separation of the interest of "evacuees" from those of "non-evacuees" in "composite properties."[23] This legislation particularly affected joint family or ancestral homes where an array of kin lived together but one or more of the part-owners of the property had left for Pakistan. The "separation of interests" between "evacuee" and "non-evacuee" entailed the actual physical division of the property "by metes and bounds" by the custodian. In cases where such physical division of a property was not possible, the "non-evacuee co-sharers" had the option to buy the "evacuee share," but if they were unable to do so then the entire property was auctioned. This meant the displacement of even those who were "non-evacuee" under the law. These provisions were also added to the Pakistani laws.

A realization of the institution's exclusionary power was felt early in its application in India. In 1948 G. D. Khosla was appointed to look into the workings of the Custodian of Evacuee Property because of the "unprecedented nature of the business."[24] I have already quoted his conversation with Gandhi on the subject of "empty" Muslim houses in Delhi. In February 1948, Kazi Syed Karimuddin pointed out to the Indian Assembly that the evacuee property laws were "causing great hardship to the Muslims of Delhi and particularly to the *pardahnashin* [veiled] ladies," but received the short reply that these laws had been promulgated to "mirror" Pakistan's, and this retaliatory logic served to silence its local effects.[25] However, in the ensuing years evacuee property's important role in the discourse of rehabilitation for the well-being of the putative nation was so powerful that it justified the institution and led to the widening of its captive net. In addition, the controversial resignation in 1951 of Achhru Ram, the custodian general of evacuee property, marked an attempt to check its excesses.

Ram was asked to resign by A.P. Jain, the minister of rehabilitation, because Ram gave two contradictory judgments on the status of a Mr. Chhatriwala, as to whether he was an evacuee or not. In a judgment on September 6, 1950, Ram had declared Chhatriwala as not an evacuee because he had gone to Pakistan before the introduction of the permit system and had returned. As a result, his property which had been declared evacuee was returned to him. But in another judgment a year later, Ram declared him once again an evacuee, taking the position that his earlier view was not binding. Although this capriciousness was almost built into the application of evacuee property laws, the demand for Ram's resignation came as an attempt to restrain these powers of the laws.

Ram, in his letter of explanation to Jain, wrote that he had accepted the office of custodian general "in response to the touching appeals received from hundreds of my displaced brethren . . ." The fact that the custodian saw his role as primarily concerned with his "displaced brethren" (including only Hindu and Sikh refugees) reflects the divisive shift in the practice of the institution. This is also reflected in an ordinary legal guide on evacuee property, which remarks that its purpose was for "this property . . . ultimately to be used for compensating the refugees who had lost their property in Pakistan."[26]

Jain, in turn, reiterated the original conception of evacuee property, that the task of the custodian was to consider "yourself as much interested in the persons on whose behalf you have held the property" that the "title of the property continues to vest in the evacuees," even if it is allotted. However, the analogy that Jain drew to make his point was that the Custodian of Evacuee Property was meant to function like the Custodian of Enemy Property appointed during the Second World War.[27] This analogy, equating "evacuee" with "enemy," is noteworthy for placing the South Asian custodian in a comparative history of mass displacements in the mid-twentieth century.

The Custodian of Enemy Property was established in Britain during the years of the Second World War, from 1939 to 1945. It was a part of the "trading with the enemy" legislation which allowed the British government to take over the properties of "belligerent enemies" in Britain, which included citizens of Germany, Hungary, Romania, and Bulgaria, as well as "technical enemies," which included citizens of Czechoslovakia and Poland. This institution took over the properties of 220,000 people, and a more recent recognition of its abuses has led to British legislation to compensate its victims.[28]

However, the subcontinent's legislation has closer, disturbing parallels with the Israeli state's Custodian of Absentee Property. It was not only nearly contemporaneous to the South Asian institution; it may also have been to a certain extent self-consciously modeled after it. Accounts of the custodian's office in Israel have argued that the legislation served to "empty" the land of Palestinian Arabs and construct the myth of a voluntary exodus. In Israel, the Emergency Regulations on Property of Absentees were passed on December 2, 1948, and were later converted into the Absentee Property Act of March 2, 1949. According to this Israeli legislation, Arabs not present in their homes on November 29, 1948, were declared "absentees" and their properties were appropriated, even if they had only gone to a neighboring town. Although in the original evacuee property legislation in India and Pakistan the same definition of evacuee made sense—most of the displaced moved to camps in a state of emergency and uncertainty—the later use of this definition in places like UP and Bombay where Muslims owned considerable properties meant internal dispossession of some scale. The Israeli legislation preserved the rights of ownership while restricting transfers, and a Development Authority was established to then allot the "empty houses" to Jewish immigrants for up to six years. The South Asian custodian was set up on similar lines, and a rehabilitation commissioner performed the role of the Development Authority. However, later, and unlike the South Asian institution, the Israeli legislation was changed and the Development Authority was allowed to sell the properties to the Israeli state, the Jewish National Fund, and other organizations. As further changes were made in the Israeli laws, it produced Arab Israeli citizens who came to be classified as "present absentees," parallel to the South Asian "intending evacuees."[29]

Similarly, the effects of evacuee property in "emptying" out religious minorities and producing internal dispossession cannot be underestimated. However, the realization by the Indian state that Muslims were being dispossessed while living in India led at first to removal of the "intending evacuee" clause in 1953 and then the final abrogation of the law in its entirety in 1954.[30] A long and important debate took place in the Constituent Assembly on August 11, 1952, when Jain first proposed the removal of the "intending evacuee" clause but faced considerable resistance. This debate locates the discursive effects of evacuee property in the making of new nations.

Jain had to walk a tightrope in proposing the removal of the "intending evacuee" clause: he was arguing for Muslim inclusion while at the same time appearing to protect the interests of (non-Muslim) refugees. Jain made a long presentation on the history of the evacuee property laws as he built the case that "we have taken care that while the evacuee pool does not suffer, at the same time if any provision of this bill discriminates against any citizen of this country, whatever may be his caste or creed or religion, then such provision needs modification":

> It does good to nobody. It does not add anything to the evacuee property [compensation] pool. At the same time it does a lot of harm to one section of our people. In fact, I have been of late receiving a large number of representations and come across some heartrending cases in which some Muslim citizen of India wanted to sell his property but people were afraid to buy it or at any rate were not willing to pay the full price for it because they thought that that citizen may be declared an intending evacuee or because the transaction may not be confirmed under section 40. . . . The chief minister of Saurashtra

> wrote to the prime minister that there was a certain Muslim in that state who wanted to sell his house to maintain his cattle because there was scarcity of fodder but no purchaser was forthcoming because nobody was sure whether that Muslim would not subsequently be declared an intending evacuee and the sale may not be confirmed. There was the case of a nationalist Muslim—a person much devoted to the motherland as any member here—who even refused to attend the marriage of his relatives in Pakistan, who wanted to mortgage but, found difficulty in doing it. That state of things, I submit, is no good. . . .[31]

Jain presented the ways in which "Muslim citizens" were being discriminated against by the all-encompassing "intending evacuee" clause, but his argument that Muslims were "our people" and deserved fair treatment was met with considerable resistance from Sardar Hukam Singh. Singh derived authority for his argument from the "lofty ideal" of nation itself, in which "what is best for my country, what is best for the citizens of this country" gave him legitimacy. In terms of this "lofty ideal," the "question of evacuee property and the compensation that they have to get [we]re very intimately connected with the fate of the refugees." The economy of rehabilitation was centrally based on the value of evacuee property, and Muslim houses and businesses could not be separated from the compensation pool. Thus acquiring as much evacuee property as possible had a driving economic imperative. He argued that refugees had been led to believe that Muslim evacuee property would contribute 350 crore rupees, but this amount was now reduced to 50–70 crore because of a "liberal attitude" toward Muslims like the Chhatriwalas to whom properties had been restored. Jain argued that only forty-two evacuee properties had been returned to owners in cases where it was found that the "evacuee" had not really left India, but Singh contested these seemingly paltry figures.

The argument between Jain and Singh over numbers and the value of evacuee property was most revealing when it turned to "Muslim zones" in Delhi which were outside the jurisdiction of the custodian:

> SARDAR HUKAM SINGH: Then, there is another thing. There are in Delhi alone about 3,500 houses, I am told.
>
> SHRI A.P. JAIN: I might correct you. There are only 121.

SARDAR HUKAM SINGH: I am told that there are 321 . . .

SHRI A.P. JAIN: No, 121. Which houses, you mean in the Muslim zones?

SARDAR HUKAM SINGH: Exactly? 3,500 according to my information, which must be wrong, I say. But I cannot believe they are 121. The custodian is not allowed to go there. Possession has not been taken. The Jamiat is keeping possession of them and distributing as it likes. It is not permitted that any Hindu or Sikh might go inside that. There are Muslim zones for the past five years and that is being continued up to date. What right have they? Is this loyalty to India that they can keep those doors closed? Those zones are closed to everybody. Even the custodian cannot go and take possession of them. People are lying on the streets, but these houses must be kept intact and we should wait till the right owner comes!

We saw in the last chapter how Muslim zones were described as mini-Pakistans by the deputy commissioner of Delhi, a view linked to the implication that Muslims in India were a "fifth column" for the Pakistani state. This had helped legitimize a permit system to prevent Muslims from returning to India. Thus Singh's perception that Muslim zones equaled Muslim disloyalty had prior underpinnings.

The debate on the legitimacy of evacuee property quickly became not only about rehabilitation economics, but also about questions of "loyalty" and whether Muslims were being pushed out or wanted to leave India. Singh argued that there were two sets of Muslims: "honest Muslims" and others. An "honest Muslim would [not] be threatened and be obliged to leave this country" because of the Custodian of Evacuee Property. But the others, "those persons who had no intention of living here," were to be encompassed by the law. Importantly, for Singh the Muslims "who had no intention of living here" included those who had families in Pakistan. These others had not only sent their wives and children away, and taken advantage of allotments of evacuee property there, but were running businesses and maintaining their children there. The fact that they might be "carrying on their business there and they are good citizens here" was deemed inadmissible. Although there were limitations on remittances for families between India and Pakistan, Singh assured the Assembly that "there is no check on the large amounts that are going out." This "great flow of money" between Muslim families in India and Pakistan, made possible by earlier "liberal" evacuee property laws, was a direct threat because "[u]nder that law I can only say that even the builders of Pakistan had been receiving large amounts from our country." Thus financially crippling Muslims living in India with evacuee property laws was seen as having a positive effect in actually undermining the Pakistani state.

If this institution of the Custodian of Evacuee Property, the cornerstone for refugee rehabilitation in both postcolonial states, can be examined in comparison to the better-documented Israeli parallel, then it may be possible to begin accounting for a long Partition of displacements, produced not just by civic violence but through planned rehabilitation in both states. On the one hand, the custodian served to "push out" or "empty out" those constructed as minority religious communities, as if their displacement constituted voluntary migration. On the other hand, evacuee property produced large-scale internal displacements, particularly in India where a far larger number of Muslims remained. By making citizens into "evacuees" and "intending evacuees," it functioned like an internal border, pushing marked groups into margins within the nation by demanding of them "loyalty" even in the face of persecution.

EVACUEE PROPERTY IN DELHI AND UP

After evacuee property laws were abrogated by the Indian state in 1954, they became a part of the nation's history that needed to be effaced and written over. As a result, in 1961 the Ministry of Rehabilitation produced a brochure on evacuee property[32] outlining its history as one acceptable to the nation, the story of "an abnormal law" "necessitated by an abnormal situation created by the Partition," but followed with "humanity and justice." This brochure was circulated to its diplomatic missions around the world, and instead of projecting an Indian perspective in opposition to that of the Pakistani state, the Ministry of External Affairs noted that it aimed to show "the humane manner in which this abnormal law has been dealt with and the various concessions that have been given to Muslim nationals in India."[33]

Thus the international relations brochure focused not on the number of persons declared "evacuee" or the value of properties declared evacuee, or its relationship to the compensation pool, but rather on the number of properties that were restored to Muslims who had initially left and had then returned. This included the Meos of Alwar and Bharatpur, who had initially left for Pakistan but had returned by October 1949, as well as those who returned under the Nehru-Liaqat Pact of April 8, 1950 (which I shall discuss in next chapter).[34] Since these Muslims had left, the evacuee property laws encompassed them, but on their return a "humanitarian" view was taken by the Indian state. In addition, when the law was repealed persons in certain categories were asked to submit applications for restoration, and the 8,000 applications received were dealt with by special officers and district and sessions judges appointed for the task. Also, the brochure did not focus on how those declared "evacuees" had to prove they were "non-evacuees," but did mention that adjudication after 1954 no longer required "ration cards as evidence of continuous stay, and where original deeds were not available then other revenue records, municipal records etc. were allowed." In sum, it emphasized that properties worth 10 crore had been restored to Muslims. Here are two excerpts from the brochure:

> In processing these applications the human aspect has all along been kept in the forefront . . . [If] those decisions though legally correct would cause considerable hardships to the evacuees or their dependents, the government to mitigate hardship in such cases has given ex-gratia grants to the persons concerned on humanitarian grounds.

> *Judicious Use of Law and Human Aspect:* This law was a necessary evil which both India and Pakistan had to follow to meet the abnormal situation. India has tried to minimize the effects of this law by following liberal and humane policy in regard to the release and restoration of evacuee property . . . In retrospect it can therefore safely be claimed that India made a judicious and liberal use of even this abnormal law despite various internal as well as external stresses and strains.

The history of nation is rarely represented as one of exclusion and prejudice, so this official history of evacuee property in India is not exceptional. While evacuee property laws were recognized as "abnormal," such that "legally correct" decisions based on this law required mitigation, the state claimed to have "minimized" its effects with its "humane policy."

Here a "humanitarian" view emerges as the state's response to its own bureaucratic violence.

However, the rewriting of the contentious history of "Muslim zones" of Delhi is particularly significant for it need not have been included in the brochure at all, given that these zones were outside the jurisdiction of the custodian. Yet by including them, they served to counter any charge of Muslim discrimination:

> Disposal of Properties in Predominant Muslim Areas of Delhi: In the matter of sale of evacuee property in the predominantly Muslim areas in Delhi the concessions which have been given to all Muslim occupants of these properties are not even available to the displaced persons. Such properties are offered to the Muslim occupants at reserve price irrespective of whether their value is up to Rs10,000 or more. In the case of displaced persons, only properties up to the value of Rs10,000 are offered at reserve price, while those of higher value are invariably sold by auction. The Muslim occupants can pay the price of the property in installments and the balance in seven annual equated installments in cash or by association of compensation claims. The relations of the occupants can purchase property provided they are residing with the occupants. In case the Muslim occupants do not wish to purchase the property it is offered to some registered body of Muslims like Jamiat-e-Ulema-e-Hind. It is also referred to any other Muslim provided he is nominated by the said body.

Muslim zones were dramatically transformed in this narrative, for they were no longer a marker of "Muslim disloyalty," nor were "empty houses" there a source of struggle. All dissent and disagreement was wiped out and replaced by an extraordinary story of Muslim privilege in the new nation.

This document of the state's humanity toward Muslims becomes all the more poignant against the other layers of silences that accompany it. Secondary sources that I draw upon here are largely from the 1950s and focus entirely on the intergovernmental dispute over the value of evacuee property and the intransigence of Pakistan in not paying its part in the compensation pool.[35] After the law was abrogated and the intergovernmental dispute rendered void, the Custodian of Evacuee Property was no longer to be a subject of inquiry. In addition to that, most of the documents on evacuee property in the Delhi State Archives were destroyed in the 1960s. The index of the commissioner's records lists files on the hundreds of properties that came under the custodian's net, but simply provides a date for when they were destroyed. In addition to individual case files, files covering correspondence, procedures for taking possession of properties left by Muslims, allotments of houses to refugees, and distributions of land evacuated by the Muslims in Delhi province, as well as complaints, and petitions have mostly been destroyed.[36]

Thus I examine here some fragments from memories, newspapers, and a few files and court cases to provide alternative stories of the Muslim experience of the institution. To begin with, there are some traces of individual attempts to exchange properties outside of the planned intergovernmental frame and these are important to recover from under the hegemonic two-state ordering of place. For instance there were some people who had decided to migrate prior to Partition, and they, in anticipation of their migration, arranged an exchange of properties on an individual basis. I interviewed a member of a divided family whose father had arranged such an exchange of their home in UP with that of a Punjabi Hindu family in Lahore and after migrating had initially moved into that house before finally resettling in Karachi. The petition of Vas Dev Varma to K. C. Neogy (the first minister of rehabilitation) concerned such an exchange, of a shop in Delhi with his own in Lahore. He found the former looted on his arrival in Delhi in October 1947.[37]

It is possible that such exchanges were arranged by property "specialists" (see figures 4.1 and 4.2), for although transfers of property came to be restricted by evacuee property laws, after the Karachi Agreement there was an announcement that exchanges would once again be allowed, and *Al-Jamiat* began to carry a large number of advertisements by businesses and consultants for the exchange and sale of property. Below are some of the advertisements for "*tabadala-e-jāedād*" that appeared in *Al-Jamiat*:

> *Tabadala-e-jāedād:* To buy or sell, immediate advice will be given. Karachi, Rawalpindi, Lahore, in almost every city of both countries, properties worth arabs are with us. In nearly every city of Pakistan and Hindustan we have an office or a representative. General Manager: Raghu Ram Dhoon and Co., corner of Ballimaran and Chandni Chowk, Delhi.[38]

تبدیلی جائیداد

ضروری اطلاع

سٹی ہائی اسکول

FIGURE 4.1 Advertisement for "tabadala-e-jāedād" (property exchange), *Jang*, December 11, 1947, by Ahmad Ali, Adamji Abdul Ali Building, Karachi.

Farookht aur Tabadala-e-jāedād: To buy or exchange property. Lahore's famous property dealer, Mohan Co., A Block, Connaught Place, Delhi. Get exchange/transfer forms immediately from him. With the best of properties approved, they are in an excellent position to offer you services. This month their offices are opening in Lahore, Karachi, and Rawalpindi. Phone number 8150.

Tabadala-e-jāedād: Do you have any property in Pakistan? Contact Lala Moti Ram Bhalla, property dealer.

Khaas 'Ailān [special announcement]: Muslims of Hindustan. One [who is] informed of the sale of their *jāedād* or its transfer—Syed Ahmed Farid Ahmed saheb, government auctions, expert on property exchange in India and Pakistan, Bazaar Matia Mahal, Jama Masjid, Delhi. Provide all details so that according to the new ordinance, you can be guided. Syed Moinuddin saheb Haqi, B.A.[39]

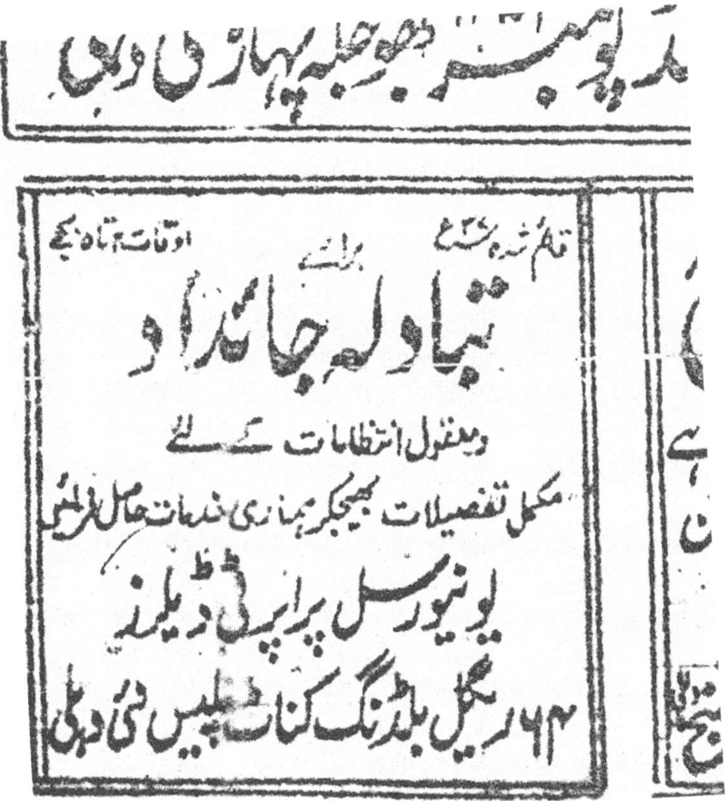

FIGURE 4.2 Exchange of properties, *Al-Jamiat*, February 6, 1949. Universal Property Dealers, 64 Regal Building, Connaught Place, Delhi.

In addition Hindu and Sikh refugees placed personal ads in *Al-Jamiat*, so that Muslims of the city who were migrating to Pakistan could contact them. One such advertisement announced:

> In Bannu we wish to exchange the following properties to Amritsar or some big city of Hindustan: 1) One residential bungalow, 2 floors, 14 rooms, with electricity and water, building of uptodate design, value Rs.60,000.

These advertisements suggest an entrepreneurial spirit that sought to informally resolve a situation in which people had been forced to move but their properties had been left behind. It is difficult to assess how successful these specialists were as middlemen between two states, how they functioned, and if they were trustworthy. But their entrepreneurial spirit was eclipsed by planned rehabilitation in which all individual properties became part of a collective compensation pool, and these advertisements came to be overshadowed by transformations in the evacuee property regulations that followed the Karachi Agreement.

Soon long lists started to appear almost daily of Muslim houses which had been declared "evacuee" by the Custodian's Office. Sometimes they were several pages long and dominated the newspaper, even if it carried other stories in its headlines. Its impact must have been quite substantial, for shortly after the lists started appearing, Jamiat-e-Ulema-e-Hind (JUH) began running announcements to "Delhi's Muslims who have not gone to Pakistan, and do not have any intentions to do so, but that their properties have been taken over illegally by the Custodian," to report the *najaiz qabza* (illegal seizures) immediately to Aruna Hall in Urdu Bazaar.

In addition, *Al-Jamiat* announced free legal help at Jama Masjid for those Muslims of Delhi who had been declared "evacuee"[40] (see figure 4.3). Another announcement ran as follows: "For those who are outside Hindustan and have been declared *muhajir*, or those whose part property has been declared *muhajir* or that person who has been declared *muhajir* and his home or business has been allotted by the custodian, please come to the following address: Incharge Office of Legal Help Committee, Jamiat-e-Ulema-e-Hind, Galli Qasim Jan, Delhi."[41] As show cause notices were served on Delhi's remaining Muslims which classified them as "evacuee" or "*muhajir*" (both the English term and this Urdu translation were used), the JUH attempted to organize a response, for this meant more than just a loss of property—it also meant a loss of belonging in a nation that many had chosen to stay in despite the September violence and its aftermath.

Although JUH was at the forefront in the struggle against the institution of evacuee property, *Al-Jamiat* was remarkably cautious in criticizing the Custodian's Office. Given that debates on the validity of evacuee property laws were so intertwined with questions of Muslim loyalty, JUH's cautious tone is understandable, as it had to contest discrimination without appearing too critical of the Indian state. It of course noted that the custodian had taken over not only those properties that were "truly evacuee" but also the property of Delhi's current Muslim residents. However, it suggested that in many of these cases the custodian did not know of this dispossession.[42] In another editorial, *Al-Jamiat* argued that joint

کسٹوڈین کے قبضہ میں آئی ہوئی جائیدادوں کے متعلق ضروری اعلان

مسلم انٹر کالج میں جلسہ

FIGURE 4.3 Important announcement regarding properties that have been taken over by the custodian, *Al-Jamiat*, February 7, 1949. The ad requests that people register with the legal help for JUH in Galli Qasim Jan, Delhi.

family homes were being taken over because of "mistakes" and a "lack of carefulness and lack of information" on the custodian's part. This could be interpreted as a strategy for negotiating with the custodian's office, for in its editorials it appealed to the custodian that it was his moral duty to help Muslims because they too were Indian citizens, and prodded the government by asking if it was taking its revenge on Pakistan's Muslims through Indian Muslims. "If not," the editorial stated, "then it should protect the property of Muslims."[43]

On the other hand, *Jang*, in Karachi, was far more vocal in denouncing the Indian custodian's office and its "victimization" of Muslims (*Jang* was predictably silent on the custodian's practices against Hindus in Karachi). However, while *Jang* may have exaggerated its portrayal of Muslim persecution, it did record Muslim experiences with evacuee property, particularly as those affected by it started coming to Karachi. For instance, when *Jang* raised the alarm that the "Hindustani permit office [staff] are spies for the Custodian's Office" it was not inaccurate in its perception of the permit system's surveillance component. It stated that certificates that had been awarded to Muslims for returning from Pakistan to India in August 1949 were cancelled in large numbers by the Indian High Commission, such that those who had come to Pakistan for purposes of visits only were unable to return, and in the meantime their properties were taken by the custodian. *Jang* narrated stories of individuals to corroborate its claims, such as that of a person who went to India's permit office in Lahore on August 28, 1949. By the time the man reached Delhi on September 6, his property there had already been declared "evacuee" and his family had been removed from the premises by the police.[44] Over the next few years, *Jang* coined the term "custodian-gardi" to describe the institution's "merciless behavior towards Muslims," but its particular concern for Muslim dispossession as a result of evacuee property laws was partially tied to the fact that large numbers of Muslims were migrating to Pakistan[45] and this was fueling an important debate, discussed in the next chapter, on restricting the entry of these Muslims.

The chief commissioner's files on the growing practice of *pagri* among Muslims are quite revealing of the effects of evacuee property not only on Muslims who owned property but also on those who rented from Muslim landlords whose properties had been declared evacuee. *Pagri*, as explained earlier, was a practice of circumventing urban rent restrictions under colonial rule, and here became an important means for circumventing restrictions on transfers imposed by evacuee property laws. These restrictions included obtaining permission of the custodian to sell, transfer, or rent out any property, even to another family member or friend, and permission from the custodian was often difficult to obtain. Since the "legal" route was made arduous, the "illegal" system of *pagri* gained importance. As the custodian of Delhi noted, in predominantly Muslim areas the occupant of an evacuee property house would "pass it on" to another person against payment of *pagri*. The new occupant paid the *pagri* "because he has little to fear of eviction, particularly as present occupants of evacuee properties are being confirmed and their occupation is not to be disturbed."[46]

The chief commissioner remarked that this form of "illegal gratification" was pervasive among Muslims of the city, particularly when the custodian began to collect rents on the properties under his jurisdiction, including rents in arrears. Most Muslims were unable to pay "even in installments the huge amounts of arrears and therefore consider[ed] it more advisable to quietly surrender the house on payment of illegal gratifications to others, mostly refugees." This included Muslims in "mixed areas" who were giving up their houses on *pagri*, and moving into "Muslim zones." The situation in "mixed areas," the commissioner noted, was "deteriorating and the cases of attempts at forcible occupations during the past month have increased."[47] If a house became occupied by a "refugee," then it became almost impossible for the prior Muslim occupant to reclaim it by "legal" means, and so leaving "voluntarily" with a payment of *pagri* would have been an inviting option. The chief commissioner added that there were many cases in which the people did not want to leave their houses but did so "on account of ignorance," for there were "regular gangs of *pugree* dealers in different wards and the whole thing goes on like anything." Finally, the official comment that this was resulting in Delhi "losing its secular and human character" captures the growing internal displacement and ghettoization of Muslims in the city.

In 1952, *Al-Jamiat* once again urged its readers to pay their rents to the custodian without waiting for a rent collector to come by. This was because the "custodian's strictness" in collecting rent from properties declared evacuee was resulting in "worry" and dispossession. The custodian had not collected rents in a long time and then was making sudden lump-sum demands which Muslim renters were unable to pay. *Al-Jamiat* noted that Jamiat-ul-Ulema's legal group was looking into this "strictness" but the paper asked readers to make the rent payments as soon as possible. It suggested that it was "the wish of the custodian department to overlook collection for a long period of time and then to make a sudden demand, forcing the person to be unable to pay and therefore leave his premises."[48]

Embracing both propertied and tenant Muslims alike in a place like old Delhi, where Muslims used to own a significant portion of the houses passed down over generations, Salim saheb's recollection of the "strange sight" at the custodian's office describes how the institution transformed the lives of the city's Muslims:

> *Taqseem ke ba'd jahan aur bahut masa'il paida hue. Is men sab se ziyada tarakun custodian department ka tha. Taqseem ke ba'd custodian ka idara Rehabilitatoin Ministry ne qaim kiya. Aur us ka kam tha ke tamam jane wale musalman muhajireen-e-Pakistan ki tamam jāedadein zabt kar li. Acquire kar li. Ye kam itne baṛe pehmane par hua ke jo log Pakistan nahin gae the aur yahin pe rehaish-gazeer the, un ki jāedadein bhī tamam custodian ne acquire kar li. Aur ye pareshani is had tak baṛh gaī ke us men kuch siyasi jamaton ko hissa lena paṛā. Aur us kī āwaz uṭhani paṛi. Is zamane men JUH ke aqabireen aur qaideen bahut mutarib the. Aur un ne ye masla apne hath men le kar custodian aur sarkar se bātcheet karte rahe aur ye yaqeen*

dilate rahe ke ye to Pakistan nahin gae. Āp un ki jāedād ko kaise acquire kar rahe. Is silsale men woh mukhtalif qasm ke suboot mangte the ke nahin gae to us ka bhī suboot dejye. Aur us zamane men us ka suboot mohaya karna ye dushwar gazeer marahil tha. Natīje men das sal se le kar bees sal tak lag gae case men. Aur logon ne bahut mushkil se–jo Pakistan nahin gae the–apni jāedādein chuṛwāī. Lekin be-shumar properties āj bhī hai jin ka faisala āj bhī nahin hua. Woh custodian men hain. . . .

Suboot ek to ration card aur dusra ye keh kisī gazetted officer se āp tasdeeq karae aur aise gawa pesh kījye jin ko sarkar jantī ho. . . . Kisi ko bhi nahin choṛa tha. Kisi ka fesala das sal ba'd hua. Kisi ka pundra sal, kisi ka pachees sal . . . jitne bhi ye malik makān the, ye jāedād wale log the. Subha uṭh ke nashta kar ke apne custodian ke daftar chale jate the. Sham ko panch baje āte the. Wahan pe ek mela sa laga rehta tha. Jaise ke Dilli ke sāre musalman custodian ke office men khaṛe hai. Ajeeb manzar hota tha. Is ki bahut sari misale ke koī kisi ki enquiry hoti hai ya koī poonchney āta hai ke woh kahan hai. To un se yehi kaha jata tha ke tum custodian ke daftar chale jāoge to wahi mil jāenge. . . . Ghar men rehte the aur case laṛte rehte the . . .

After Partition, as many problems arose, the most difficult was that of the custodian department. After Partition the institution of the custodian was established by the Ministry of Rehabilition. And its job was to confiscate the properties of all those Muslims who went to Pakistan as *muhajirs*. To acquire them. This work was done on such a big scale that people who had not gone to Pakistan and were living here, their properties were also acquired by the custodian. And this worry increased to such an extent that some political parties had to get involved and raise a voice. At this time JUH's leaders played a role. And they took up this problem with the custodian and the government and began talking and making them believe that these people have not gone to Pakistan, how can you acquire their properties. In this regard they asked for different kinds of proofs to believe that you have not gone to Pakistan and this was a very difficult process. As a result cases took ten years, twenty years. And these people who did not go to Pakistan had to face great difficulties to get their properties released. But even today there are many properties for which the decision even today has not been reached. And are with the custodian. . . .

[Later in the interview]

> Proof, one was a ration card, and the other was affirmation from a gazetted officer and presenting witnesses which the government knew . . . no one was left. Some decisions took ten years, some fifteen, some twenty–five . . . all those who were owners of houses, those with properties. They would get up in the morning, eat breakfast, and go to the custodian's office. In the evening at five o'clock they would come back. There would be a *mela* there. As if all of Delhi's Muslims were standing at the custodian's office. It was a strange sight. There are many examples. If there was an inquiry for someone, or if someone asked where is he. Then he would be told to go to the custodian's office and you can meet him there . . . they would live in the house and fight the case.

It is here that the disciplinary effect of evacuee property is most evident, for it was not sufficient for Muslims to go to the custodian's office and claim that they had not left for Pakistan and that a mistake had been made on the government's part. As "evacuees," they were deemed to have "migrated" to Pakistan, and the burden of proof lay on them to establish that they had not gone or did not have any future intention of going to Pakistan. This process of proving, as Salim saheb put it, was an extraordinarily long one, requiring ration cards, municipal records, and other documents presented to show that they had not gone to Pakistan and were all the time living in India. To produce "witnesses which the government knew" meant patrons had to be found within the state bureaucracy to vouchsafe for their character.

While evacuee property cases joined permit cases to embroil Muslims in India in a litigious, exhausting process of establishing national identity, there was a key difference between them. While permit cases were centrally about contesting citizenship and involved deportations, in evacuee property cases one could "live in the house and fight the case," be considered a citizen and declared an evacuee at the same time. A legal guide on evacuee property explained why this was possible. Citing cases, Goyal noted that the law "does not provide for declaring a person as evacuee. Section 7 provides for declaration of property as evacuee property, though declaration of its owner as evacuee is implied." Thus the clause "leaves or has left" for Pakistan implies "some amount of permanent stay or residence outside India but not to the extent of completely abandoning Indian domicile."[49]

Nehru noted that "the pressure of the evacuee property laws applies to almost all Muslims in certain areas of India. They cannot easily dispose of their properties or carry on trade for fear that the long arm of this law might hold them down in its grip." Although in Delhi almost all Muslims were declared evacuee,[50] in other parts of India there were many ways in which Muslims came to be declared "evacuee." Often it hinged on an "informer" to make a case to the custodian's office, and the burden of proof to show a complete absence of intention of going to Pakistan fell on the person. The fact that the "informer" might be a "displaced person" interested in being allotted the property was not held against the informer. Thus one finds the court case of Aboobaker Abdul Rahman of Bombay, after Tek Chand Dolwani, a "displaced person" from Sind, became an informer for the Custodian's Office. Dolwani "informed" the custodian that Rahman had gone to Pakistan and was therefore an "evacuee," and asked that Rahman's Imperial Cinema be allotted to him. When Rahman appealed on the grounds that he was a resident of Bombay and had not migrated to Pakistan, he was declared not to be an "evacuee," but on the next day was declared an "intending evacuee." Rahman had one adult son in Pakistan, and another adult son and daughter in Bombay when he died three months later while still contesting the dubious title of "intending evacuee."[51] Dolwani insisted that the dead man be declared "evacuee" so that the property could then be allotted to him.[52]

However, going to Pakistan, including even for a visit, was not the only crime that could result in one's being declared "evacuee" or "intending evacuee." An informer could describe a person as a "Muslim Leaguer" and thereby have a basis for the property becoming evacuee. In the case of Kaiser Saleem of Churiwalan,[53] old Delhi, it was his father who had migrated to Pakistan and, according to the informer, was a "notorious Muslim Leaguer." This resulted in the son's printing press and bookshop being declared evacuee property.

Muslims could be "punished" for having gone to Pakistan for a "visit" or for having familial ties there, but in the case of Hakim Dilbar Hasan Khan[54] neither was a reason for being declared evacuee. It is curious that his file survives from the largely destroyed records of evacuee property for it reveals how "evacuee" ceased to have anything to do with the specifics of the law itself. The custodian's complete juridical authority to decide if someone was evacuee or not (the courts could decide other issues, but not this fundamental one) not only allowed for the widest interpretations but was also used to discipline the participation of Muslims in the public sphere.

Hakim sahib, an *unani* physician, applied for the restoration of his house, which had been declared evacuee, arguing that he had never gone to Pakistan. The assistant custodian wrote that he had seen Hakim sahib's landlord and ownership deeds, as well as his ration cards, and had also examined witnesses, all of which verified that the Hakim indeed had not "migrated" to Pakistan nor acquired any right or benefit in the evacuee property there. In addition, Randhawa, the deputy commissioner of Delhi, gave Hakim sahib a testimony of his good character as he acknowledged his help during the Partition violence. Randhawa described the Hakim as "a very sedate and sensible person with a strong common sense and I am grateful to him for the cooperation he has given." It was also noted that all of Hakim sahib's family, with the exception of one son-in-law, were living in Delhi.

Yet all this was not enough. A CID inquiry revealed that he had been "a staunch Muslim Leaguer before Partition and delivered a number of anti-Congress and anti-Hindu speeches." In addition, he had been arrested on November 11, 1948, for "his prejudicial activities," though he was released on the intervention of local Congress and Jamiat workers. Thus although the Hakim was, by definition of the law, not an "evacuee," the Ministry of Rehabilitation decided that it was "not desirable that his property should be restored to him."

This decision is evidence of the ways in which questions of loyalty not only operated at the level of discourse but were also enforced through institutions and practices of the state. This made Muslim participation in public and political activities extremely cautious and carefully aligned within a national frame. It became common to include, in petitions and applications, statements like those given by Abdul Wahid, who was reduced to living in the Masjid Moulvi Abdul Wahab, a mosque built by his family: he stated that "throughout the time we have been Congress-minded and have been helping the Congress. We have never been members of the Muslim League nor have been taking any part in any other communal section."[55]

Joint family properties, not uncommon, were particularly affected by the Evacuee Interest (Separation) Act of 1951. A professor of Urdu from UP told me of how his family was physically evicted one afternoon, when police came to seal their ancestral family home as evacuee property. He was only a boy at the time, but recalled the day as one of the most powerfully inscribed of his childhood memories. The house had been declared evacuee because it had been passed down as a joint property for the use of four brothers: his father and three uncles. While two of his uncles migrated to Pakistan, and according to him received handsome allotments there, they were rendered literally homeless. After being pushed out of the house with only the clothes on their backs, they waited in the house of a neighbor until nightfall. With police locks on their door, the boy climbed through an open window to remove some of his family's belongings from the house. Although after more than a decade of fighting a court case the family home was restored to them, the years of dispossession could not be meaningfully mitigated.

The file on the joint family home of Habib Rahimtoola, the Pakistani high commissioner to the United Kingdom,[56] survives in part because it entered the Ministry of External Affairs record. His family property in Bombay was owned by him and his three brothers, all of whom remained in the city; his mother and other relatives lived in the actual house. The correspondence between the custodian and the Ministry of External Affairs repeatedly emphasized the necessity of following the letter of the law, and assurances were given to Rahimtoola that his mother and other residents of the house would not be removed from the house. His brothers would have the option of buying his share of the property, and even if auctioned, the new owner would have to recognize the present residents as his tenants. However, the emphasis on handling the case "with care," and following the letter of the law, makes it obvious that this was consciously not always the case.

For *Jang*, the Separation Act was a "new storm blowing in India" which was resulting in more *muhajirs*. It cried out that in UP, Muslim *khandani* or ancestral houses were being divided such that it was leading to Muslim displacement. It argued that once "evacuee" and "non-evacuee" interests in a *khandani* house were separated, the non-evacuee part went to *sharnatis,* non-Muslim refugees, and the house as a whole became useless for the Muslims who lived there. In these houses, it argued, there was only one toilet and one bathroom:

> How is it possible for one toilet and one bathroom to be shared with a West Punjabi Hindu or Sikh family and a traditional Muslim family, when their cultures are so different? How can they live in one house? Naturally there will be a clash between them and the government will take the side of the *sharnatis* against the poor

> Muslims. Thus the Muslims will have to leave the house and sooner or later will have to migrate to Pakistan. So thus on appearance the government of UP's law is completely fair and reasonable, and respectful of rights. But in practice its consequences and effects can only be assessed by those who have an experience of such situations and are familiar with present-day conditions in India.[57]

The evacuee property laws and the Separation Act also encompassed family endowments or *waqf-e-aulad*, and the appointed caretaker or a *mutawalli*, or one of the *mutawallis*, was declared "evacuee."[58] There are numerous court cases related to *waqf-e-aulad* and evacuee property, given that they required interpretation of rights through codifications of Muslim law. One example is that of a *waqf* established in 1913 in UP where two brothers were *mutawallis*. While Ali Ahmad was appointed a *lambardar* in 1918 in respect of the property, the younger brother, Ali Asghar, joined military service, had little interest in the property and then later opted for Pakistan. As a result the *waqf* was declared evacuee and its management was taken over by the custodian. Ali Ahmad, who must have been over fifty-two years of age at this time and had managed the lands all his adult life, and may have remained in India because he was tied to the land, lost his livelihood. His appeal to the courts was to simply have the management of the *waqf* returned to him; he argued that he would give half the income from the land to the custodian if only he could be its caretaker.[59]

From propertied individuals, to tenants, to joint family households, to caretakers and beneficiaries of endowments, Muslims particularly across north India had to contend with evacuee property laws, which, as was widely noted at the time, internally displaced them, economically disenfranchised them, and made it very difficult for them to participate not only in the economy of the nation, but also in its political life.

EVACUEE PROPERTY IN KARACHI

In Karachi, evacuee property laws were not applied until 1948, when the West Pakistan (Protection of Evacuee Property) Ordinance was passed to encompass all of West Pakistan. This was because of a perceived absence of violence in the city.[60] Therefore, the Rent Controller's Office had managed allotments of "abandoned" Hindu homes and businesses to *muhajirs* under the Sind Economic Rehabilitation Ordinance.[61] When evacuee property laws went into effect, the Rent Controller's Office also undertook the role of the custodian. In Pakistan, as in India, "the administration of evacuee property was considered an integral part of the rehabilitation policy of the government of Pakistan and such properties were managed as part of the rehabilitation scheme of the government."[62]

In Pakistan, as I have already mentioned, government records were difficult to find, in part because no one seemed to remember where they had gone. With the almost total departure of Hindus from West Pakistan, there are also no counter-memories and few signs of struggle left in the city's *muhajir*-dominated culture,[63] and no political imperative to question this amnesia. However, the Custodian of Evacuee Property is widely remembered, but in an unexpected way—it is remembered as the first site of the nation-state's corruption. The comment that "evacuee property corruption *ki jaṛ hai*," evacuee property was at the root of corruption in Pakistan, was repeated several times, and stories of usurpation by a few people of such a limited and essential resource as housing were commonplace.

Corruption as an originary narrative is vastly evocative. Yet there were material reasons for this memory of corruption. Sindhi Amil Hindus of Karachi were by and large economically well-off, and thus they "left" behind valuable properties. In addition, as I discussed earlier, *muhajirs* arrived in vastly different material conditions. There were *sarmayadar muhajirs* and *tabah-o-barbād muhajirs* who lined the footpaths of Karachi. As a result the Rent Controller's Office was the site of *muhajir* anger, frustration, and disappointment with the homeland that they had come to, and the city came to be dubbed as *"Darulkhilafah Pakistan: Karachi-jahan makān nahin milta* [capital Pakistan: Karachi—where you can not get houses]."[64]

I want to recover here some traces of the Hindu experience of evacuee property in the memory and record of corruption. In a Constituent Assembly debate on the amendment of the laws to mirror Indian legislation, Dr. I. H. Querishi argued that Hindus in Karachi sold their properties for large amounts of money before they left, given the earlier absence of evacuee property laws in Karachi, while on the other hand Muslims were arriving in Pakistan completely dispossessed. This view is important for it gave legitimacy not just to the legal, but also the extralegal dispossession of Hindus in Karachi.

I had heard of Maulana Abdul Quddus Bihari from a number of divided families I had spoken with. But it was a young assistant at the *Jang* office, who was taking great interest in my research, who was emphatic that I interview Maulana Bihari's family (for he had already died). "*Un ke baṛe khidmāt hai, un ne muhajiron ke liye bahut kuch kiya hai* [His services are many, he did a lot for *muhajirs*]," was how he described him to me. The fact that Bihari has been passed down in memory as a *muhajir* hero is particularly significant.

However, when I began to encounter him in record, I was taken aback to find that Bihari's fame lay largely in "uncovering" properties of Hindus who had "left" and having them declared evacuee. But he was more than just an "informer" for the Rent Controller's Office. What distinguished him was that he represented himself as a dynamic and honest champion of national interests, and this allowed him to supersede the authority of the rent controller, which he represented as a weak, ineffectual, and corrupt institution.

As early as 1947, he entered police records for removing the lock from a Hindu shop near Boulton Market and replacing it with his own. This was, not surprisingly, recorded as having "caused a slight panic among the Hindus of the locality."[65] It is evident that his actions were considered as "aggression" by some and "initiative" by others, but it is his "initiative" that is remembered. Later, he took "initiative" in taking Hindus to court to have properties recognized as evacuee.[66] His fame grew in particular with the Palace Hotel court case he initiated, and which was covered in *Jang* as a saga on a regular basis for the length of the court case. Minute developments in the case were reported (and presumably read with avid interest).[67]

The Palace Hotel was owned by a Hindu and had a Hindu manager, and Bihari "exposed" the fact that the earnings of the hotel were "not in Pakistan": its shareholders had not received any money, nor were there any funds in its Karachi bank account. Given that it would take more than passing interest to find out such financial details, there must have been some questions raised as to his intentions in undertaking such a task. He thus published his mission statement as a letter to the *Jang*:

> This incident is entirely sad . . . [T]he non-Muslim manager came under suspicion when not a cent of such a big hotel's earnings of the last five years was in Pakistan, and that instead the hotel is indebted to the bank. I don't know what our special police and income tax

> people are doing, where they have been sleeping. About this incident it is important to tell that in 1949 since the department of the custodian has come into place, and since I have struggled to expose the loot and lies and concealments of evacuees, at the same time I have kept the government informed in writing that whatever property I get deemed evacuee, I will not put in a request for its allotment. Thus, with thanks to God, up to now I have not taken an allotment of any evacuee property nor do I plan to. Abdul Quddus Bihari.[68]

Over the course of the trial, which ran for months, Bihari used this platform to reprimand the government for their apparently lenient views on taking over evacuee property. He demanded that the government apply the laws to their fullest, and that a full-time custodian (and not the rent controller, who had other duties) be appointed who could keep an "updated list" of all evacuee property. Bihari insisted that Hindus who had sent their wives and children to India had bribed officers in the Rent Controller's Office in order to hold on to their properties, and he appealed not only to lawyers but to people in general to take the initiative against them.[69]

Extralegality, legality, and illegality were not unique to the practices centered on the Rent Controller's Office, but it is how power and discourse get articulated that produces a notion of corruption. Bihari was a hero, while the Rent Controller's Office was corrupt. However, it was considered corrupt not because of its treatment of Hindus. This is evident in a Constituent Assembly debate in which Seth Sukhdev narrated an incident involving "Officers of the Custodian" who came to the residential premises of Seth Bhagwanlal Ranchordas.[70] Ranchordas was occupying a part of his own building while tenants occupied the rest. Ranchordas and the tenants were all ordered to leave the premises within half an hour and were allowed only to remove some of their bedding, clothes, and cooking utensils. After sealing the building, the assistant custodian had moved into a part of the building with his own family. Dr I.H. Querishi replied to Sukhdev's concern over the abuse of the custodian's power by pointing out that on appeal to the custodian, the actions of the assistant custodian had been declared illegal. The law had been enforced. However, Querishi added that a Mr. Acharya, an advocate who was a single tenant in the building, of his "free will" allowed the assistant custodian, who had a large family, to move into his home. This was not considered corruption, although, needless to say, it is questionable how "free" Mr. Acharya was to make such an offer.

Corruption in the Rent Controller's Office was also pointed out when a scheme for "rationing" houses was proposed by the Ministry of Rehabilitation to deal with the city's housing crisis. The scheme came under the guise of the Sind Rent Restriction (Amendment) Bill, and as the then minister of rehabilitation, Khwaja Shahabuddin told the Constituent Assembly, "[i]t has been found that there are persons who are staying here alone but occupying a very large accommodation" and this bill was meant to give the rent controller "the necessary authority to utilize the space."[71] The bill envisioned single occupants of homes, people such as Mr. Acharya, but not only Mr. Acharya, sharing with refugee families by dividing those houses up between several families.

Kamini Kumar Datta immediately raised the question of whether this legislation was meant to single out Hindus, and Shahabuddin replied that although certain buildings in the city were reserved for "permanent residence" of the city's Hindus, most of these permanent residents had gone and only one or two people were living, and so a "large space" was unoccupied. Shahabuddin argued that "we are pressed for accommodation, but should these rooms and that accommodation, although it is not occupied by Hindus, be allowed to remain vacant? Muslims as untouchables should not be allowed to occupy them and have a shelter?"

It was pointed out in the course of the debate on the bill that the proposal was meant to conceal the corruption of the Rent Controller's Office since it had allotted large properties to small families with money, leaving others still homeless. However, resistance to this scheme came out of practical concerns, as well as fears of a different kind of corruption. Khuhro pointed out that this was a "drastic measure": "supposing there is a flat consisting of three rooms and the rent controller decides that the inhabitants of that flat, who may be ten or twelve, should live in two rooms and one room should be spared for some other family. It will be most inconvenient for the people who will be occupying that flat, because in most of these flats and tenements here there is only one kitchen and one bathroom. How will these people with their families be able to share these bathrooms and kitchens?"

Hashim Gazder[72] was alarmed that this scheme meant "*purdah-nashin*" Muslim women would have to live alongside "*na-mahram*" men.[73] Gazder found an analogy in the Second World War, arguing that although in war-bombed London the government forced people to take in families through a system of billetting, this resulted in thousands of "bastards." Governments in Europe were forced to make laws for these "war babies which no one wanted." Outraged, he argued that such a scheme went against "the sentiment of Muslims" and that "Muslim society is not prepared to go to this depth of degradation."

Despite Gazder's sentiments, the bill was passed and the scheme was experimented with, although in a limited way.[74] Initially, according to *Jang*, it was received with optimism by *muhajirs*, largely because it was promoted by the administrator of Karachi, Syed Hashim Reza,[75] who was highly respected amongst them. He announced that according to the scheme a three-room apartment would be required to accommodate twelve people. Wherever there were fewer people in an apartment, they would have to take in more people, since the government was not in a position to undertake any large building scheme. The Jamiat-ul-Muhajireen supported what it dubbed the "Hashim Reza Scheme," for it was viewed as a check on the corruption of the Rent Controller's Office in allotting houses in excess of people's needs.[76] However, eventually the scheme was denounced as creating *"murghi-khanas"* or chicken pens.

In Karachi, although the custodian's task was taken over by the Rent Controller's Office, a separate rehabilitation commissioner was appointed who was assigned the task of making allotments. This post went to the administrator of Karachi, and therefore Hashim Reza was the rehabilitation commissioner until 1952, when he left both posts.[77] Figure 4.4 is an example of the allotment notices that appeared on a regular basis in the *Jang* newspaper.

In his autobiography he writes that, overwhelmed by the responsibility of making allotments, he established a Rehabilitation Board to make collective decisions. Originally from Lucknow, and particularly fond of Urdu poetry, he narrates their decision-making with charm and humor. He writes that it was the decision of the board to allot businesses to those who used to carry on that business in India:

FIGURE 4.4 (*opposite page*) Notice of allotments made by the Rehabilitation Board of evacuee property, *Jang*, January 15, 1950. It lists names of persons and the address of the property that has been allotted to them.

نوٹس

وفاقی دارالحکومت کے علاقہ میں متروکہ جائدادوں کے الاٹمنٹ کے لئے جو بورڈ بنا تھا اس نے حسب ذیل درخواستیں دینے والوں کو ان کے ناموں کے سامنے لکھی ہوئی متروکہ جائداد الاٹ کردی ہے۔ الاٹمنٹ آرڈر اس وقت دیئے جائیں گے جب ڈپٹی ری ہیبلیٹیشن کمشنر اور الاٹمنٹ بورڈ کے سکریٹری صاحب ان کی درخواستوں میں لکھی ہوئی باتوں کی تصدیق کریں گے۔

محمد عثمان ولد شیخ محمد حسن لدھا بائی بلڈنگ پنچر ہاؤس بندر روڈ۔ کراچی۔	جوہنی سٹورز الفنسٹن اسٹریٹ صدر، کراچی۔
میسرز افتخار احمد ایس۔ اے۔ خالق ۱۸/[illegible] - بہار کالونی کلیٹن روڈ کراچی نمبر ۵	نند داس پارکداس کتب فروش - رامباغ کراچی کی دوکان
ـ عبدالرحمٰن گرین مینشن [illegible] روڈ [illegible] کوارٹر کراچی اور محمد یوسف - مالک میسرز عیسیٰ بھائی نور محمد صالح محمد اسٹریٹ بالمقابل گوردھنداس مارکیٹ کراچی (دوکان میں دونوں شریک ہونگے)	میسرز بہاری مل جگامل صالح محمد سٹریٹ کراچی کی دکان نمبر ۵/۴۳
۴ـ ایس اعجاز حسین معرفت میسرز ایم۔ اے۔ خالق اینڈ کمپنی ۲۸ - شیوا جی گرشاری بلڈنگ بندر روڈ - کراچی	پروگریس سٹورز بندر روڈ کراچی۔

(ایم - اسحاق)
کلکٹر اینڈ ڈپٹی ری ہیبلیٹیشن کمشنر اور
سکریٹری الاٹمنٹ بورڈ برائے علاقہ وفاقی دارالحکومت کراچی

> I recall the allotment of an evacuee shop of hats and caps situated in Saddar. There were 1,000 applicants for this shop, each claiming to have abandoned shops containing thousands of hats and caps in places like Calcutta, Bombay, and Madras. The claim of one of the applicants was very modest. He was a refugee from Delhi. In his application he stated that he owned a small shop in Delhi which was located on a small street. The number of hats and caps in his shop was less than a hundred. When the mass killings of the Muslims of Delhi took place after Partition . . . he was advised by his friends to move to the Purana Qila and go to Pakistan. He argued that the Hindu and Sikh militants had looted big shops; his own shop was too insignificant to attract anyone's attention. And yet when he was driven away from his shop at the point of sword, he had to migrate to Pakistan and wended his way to Karachi. At the end of his application, he quoted a verse of Mirza Ghalib:
>
> *Hum kahan ke dana the, kis hunar men yakta the*
> *Besabab hua Ghalib dushman āsman apna.*
>
> Wisdom I possessed not, nor skilled was I
> For no reason, inimical became the sky.

The members of the Rehabilitation Board were unanimous in allotting the shop to the Delhi refugee, much to the disappointment of the remaining applicants who complained to the press that the allotment had been made not on merits but on Mirza Ghalib's verse! He added that as a result they began to receive more and more poetical petitions, such that he had to issue a press note that applicants should not incur double fees of both petition writers and poets.[78]

Yet as charming as Reza's account is of the process by which the registration of claims as "displaced persons" was formalized, the accounts narrated to me were of a far different nature. Abida apa explained to me that on registering a claim of property left behind in India, and presenting deeds or other proofs showing the value of that property, "units" were issued to the "displaced person." Further evacuee properties were auctioned, and a "displaced person" could bid with the "units" that they had for an equivalent property. However, she remarked that the process was so full of corruption that "an ordinary person" like herself had no hope of obtaining a property by such means. Therefore she sold her "units" on the black market. There were people who had two "units" but wanted to get a property that was worth four or six "units," and did so by buying the extra "units" from someone like her. Furthermore, she argued that you had to have "contacts" to actually get a property and take possession of it.

Abida apa's experience was repeated to me by many other people, but no one admitted having obtained an evacuee property allotment. (For instance, Salim saheb in Delhi had told me that his sisters who went to Karachi "got claims" for the property that they left behind. But when I interviewed them in Karachi, they stated that they did not.) Corruption was always elsewhere. Also, the large number of court cases on evacuee property were not claims by Hindus whose properties had been declared evacuee, but rather were mostly competing claims of "displaced persons" requiring adjudication. There were also competing claims made by Sindhi and other Muslim *ansār* residents of Karachi on evacuee property as well. Thus a *Jang* editorial argued that 5 percent of evacuee property should be given to "*ansār* brothers" but the rest to *muhajirs* only. The paper complained:

> Allotments have been made such that there are those who are being shunted around, and no one asks them, and others who are occupying large properties that exceed their needs. This corruption in evacuee property must stop. After all, it is such a shameful and sad state of affairs that those people who in India owned properties worth lakhs, in Pakistan are being shunted around . . . [I]n opposition there are those gentlemen who have gotten that which far exceeds their rights and today are living like nawabs.[79]

It is clear that through displacement and evacuee property the social order for *muhajirs* changed, and old relationships between class, descent, and property became disordered. This sense of disorder, that there were those who were living like nawabs who had no cultural or historical entitlement to do so, is also why evacuee property came to be identified with corruption, a symbol of moral disorder. Moreover, as Muslims from India, *muhajirs*, continued to come to Pakistan, as I discuss in the next chapter, the government argued they were coming with greed for allotments, further adding to anxieties about corruption.[80]

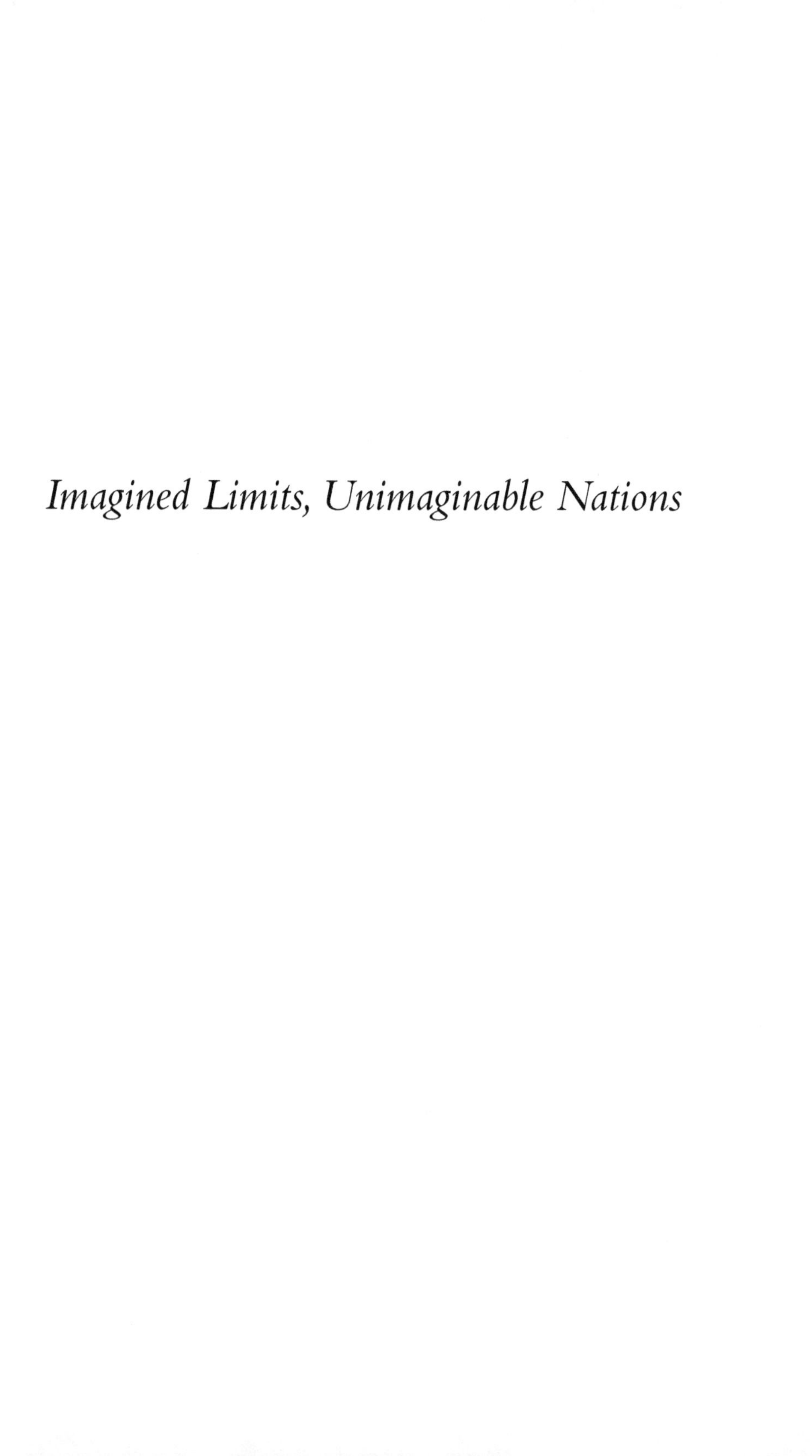

Imagined Limits, Unimaginable Nations

5. *Passports and Boundaries*

Our country is mapped by abandoned highways . . .
The future shriveled to this one place.[1]

If the permit system was meant to bring closure to Partition's displacements, it was not an effective measure for the Pakistani state. The discursive claim of being a Muslim homeland meant that when an "illegal" border crossing emerged in the Sind desert, at Khokrapar, and thousands of Muslims from India, particularly from UP, began to pour through it, the state was unable to acquire the legitimacy to seal it. Thus, just as the permit system was instituted by the Indian government to stem the return of north Indian Muslims back to their homes, the passport system was introduced between the two countries in 1952 at the Pakistan government's insistence, to curtail the "flood" of UP Muslims into the proclaimed homeland.

It had been possible to introduce permits without much debate in Pakistan since they were perceived to be an Indian-initiated restriction. After the permits came into place, people continued to hope that the permit system across the western border would be either brought to an end or that its extraordinary restrictions would be eased. Instead permits were replaced by passports, a technology that was the introduced on both the eastern and the western frontier with India. In this chapter I examine the debate spawned by Khokrapar over restricting the entry of Muslims from India that led to the shift from permits to passports.

From the perspective of the present and its ubiquitous use of passports, it would seem that the passport system would be a more familiar technology than that of permits, given its antecedent in the British Indian passport. However, an ordinary Indian legal guide, *Law of Foreigners, Citizenship, and Passports,* noted that the term *passport* emerged in an English statute in 1548 as a license given by a military authority to a soldier on furlough. It noted that its alignment with "nationality" emerged in the nineteenth century although passports as a rule were not required for crossing a frontier. "Only since the First World War has the passport system in its modern sense been introduced in most countries, i.e., the system whereby aliens who wish to enter a foreign territory are required to produce a passport issued by the authorities of their country of nationality."[2]

The passport has a history as a travel document, but shifted from being a travel document, a means to control movement, to also becoming a certificate of citizenship, a means to establish state-bound national identity, and this shift needs to be located rather than presumed. The British Indian passport not only had extremely limited usage, its carrier was marked as a subject of the colonial state. Thus the India-Pakistan passport emerged in important ways as a new kind of document, and was probably the first of this technology to be widely used in the region. Its history, on the coattails of its predecessor, the permit, suggests an uneasy relationship between controlling movement and determining citizenship in the making of a post-Partition national order. It required declaring territory of the "other" state as "foreign" and distinguishing between "citizens" and "aliens." It is therefore not incidental that it was as late as the Passports Act of 1967 in India when the status of passports was made clear, as both an "essential political document" for "safe travel" but also "an aid in establishing citizenship" and "evidence of the holder's nationality," thus securing a relationship between travel, citizenship, and national belonging.[3]

The indeterminate relationship between passports and citizenship in fixing national belonging in the subcontinent's history is evident in this excerpt from my interview with Salim saheb:

> *Main gayā thā [Karachi] bawan, trepan men. Do sal raha hun Pakistan. To wahan par sab ke pas achhe flat the. Achhe makān the. Aur baqi Quaid-e-Azam ke mazar ke pas jhonpṛiyan paṛi huī thī. Bahut tadād men. . . .*

> *behnon ke pas gayā thā. Main ne socha ke main wahan reh jāun. Is liye yahan hum rehte the. Ek nafsiyati masla bhi hai. Walid bahut sakht the. Na kahi bahir jane dete the. Na ghumne. Na kisi ke sath ja sakte the. Wahan jo hum ko azadi mili. To permit wormit tha. To passport banaya. Ḍehḍ do sal bād walid zabardasti, hamare walid le kar āe the. Agar main wahi reh jata to goli maṛ di jati. Congressi hone ki wajah se bahut tane milte the. Ye muhajir tehrik werik chali na us men kuch na kuch hissa leta. Māṛ diyā jatā. Wapas āne ke bād do sal key bād Pakistani passport cancel hua. Do teen char sal ke bād. Main Pakistani passport se wapas āya. . . .*

> I went [to Karachi] in '52, '53. I have stayed two years in Pakistan. There everyone had good flats, good houses. And the rest were in shanties around Quaid-e-Azam's tomb. In large numbers . . . I went to my sisters. I thought I would stay on there. Because here we lived. There was also a psychological problem. Father was very strict. He didn't allow one to go anywhere, not to visit any place, not to meet anyone. There I got freedom. There was a permit wermit. I then made a passport. After one and a half or two years father forcefully, father brought me back. If I had stayed on there I would have been shot. I used to get chastised for being a Congressite. This *muhajir* movement wovement that started, I would have taken part in it. Would have been killed. After coming back, after two years the Pakistani passport was cancelled. After three or four years, I had returned on a Pakistani passport.

In my second interview with him, several months later on another visit to Delhi, when I specifically asked Salim saheb about his stay in Pakistan, he denied ever having gone to Pakistan. When I discussed this denial with a friend who lived in Salim saheb's *mohalla*, she said that she had heard that Salim saheb had been in love with a girl who had migrated with her family to Pakistan. Moreover, this woman had come to visit Delhi recently and her behavior, for she had become a "madame" and a "fashionable type," had disgusted him. She conjectured that Salim saheb might have gone to Pakistan in his youth to pursue his "love-interest," but now wanted to distance himself from this past.

During my interviews with Salim saheb, his wife had always been present. This piece of "gossip" reminded me of a discussion I had had with them of cross-border marriages. It was his view that there were still cross-border marriages, but in most cases the men came from Pakistan to look for girls here. This is what Salim saheb had to say: "*Ek bāt hai. Pakistani Hindustan ki laṛkiyan ziyada pasand karte hai. Is liye wahan ki laṛki itni taraqi kar gaī hai, itni fashion parast ho gaī hai, woh qabo men nahin ārahi hai. Woh qabo men nahin rahi hai shohar ki.* [Pakistani (men) prefer girls from India. This is because girls have progressed/modernized so much there, have become so fashionable, that they cannot be controlled. The husbands cannot control them.]"

I make this connection between gossip about Salim saheb and Salim saheb's opinion of Pakistani women from a conversation on cross-border marriages, not at all to propose the truth of the gossip[4] but rather to draw out the consanguineous and affinal imaginaries which functioned across Karachi and Delhi, which made Indian Muslim/*muhajir* a fluid identity and one in which "citizen" and "alien" had to be constituted.

Salim saheb went to Pakistan as a youth, for he had sisters who lived there. He wanted to live in Karachi because his sisters seemed to live well there and he had an authoritarian father here in Delhi. For the short time he was there he was a *muhajir*, but his sense of community with that identity was such that decades later he could speak of the Muhajir Qaumi Movement as if he would have been its member, although he had to return and was an Indian Muslim again. He may or may not have gone to Pakistan in pursuit of a beloved, and may have returned because his feelings about her changed or she did not return his feelings. He went on a permit from Delhi to Karachi, but returned to Delhi on a Pakistani passport, which was later "cancelled." His speech and silence on his visit to Pakistan could have been produced by personal disenchantment or political process, but it was constituted by an array of emotional ties that crossed boundaries of new nations, and a sense of danger that came to be constructed around those ties in the emerging national order.

In this chapter I examine the debates that led to the shift from permits to passports.

TO DAM THE DELUGE

A "*Selāb-e-Nu*," or Noah's Deluge,[5] began to animate public debate in Pakistan soon after the discordant Karachi Agreement on evacuee property in 1949. Numbers were once again extremely powerful in shaping the perception that a flood of Muslim refugees from UP were pouring into Pakistan over Khokrapar, and I include my tabulation (table 5.1) of

TABLE 5.1 Enumerating the Deluge

Source	*Date*	*People coming through Khokrapar*
Khwaja Shahabuddin in Constituent Assembly	Feb. 23, 1949	5,000 every month
UKHC to CRO[1]	March 12–18, 1950	4,500 in three weeks
Constituent Assembly	March 29, 1950	111,615 in previous six months
Jang	April 16, 1950	5,000 in 24 hours
UKHC to CRO[2]	April 16–May 6, 1950	3,000–4,000 every day
Dr. I.H. Querishi in *Jang*	May 6, 1950	4,000 every day
Constituent Assembly	Sept. 30, 1950	79,762 in six months prior to the Nehru-Liaqat Pact
Dr. I.H. Querishi in *Jang*	Nov. 25, 1950	3 lakhs, 19,000 since Nehru-Liaqat Pact
Selab-e-Nu, "Noah's Deluge," *Jang*	May 20, 1951	25,000 in two months
Karachi administration in *Jang*	July 2, 1951	5,000 every month
Constituent Assembly	Nov. 20, 1951	118,809 in Jan.–Sept. 1951
Administrator of Karachi in *Jang*	Jan. 13, 1952	5,000–10,000
Radio Pakistan in *Al-Jamiat*	July 20, 1952	13,206 since Ramazan
Jang	Sept. 18, 1952	15,000 in Aug. 1–Sept. 15, 1952
Jang	Oct. 17, 1952	6,000 in first week of Oct. 1952
Jang	Dec. 4, 1952	1,788 in Nov. 1952
Constituent Assembly	March 12, 1953	441, 721 "illegal entries" since 1948, introduction of permit system
Constituent Assembly	Sept. 24, 1953	27,726 "illegal entries" Oct. 18, 1952–Sept. 13, 1953

1. United Kingdom High Commission to Commonwealth Relations Office, March 12–18, 1950, IOR L/P&J/5/331.

2. United Kingdom High Commission to Commonwealth Relations Office, April 16–May 6, 1950, IOR L/P&J/5/331/22300/1949.

the repeated enumerations that fed this swelling discussion on Muslims in India and Pakistan's relationship to them.

While the Pakistan government limited the issue of permits to Karachi to restrict the entry of Muslim refugees from India, those who had been denied permits or could not wait for one, or did not want to bother with obtaining one, entered Sind through Khokrapar.[6] While the Indian government policed this crossing so that entry from Pakistan into India was not possible through Khokrapar, on the Pakistani side an array of semi-official and unofficial services provided for the Muslim refugees. This included camel rides by local villagers to cross forty miles of desert from the no-man's-land to reception camps, as well as a train service from Khokrapar to cities in Sind. This turned the flow of refugees into what would once again be called "one-way traffic," and much of the debate in Pakistan centered on whether the Pakistani government could legitimately close this border crossing by policing or arresting Muslim refugees from India.

In the early months of 1950, this "flow" was perceived to have increased dramatically, as a result of the combined effects of evacuee property laws and of "communal disturbances" in UP. This increase in flow of refugees into West Pakistan coalesced with "disturbances" in divided Bengal and Assam, and the displacement of thousands across the eastern frontier.[7] Divided Bengal, as we have seen, was always considered exceptional because religious minorities on both sides of the eastern frontier were seen to balance each other, albeit precariously. Therefore permits and evacuee property laws were not applied in this region. However, now the seemingly large-scale movement of people across this eastern border alarmed both governments. In order to avert the kind of massive displacements that had taken place earlier in divided Punjab, the two governments forged an agreement on April 8, 1950, called the Nehru-Liaqat Pact.

The Nehru-Liaqat Pact, also referred to as the Delhi Accords, was a landmark agreement, even though it was largely an attempt to reassure religious minorities on both sides of Bengal and reverse displacements there. The agreement was broadly for the protection of minorities as a whole, and therefore encompassed all of India and Pakistan. It assured minorities of "freedom of movement" as well as "complete equality of citizenship" and "equal opportunity" to participate in public life, hold political office, and serve in their country's civil and armed forces, and was to be enshrined in the constitutions that were being drafted by the two states.

After this agreement, Liaqat made a presentation to the Constituent Assembly on April 10, 1950, in which he pointed out aspects of the agreement to allow for those displaced across divided Bengal to return to their homes. In addition to assurances of "freedom of movement," he noted that those who returned before December 31 to their homes would not only have their properties restored to them, but would also be rehabilitated by the two states. This meant that, unlike the displaced across the west, "non-Muslim refugees" would be included in "rehabilitation" in East Pakistan, and "Muslim refugees" in West Bengal. As a result, after the Nehru-Liaqat Pact it appears that most of the displaced returned to their homes.[8]

Although the Indian constitution was unambiguous about consecrating "equal citizenship," this was not the case with the Objectives Resolution that had been passed earlier as a framework for the Pakistani constitution. It stated that it would ensure "principles of democracy, freedom, equality, tolerance, and social justice *as enunciated by Islam*," leaving open what the Islamic interpretation would be.[9] Liaqat, after signing the Delhi agreement, attempted to quell anxieties around "equal citizenship" in the Pakistani state when he stated that "some fears have been expressed from time to time by those who have an imperfect understanding of the concept of an Islamic state that such a state will be a theocratic state and that it may not be guided in its policy by principles of equal status, rights, and citizenship in respect of the minorities who reside in it. Such fears are entirely baseless." Although Liaqat was apparently upholding Jinnah's position of August 11, 1947, on equal citizenship, the varying contending positions on what the role of Islam should be in the new state made his reassurance tentative at best.[10]

The effects of the Nehru-Liaqat Pact on the eastern frontier is still in need of research. Although it seems that large numbers of the displaced there returned to their homes, the introduction of the passport system two years later, the first restrictions on movement across that border, was a reversal of the agreed "freedom of movement" in the Nehru-Liaqat Pact and led to a substantial exodus of Hindus from East Pakistan.

However, *muhajir* aspirations in West Pakistan around the pact were of a different order, and this is suggested by a satiric dramatization of the meeting of the two prime ministers by the poet Rais Amrohi. Below is an excerpt from this dramatization as it appeared in *Jang*. The stage opened onto the Government House in Delhi, where after warm greetings and witty poetic exchanges, Nehru told Liaqat to come to the "real problem":

LIAQAT: *Asal masla ye hai ke donon mulkon men aqliyaton ko hifazat ka mukamal yaqeen dilaya jāe aur jis tarha āp barabar ye aillān karte rehte hain ke mashriqi Pakistan ki aqliyaton ki hifazat ki zimedari Bharat par hai. Is qism ke aillān ko khatm kiya jāe aur ye tae kiya ja'e ke har mulk ki aqliyat sirf usi mulk ki shehri hai. Kisi dosre mulk ko haq nahin hai ke woh us ke mu'amalāt men khwa-ma-khwa ṭang aṛata phere.*

RAJENDRA PRASAD: *Magar bhai, ye kyon kar ho sakta hai ke hum porbi Bengal ke abhage hinduon ko bhul jāe. Kiya woh Bharat ke shareer aur roh ka ek ṭukṛa nahin, jise zabardasti kāṭ kar alag kar diya hai.*

LIAQAT: *Aur agar Pakistan bhi Bharat ke char crore muslaman ka sarparst ban kar har moqeh par āpke mu'amalaat ki baz parst karta rahe to āp ko shikayat to na ho gi. Kiya Bharat ke musalman hamare bhai nahin hain, kiya un se hamara jisam aur roh ka rishta nahin hai? Yaqeen kijiye ke porbi Bengal ki aqliyāt se āp ko jo dilchaspī hai main us ke insanī pehlu ki qadr karta hun. Main khud isī dard men mubtala hun jo doctor sahib āp ko mubtala-e-gam kiye hue hai. Main khud ek muhajir hun aur mujhe mālum hai. . . .*

LIAQAT: The real problem is to make the minorities in both countries believe in their complete protection. But the way you keep announcing that minorities in East Pakistan are the responsibility of India: this kind of announcement must come to an end and it should be decided that every country's minorities are citizens of that country. No other government has the right to unnecessarily interfere in their matters.

RAJENDRA PRASAD: But my dear brother, how can this be that we forget the entire Hindu population of East Bengal? Are they not part of the single body and spirit of India that has been by force cut and separated.

LIAQAT: And if Pakistan too becomes the caretaker of the 4 crore Muslims in India and interferes then will you not complain? Are the Muslims of India not our brothers also? Don't we also have a relationship of the body and spirit with them? Believe me, the interest you have with East Bengal's Hindus, I appreciate its humanity. I too am dealing with the same pain that the Doctor sahib has. I am myself a *muhajir*. . . .[11]

From a *muhajir* perspective, the "real problem" was not just to reassure religious minorities, but also to resolve the very question of where they belonged. Amrohi portrayed the Indian state's relationship to Hindu and Sikhs in Pakistan as part of the "body and spirit" of the Indian nation, while Liaqat, representing the Pakistani state's position, desired a severance of this relationship by declaring them citizens of the Pakistani state and therefore its responsibility. At the heart of this severing lay the critical question of Pakistan's relationship to the 4 crore Muslims that remained in India.

If they were indeed to be regarded as part of the "body and spirit" of Pakistan, could the Pakistani state legitimately restrict their entry? The Nehru-Liaqat Pact provided the Pakistani state with an agreement which appeared to secure Muslim rights within India, and could be used to argue that as a result there was no imperative for Muslim flight from India to Pakistan.

As part of the agreement, the Indian government agreed to take back, in addition to the Muslims displaced in the east, Muslims from UP who had left for Pakistan between February 1 and May 31, 1950, and restore their properties to them. We have seen how the restoration of properties as part of the Nehru-Liaqat Pact was included in the Indian government's 1960s foreign relations brochure on evacuee property. As a result of this promise, some 95,000 out of an enumerated 135,000 Muslims that had come to West Pakistan in that specified period registered to return to their homes in India. A year later, on June 15, 1951, Liaqat Ali Khan personally saw off 1,500 *muhajirs* at the train station who were returning to their homes in UP.

However, all those who registered in West Pakistan to return home were not allowed back by the Indian government, for this was a time when evacuee property laws were being expanded with the introduction of the "intending evacuee" clause, and the *Mahada-e-Dilli* was largely meant to reverse displacements across West Bengal and East Pakistan. It seems that only about 23,000 people were able to return out of the 95,000 that had registered to do so. One newspaper article noted that as a result "thousands of those who had registered for repatriation are in a state of suspense; they cannot be rehabilitated in Pakistan nor has it been possible to send them back to India due to the dilatory methods of the Government of India."[12]

However, the Nehru-Liaqat Pact gave the Pakistani government a basis for threatening to close the Khokrapar crossing and insist that all movement between India and West Pakistan be regulated by permits only. To make the threat of closing this desert crossing effective, the government announced that all services functioning at this border post would be stopped after May 1950.[13]

However, as we shall see, the Nehru-Liaqat Pact did not produce the kind of closure that the Pakistani government may have hoped for, as *muhajir* opinion on restricting the entry of Muslims from India was so strong that the government was unable to actually police or criminalize those who continued to enter "illegally" via Khokrapar.

KARACHI IS "FULL"

A refugee census carried out in Karachi in May 1948 had shown that there were some 470,000 Muslim refugees in the city. It was against this statistical backdrop that Khwaja Shahabuddin, then minister of refugees and rehabilitation, noted with alarm that 5,000 refugees were coming every month through the Khokrapar crossing, and that most of them were heading to Karachi. The Khokrapar refugees thus came to immediately represent a rehabilitation crisis, adding to the already difficult housing problem in the city. Shahabuddin announced that "[i]n regard to prevention of further influx into Karachi, the public has been warned through the press and over the radio that Karachi can accommodate no more Muslim refugees."[14]

The notion that Karachi was "full" had been expressed by Sindhi leaders since 1947, but their cries had been dismissed as mere provincialism and contrary to the spirit of the nation. In 1948, the city was separated from the province of Sind and made into a centrally administered area. This shift was contested by Sindhi politicians, but it also meant that *muhajirs* now had greater power in the city's government.[15] It was *muhajir* Muslim League leaders in the central government, such as Chaudry Khaliquzzaman and Khwaja Shahabuddin, who were making these public statements, and this notion of "full" was tied to economics of rehabilitation.[16] By 1950, Dr I.H. Querishi, the minister of rehabilitation and also a *muhajir*, stated after touring the Khokrapar border that every day 4,000 *muhajirs* were coming and that "this is making the problem of rehabilitating the existing refugees very difficult." The administrator of Karachi, Hashim Reza, who commanded considerable respect among the *muha-*

jirs, similarly argued that because of new arrivals rehabilitation had become difficult, for as soon as the footpaths of Karachi were emptied, more homeless refugees arrived to fill them up.[17]

These repeated announcements that "Karachi is full" were meant to dissuade Muslims in India from coming, as well as encourage those that had to return. The custodian's machinations in India were considered a major reason for the ongoing exodus, and it was believed that the dispossessed Muslims were coming to get allotted properties in Karachi as "displaced persons." Therefore the government on one hand argued that such announcements were necessary to disillusion those who were coming and thus stem this flow. On the other hand, particularly after the Nehru-Liaqat Pact, government officials began to announce that because Karachi was already overcrowded, refugees in the city should return to their homes in India. Chaudry Khaliquzzaman described the coming of refugees through Khokrapar as unacceptable "one-way traffic," paralleling the Indian rhetoric prior to the permit system, and also suggested that these Muslims should return to India. It was this discourse of rehabilitation that formed the context for the thousands who registered to return after the Nehru-Liaqat Pact.[18]

However, this official discourse was met with an angry *muhajir* response, and editorials and articles in *Jang* criticized the government's position on many accounts. One article challenged the very notion that rehabilitation efforts of the government were being adversely affected by the arrival of refugees, for the government had hardly done much to begin with:

> . . . so eleven lakh Muslims have come. [But] the question is for their rehabilitation, how many houses has the government built, how many quarters has it built? Or have they settled themselves? So for the government to say that the houses are finished or the shops are finished, what has the government done to talk like this? [It has provided] no houses, no shops, no employment.[19]

In addition, the notion that Muslims were coming from India for material gain alone incensed *muhajir* sensibilities. This was countered with the view that *muhajirs* were coming in "*tabah hālat*," looted and destitute to Pakistan, and that the discrimination against them in India was so acute that it had forced them to leave their households and come with hope for better business and employment opportunities in Pakistan.[20] *Jang* used the fact that 95,000 had registered to return to India after the Nehru-Liaqat Pact to make the point that "people don't just come in the hope of getting allotted a factory, bungalow, or large house, for material gain, but because the conditions are truly bad in India, and want to return there when conditions improve there."[21]

This charge was made repeatedly against *muhajirs*, that their hearts are in India but have come to earn money in Pakistan. As one person in *Jang* responded: "*Subhanallah! Is sangdil ko kon batae ke ye ruppe kamane āne wale apne pundra lakh azizon ko Bharat men sarzameen par qurban karke aur croron ki jāedadain dushmanon ko de kar āe hain* [In God's name, who will tell the heartless that the money-earning *muhajirs* have sacrificed 15 lakh kin and given crores worth properties to the enemy]."[22]

The government's suggestion that *muhajirs* should return to their homes in India after the Nehru-Liaqat Pact, because conditions there had improved, was also attacked. Soon after Liaqat sent off a trainload of *muhajirs*, *Jang* reported that those who had gone back had been treated so badly that they were now thinking of returning to Pakistan again. Communal riots, it argued, were the Indian government's weapon for discouraging the return of Muslims, and the Pakistani government should not endanger their lives by encouraging their return.[23]

The trope of sacrifice was perhaps the most important, for as I have argued earlier, it emerged to claim an entitlement to Pakistan amid earlier attempts to limit the numbers of *muhajirs* coming to Karachi. Here it was once again used to denounce government attempts to restrict the entry of north Indian Muslims and to encourage the return of refugees. As one article in *Jang* stated, "in the making of Pakistan (*ta'meer-e-Pakistan*) the *muhajirs* of UP have played the largest role and made the most sacrifices (*qurbani*), and offered the most services. It is sad that after obtaining Pakistan there is no place for them in the world of Pakistan (*Pakistani duniya*)."[24] Another article argued that because UP Muslims had a hand in the making of Pakistan they were now being told to go away to Pakistan, and therefore the existence of Pakistan and the discrimination they faced in India were inextricably tied.[25] As a result, the argument was repeatedly made that *muhajirs* had the most right to Pakistan:

> *Pakistan par sab se ziyāda haq muhajireen hī ka hai kyon keh un ki qurbaniyon ki badaulat Pakistan 'alam-e-wujood men āya . . . Bharat men*

musalmanon ko kaha jāta hai ke woh chale jāen kyon keh un ke dil Pakistan men hai . . . aur un qurbaniyon ke sille men jahanam milī.[26]

Muhajirs have the most right to Pakistan for because of their sacrifices Pakistan's flag came into existence . . . In India Muslims are told to go away because in their hearts there is Pakistan . . . and in return for their sacrifices they have received hell.

In view of *muhajir* sacrifices, the official position, that there was not sufficient place in Pakistan for all the Muslims of India, was therefore considered immoral. It is here that a critique of *mu'amalati soch,* or literally "transactional, businesslike thinking," was launched. I earlier examined a government file that calculated "surplus" and "quotas" to arrive at the numbers of Muslim refugees that could be accommodated within the different provinces of West Pakistan, calculations that were based on the numbers of "non-Muslim evacuees" that were presumed to be departing. It was these calculations that made "one-way traffic" unacceptable to Khaliquzzaman, and it was this way of thinking that came to be denounced in Jang as *mu'amlati soch:*

[Does Khaliquzzaman mean] that it should not just be that the Muslims come to Pakistan and Hindus from here don't go? Or that Muslims from India should not go and Hindus from Pakistan must not go? Instead *hijrat* should be two ways, that if from Pakistan Hindus go then only Muslims from India should come so that the migrations stay equal? . . . *The principle which the government and Pakistan*'s *Muslim League leaders are following is the principle that in Pakistan there is only as much room as is emptied by departing Hindus.* From a businesslike (*mu'amlati*) point of view this principle is all right but given the present circumstances, can such a calculating (*nāptol*) policy be followed?[27]

"*Mu'amlati soch*" and "*nāptol,*" businesslike, transactional thinking based on measuring and weighing, or economic rationality and the basis of governmentality, were deemed acceptable for business, but not "given the present circumstances" in which people's lives were in question. An editorial the following day followed up on this critique by arguing that "the problem is not only of *mu'amla* [economy]. It is also Islamic and humanitarian and such problems therefore cannot be solved simply by *mu'amlati soch* [economic rationality]."[28] How could the space of a nation be calculated in a businesslike/economic way, when it was an ideological matter? Another article feared that "the foundations of Pakistan" were endangered by such planning by the state:

> Before this it seemed as if *muhajirs* were aliens in Pakistan, that they had no right to Pakistan, that the government had no responsibility toward them. Such statements were being made that our thoughts were upset, and we ourselves felt that the foundations of Pakistan were in danger. . . .
>
> [commenting on the statement by an Indian minister that India has space to take in all the refugees from East Bengal, even though in reality India is one of the world's most densely populated countries] *Magar jagah dil men honi cha'e mulk men nahin.* There should be space in the heart, not in the country. Indians have space in their hearts and therefore despite real shortages they are willing to settle refugees. While we Pakistanis have space and have fewer Muslims coming in comparison to non-Muslims leaving, we are crying about space. This is not because we don't have space in the country, but because we don't have space in our hearts.[29]

In relation to the Indian government's policy of accepting all Hindu and Sikh refugees that wanted to move to India, the Pakistani government's position of restricting Muslims from India appeared untenable. Space could not be a population density or land issue, for it was an ideological and emotional one. And therefore restrictions on Muslim refugees could not be justified in economic terms, for space was not tied to land as much as to the heart, or the willingness to support and make room for more people.

However, the economic calculations were not without their power. The question became *how many* Muslim refugees the land could indeed support, for if *all* Muslims from India came to West Pakistan, its population would immediately double. The Indian economic position differed in population numbers and land size, and thus could embrace all Hindu and Sikh refugees. Thus as discussion turned to a complete transfer of populations, the need for more land once again arose.

Ideas for a total exchange of populations along religious lines and the need for more land to cope with such an exchange had been proposed earlier in *muhajir* writings, even if they were dismissed as impractical. With the pact's failure in stemming the tide of Muslims coming through Khokrapar, these ideas found rearticulation.

One *Jang* editorial argued that "more land" should be demanded from India for rehabilitating these new *muhajirs*.[30] Commenting on a statement of Dr. Shyam Prasad Mukherji on a complete transfer of populations as a solution to the "minority problem," an article in *Jang* insisted that "whether the governments agree to such a thing or not, this is going on in any case, with Muslims being terrorized into migration all the time." But it added that "the transfer of populations is impossible without an agreement on land." "The time has come," the writer argued, "for those in Pakistan to make a decision on what they want to do regarding the transfer of populations."[31]

By 1952, as the government began discussing the introduction of a passport system, this notion of "transfer of populations" and "more land" found repeated articulation. It was argued that the Muslim League and Jinnah had made promises to Muslims and that these promises had to be fulfilled. The only way to do so was to ask India for more land.[32] Such a claim was justified on the grounds that the Muslims who were coming were citizens of India, and therefore had a territorial right to India which they should be able to transfer with them—moving people should be able to move land with them:

> All these people coming to Pakistan are citizens of India and the Indian government is responsible for their safety and protection. They have a right in the land of India just like Indian Hindus . . . thus Pakistan should get this land which is the right of these Muslims and which Indians are not giving to them. . . . Pakistan's original claim was the entire Punjab, Bengal, Assam, and a middle path for connecting the east and the west. . . . And the truth is that it was in view of this claim that 10 crore Muslims made sacrifices.[33]

One editorial was emphatic that restrictions on Muslim entry were ideologically "out of the question," and therefore the only way to solve the economic problem of mass migration was to have more territory:

> It is out of the question to put any kind of restrictions on the coming of Muslims from India, and as far as the danger of Pakistan's economy being destroyed is concerned, so in this matter a few things need to be kept in mind. One primary thing is that in view of this migration and if Muslims from India continue to come to Pakistan at this rate, then Pakistan has to ask India for *more land*. . . . There is one solution to the minority problem and this solution is acceptable to Pakistan, and that is that the minorities are exchanged and for the excess of Muslims who are resettled here accordingly land is given, in which the Muslims coming from India can be settled.[34]

Clearly this notion of expanding the territorial limits of the state to accommodate the proclaimed nation in its entirety was fantastical, given the kind of hostility that the Pakistan idea itself had generated among many Indian leaders.[35] Still, the fabulous aspects of these ideas are worth examining.

They testify to the force of the *muhajir* refusal to accept that Muslims in India be excluded from a Pakistani nation-state. This is not surprising, because the *muhajir*-Indian Muslim identity was but a matter of semantics and location at this time, and a large number of *muhajirs* had friends and family on the other side. So although the Pakistani government went ahead with its plans to introduce the passport system, and removed services from Khokrapar,[36] it was not able to police that crossing. This meant that though fewer people were making the hazardous desert journey, there was a continuous "trickle" through the crossing until the 1965 war between the two countries.[37]

DEBATING THE NATION

There were two important debates in the Constituent Assembly on restricting the entry of Muslims from India. The first debate, on April 7, 1952, concerned a government proposal to add a "limit date" to the citizenship laws, which had been passed in April 1951 with fairly little debate since they provided for citizenship in more or less the same manner as the Indian citizenship laws.[38]

The government brought a number of amendments to the Citizenship Bill for approval to this debate, and these are worth examining. The first amendment was to remove the domicile requirement for government servants who were posted abroad. This innocuous legislative change was important because the nationality of the Pakistani high commissioner in India, Mohammad Ismail, had come into question.[39] He was a north Indian Muslim who had not physically migrated, but was Pakistan's diplomatic representative in India. A controversy had arisen when he was quoted in a newspaper as saying that he considered himself an Indian. Thus this amendment was meant to encompass the nationality of all government servants.

The second amendment called for the removal of the registration requirement for acquiring citizenship for Muslim refugees from India, since the task of individually registering over 8 million people was considered an "impracticable demand." The amendment automatically granted citizenship to all those who had come to Pakistan *before* the commencement of the Citizenship Act on April 13, 1951. As a result, it became possible for Muslims to obtain Pakistani passports fairly easily by claiming to have arrived by this date. As we will see in the next chapter, this ease acquired significance as it became difficult for Muslims to obtain Indian passports for travel.

Legislatively this meant that all those who had migrated to Pakistan *after* the commencement of the act would be rendered "stateless," and thus a third amendment was proposed to register those who had migrated to Pakistan between the commencement of the act and January 1, 1952. Thus January 1, 1952, was proposed by the government as a "limit date" for acquiring Pakistani citizenship.

It was this "limit date" that the debate centered on, for there were two contending opinions on whether Muslims in India could in principle be prevented from claiming a belonging to Pakistan if they came after it. Sardar Shaukat Hayat Khan of the Punjab considered even this extension for conferring citizenship rights on those "who are pouring in from India" as "dangerous." He argued that "[i]f you do not stop this continuous influx, so many will come into the boat that it is sure to go down under the burden." This image of the nation-state as a boat that can rescue only a limited number of people had appeared before, so Hayat Khan was articulating wider concerns. He had sympathy for the migrants, but he argued that the economy could not shoulder their burden.

Khan also argued that if immigration was allowed, then "you must demand of the government of India extra territory in proportion to the number of Indian citizens who are being pushed across the border into Pakistan so that you may be able to rehabilitate them there." This notion of needing to expand the territorial limits of the state was therefore not just a *muhajir* imaginary; but that did not make it any more feasible.

Hayat Khan's view was opposed by Sardar Amir Azam Khan of the Punjab, who reminded the house that the All India Muslim League had stood for two objectives. First, "that the Muslim majority areas be constituted into a free and independent country," and second, "that the government be so constituted [so as to] act as a counterpoise to the government of India in securing security of life for the Muslims of those territories which will form part of the Dominion of India." He expressed the view of many when he said that "[w]e can never turn our back on those Muslims who staked their all to bring Pakistan into being, but who after the fruition of their dream were left stranded in territories which went to form part of India." He therefore opposed any policy that would "slam our doors on those who had gone all out with us in the struggle for Pakistan." H. Gurmani went further in arguing that "our concept of state is different from the popular or the modern concept of state," for in the case of Pakistan "the land belongs to God." He insisted that Pakistan had to be open to Muslims to "take refuge in this land." This meant that "we will have to increase the capacity of the boat."

Nevertheless, the government made its position clear, that it did not consider "migration to this country . . . as an unlimited process" and could not "make provision for unlimited migration for all times to come." The government provided two reasons for such a "limit date." One was that an "open migration policy" was "making conditions of life difficult for Muslims in the adjoining country," because their loyalty to India was being questioned. Another reason was to avoid "placing strain on Pakistan's economy and future well-being."

Although the government's amendments were passed by the house, these opposing sentiments meant that the question of the nation's limits was far from resolved. Thus when the legislation for the passport system was brought before the house, some of the same concerns were rearticulated. On November 24, 1952, the Pakistan (Control of Entry) Bill was discussed to "regularize" the passport and visa system that had already come into place in October that year.

Ghyasuddin Pathan, the minister of states, who introduced the bill on behalf of the government, argued that the passport system had been introduced because it would force moving people to declare their nationality, and therefore allow for a better control of "Indian citizens" coming to Pakistan, and in particular the entry of "spies" and other "undesirable elements." In addition, it would at last allow the government to know "who are the real citizens of Pakistan." He added it was "high time for all the citizens who profess to be citizens of Pakistan to decide once and for all what they are going to do."

It was Mian Muhammad Iftikharuddin who pointed out that controlling the entry of "Indian citizens" basically translated into restricting the entry of Muslims from India. He argued that although "the land and the facilities available in Pakistan are not sufficient to justify the coming of every Muslim and there are over 30 million Muslims even today in Bharat," yet he reminded the house that the Lahore Resolution of 1940 had stated that "adequate, effective, and mandatory safeguards should be specifically provided in the constitution for minorities in these units . . . where the Muslims are in minority." Pakistan had failed, he argued, to protect "our Hindus on this side," and had failed in protecting "the Muslims on that side." By declaring Muslims in India to be "foreigners" in Pakistan, the passport regulations would thus be a final failure of duty.

However, most of the debate centered on the necessity of introducing regulations on movement on the eastern border, where there had been no restrictions up to this time. One of the reasons for the government's insistence that the passport system be applied to both borders with India was the "language riots" that had taken place in Dhaka earlier that year. This was a series of demonstrations that took place in Dhaka to have Bengali recognized as a national language; the government had suppressed the protests with force. The West Pakistan perception of the growing Bengali nationalism was, as Dr I.H. Querishi put it, that it was spurred by "persons from the other side [who] have been coming and mixing up with our boys." Thus controlling the entry of such persons provided the justification for restrictions on that border.

When the imposition of permits on the eastern border had been considered, the Bengal government had opposed it on the grounds that it was impractical. With thousands of people crossing the Indo-Pak border there on a daily basis, its imposition would cause great hardship to people in East Pakistan. The same reasons reappeared here, as members from East Pakistan opposed the bill. Dhirendra Nath Dutta argued that the permit system was itself not working well, and the "remedy" was to either abolish it altogether or to improve the system, rather than replace it with another.[40] Sris Chandra Chattopadhyaya argued that there were historical and sacred connections between the two countries which demanded that freedom of movement be maintained between them. There were Muslims who went to Ajmer Sharif, and Hindus who went to Gaya, and such controls on movement would rupture these ties.

It needs to be emphasized that these controls on movement were not considered necessary by ordinary people, but rather were enforced by the state as a mechanism for necessary declarations of citizenship. Furthermore, as easy as it would become for Muslims to obtain Pakistani passports, this was not so for non-Muslims. Although there were complaints in general about the extraordinary requirements of the permit system that were being carried over into the passport system, such as requirements of photographs and police reporting (Sris Chandra Chattopadhyaya noted that "I have got a visa for all the countries in the world but no photograph, nothing of the kind"), there were specific complaints around the surveillance of non-Muslims. Seth Sukhdev narrated stories of Hindus whose papers were referred to the CID, and from whom citizenship certificates were demanded, such that "Hindus living peacefully here were considered foreigners, or I may add a little stronger word, most of them were considered Indians."

Despite considerable resistance from both sections of public opinion in West Pakistan as well as East Pakistan, the passport system was still introduced, and along with the "limit date" on citizenship, was meant to discourage Muslims in India from coming to Pakistan while subjecting non-Muslims within Pakistan to surveillance and scrutiny at the margins of the nation. Distinguishing between "citizens" and "foreigners," the passport was to resolve all the ambiguities of national identity in a divided South Asia, and produce closure to Partition's displacements.

FROM PERMITS TO PASSPORTS

In early May 1952, the Pakistani government started proposing the idea of a passport system to replace the permit system as one which would encompass both halves of Pakistan. However, the Indian government opposed the Pakistani suggestion, particularly for the east, as it saw "freedom of movement" there as critical for reassuring Hindu minorities in East

Pakistan. When the Pakistani government threatened to impose the system unilaterally, a Passport Conference was held May 17–21, 1952, in Karachi. Despite disagreements over imposing travel restrictions in the east, a Passport Agreement was reached, at Pakistan's insistence, by June 1952.[41]

As I have already discussed, restricting the entry of Muslims into Pakistan had become an emotional issue, and *muhajirs* in particular vehemently opposed it. Thus in the months preceding the imposition of the passport system, the government attempted to establish the system's necessity. In addition to holding "outsiders" responsible for the Dhaka demonstrations, the arrest of a dozen *jasoos*, or spies, made headlines in *Jang*. It was argued that Indian Muslims were being sent as spies by the Indian government by promising to return their properties that had been declared evacuee property in return for espionage. And in keeping with a need for greater national vigilance, a police crackdown in Sind on illegal travelers between India and Pakistan also made front-page news.[42]

Dr. I.H. Querishi rationalized the passport system as a means to prevent Muslim dispossession in India, for he argued that this would establish their nationality conclusively. If they came to Pakistan with an Indian passport, he argued, "the Indian government will be forced to take them back," unlike situations with the permit system where as a result of arbitrary cancellation of permits, India had snatched the right of return from thousands of Muslims.[43] In sum, by asserting a kind of closure on identity the passport system was supposed to provide greater security to Muslims on both sides of this growing divide.

In India, the passport system was pronounced as a final *talak*, or divorce, and "the formal and official burial of the Delhi Pact," which had once promised "freedom of movement."[44] However, forced to embrace the passport system in the east, the Indian government attempted to assure East Pakistan's Hindus that the restrictions there would be "softer" and that both governments would not place any hindrances on those who wished to migrate from one country to the other. In addition, those with properties or relatives on the other side would get special visas to make travel easier. Khwaja Nizamuddin, who had taken over as Pakistan's prime minister after Liaqat Ali Khan's assassination in 1951, also went to Dhaka prior to the start of the regulatory system and spoke with Hindu leaders to assure them that the restrictions would not discriminate against them.[45] Yet when the passport system was announced large numbers began to leave East Bengal, possibly in fear that it would congeal citizenship and

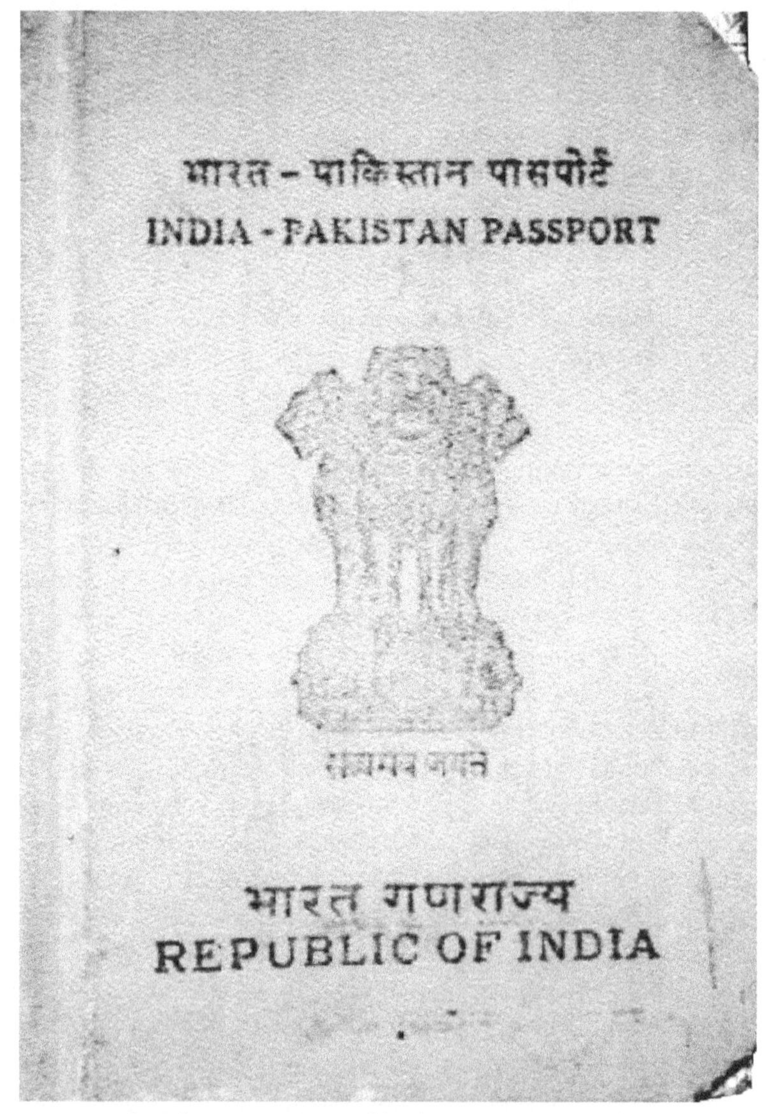

FIGURE 5.1 India-Pakistan passport issued by the government of India. These were in use until 1965, when they were replaced by international passports.

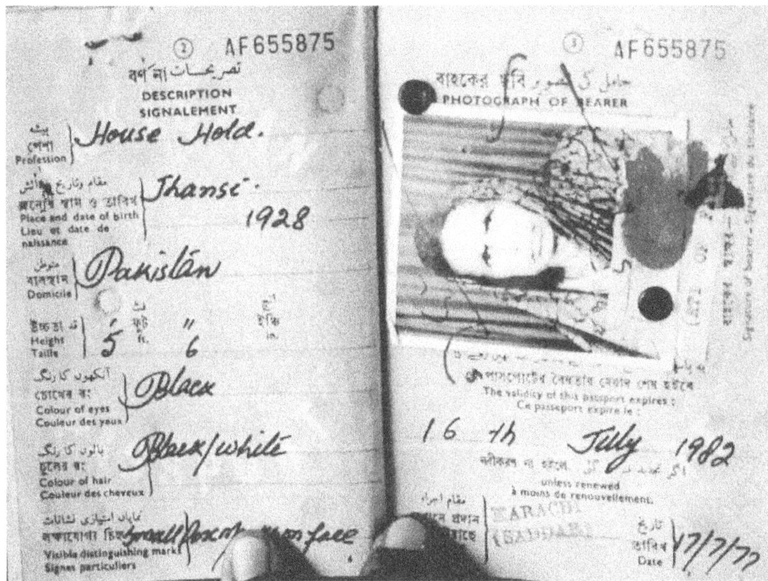

FIGURE 5.2 India-Pakistan passport issued by the Pakistani government.

nationality in a two-state order which would leave them outside the Indian nation. Thus when the Pakistani government requested that the start of the passport requirement, set at October 15, 1952, be postponed by one month, the Indian government refused out of a fear that the continued exodus would make the "situation . . . more unstable."[46]

In the west, where the transition from permits to passports was taking place with considerable confusion and chaos, people hoped against hope that it would make travel easier than the permit system. However, they feared it was only going to make the divide even deeper.[47] A letter in *Jang* made this appeal:

> The unbearable difficulties that Muslims of West Pakistan have had to bear as a result of the permit system are a painful sin in the history of Muslims in the Indian subcontinent. A son wants to meet his beloved father and he cannot meet him. A mother wants to see her only son on her deathbed and cannot see him. Delhi's permit office wants bribes, the High Commissioner's Office is merciless and follows laws blindly. So how to get a permit? Can a passport make it easier, or will our grief be heavier?[48]

However, most of the restrictions of the permit system, such as the No Objection Certificate and police reporting requirements, were transferred to the passport system as well. The permit practice of applying to visit a specific destination in the other country was continued within the visa system. In addition, the different kinds of permits were also transferred into different kinds of visas, the specifics of which will be examined in the next chapter.

As was the case with permits, the first to be affected by this new technology were families who were divided between India and Pakistan, and their letters of complaints were therefore also the first to appear in *Jang*. In retrospect, to most the permit system quickly began to appear easier to deal with than the passport system. An Ibrahim Jamaluddin from Karachi wrote to ask how he could obtain a passport for his wife and children who were in India. The permits were often issued to a head of household for the entire family that resided on the other side. But now passports were issued individually, and those individuals were required to apply by themselves to the Pakistani High Commission in India.[49] The passport system then individuated members of families, subjected them to individual scrutiny, although there were special allowances for inviting a kin for a temporary visit or permanent migration. One editorial in *Jang* outlined some of the "new" problems faced by divided families and the severe constraints placed on migration to Pakistan:

> Now to bring your families across, long procedures are required. Those who have their family in India, those people who wish to call their relatives from India, will have to use complicated methods. In the past a Pakistani citizen could get a permanent permit and call the relative; now a member of a family has to go in India to Pakistan's diplomatic office and make an application to become a Pakistani. Then it will be sent to Karachi for clearance from the Pakistani government. Once approved, this applicant will get an emergency certificate, and so instead of a passport they can show this emergency certificate and enter Pakistan. For this process to be completed it will take approximately two months. With this situation thousands of government employees and *muhajirs* will be harassed.[50]

These regulations made it difficult to bring family members to Pakistan, and those Muslims in India who had no family in Pakistan could not get that "emergency certificate" for migration. Therefore Muslims in India who wanted to come to Pakistan continued to travel to Khokrapar.

Despite the repeated announcements that the Khokrapar crossing would be closed once the passport system was in place, the government was unable to arrest or prosecute those who did come across. Services to make the crossing had already been removed, such that the six-mile journey from the border to Khokrapar had to be made on foot, and at Khokrapar the new *muhajirs* had to wait for days for a freight train to arrive and then board its empty bogies to a city in Sind. Although Dr. I.H. Querishi announced that the government did not like what were now tabulated as "illegal entries," since they compromised the controls of the passport and visa system, there was a sense that those who were coming were doing so as a result of persecution or "*ma'ashi* boycott" and were desperate enough to undertake the harsh journey. As one *Jang* editorial argued, "unless the situation in India improves, Muslims there will continue to come and it is the duty of Pakistan to give these Muslims refuge. This border therefore cannot be closed."[51]

However, as was reflected in the Constituent Assembly debates, "mixed feelings" persisted on this issue.[52] Ahmad Nadvi wrote poignantly from Hyderabad:

> I am afraid that if this migration continues at this rate and the population increases like this then Pakistan's economy will be destroyed. No country can take the burden of this kind of population growth. . . . I think about this problem every evening. Surely thinkers and analysts in this country must have some solution! I know that the minds of the country must be looking for some solution. Can they tell me what the solution is?[53]

The Indian Muslim Debate

If the continued displacement of Muslims from India spawned a vociferous debate in Pakistan, this displacement was a comparatively silent one within India itself. As Omar Khalidi notes, Nehru observed this exodus with unease in his letters to his ministers, but it never entered a public debate in the Indian press.[54] However, *Al-Jamiat,* with an entirely north Indian Muslim readership, did write about it, and its view of the Khokrapar crossing is important.

Although it was the newspaper of a long-standing, pro-Congress Muslim organization, *Al-Jamiat* had to tread a cautious path, trying to fend off questions of loyalty while still addressing the genuine concerns of its Muslim readers. *Al-Jamiat* had to discuss the exodus without reifying the charge that Muslims in India "desired/wished" to leave for Pakistan, the myth of voluntary exodus; yet it could not be too critical of the discrimination Muslims were facing, for this could demoralize its readers and encourage further exodus. This was one of the effects of being policed for loyalty and disloyalty to the nation; the need for caution placed significant restraints on speech.

This is evident in an editorial during the Ramadan of 1951, as *Al-Jamiat* attempted to counter a rumor that after Eid-ul-Fitr was celebrated many Muslims of Delhi would be leaving for Pakistan; their beddings were supposedly already packed and they were only waiting for Ramadan to be over. *Al-Jamiat* argued that this rumor was being spread by "communalists" to legitimize the harassment of Muslims and that this was pushing out thousands of Muslims into Pakistan. However, given the force of the rumor, *Al-Jamiat* began inquiries to find out if it was true, and if so, why the Muslims of the city were planning to leave. The paper found out that in Suiwallan, in old Delhi, twenty-four Muslims had been arrested, and as a result of this incident, *Al-Jamiat* said, "their spirit has been broken and they do not have hope that they will be able to live there with respect and peace and that at any time they could face injustice." However, *Al-Jamiat* reported that the incident was linked to only one police officer, "because of whom many Muslims have lost heart." Therefore the newspaper argued that only a few people were affected: the rumor was false and intended to "create an atmosphere of distrust."[55]

At the same time, *Al-Jamiat* tried to address the reality that, indeed, a large number of north Indian Muslims were leaving for Pakistan. It argued that, contrary to the *muhajir* discourse in Pakistan, Muslims were not leaving because they did not feel safe in India and that as long as they were unsafe the passage to Pakistan had to be kept open. Although *Al-Jamiat* agreed that if the Khokrapar crossing was closed it would have a terrible "psychological effect" on Muslims in India, it argued that "insecurity" was not the only reason for the departures and that the Pakistani press was misrepresenting the situation of Muslims in India:

In our view there are many different kinds of people who are going via Khokrapar. Some are those who have relatives there already and cannot get a permanent permit to go to Pakistan. Some are facing economic hardships and think that by going to Pakistan they will earn better, and then there are others whose friends/companions have opened small factories and workshops in Pakistan and they want to join the team to work there. Their interest is entirely from the business point of view.[56]

In other articles, *Al-Jamiat* tried to convince its readers that they should remain in India. Leaving was not going to solve the problem; there would still be 4 crore Muslims staying behind. *Al-Jamiat* also tried to disillusion its readers of better conditions in Pakistan:

Will they get a house when they reach there? Get employment? Get respect? Get peace? The housing situation there is such that you have to give 10,000 rupees in *pagri* to get a place and the rest of the poor, only God is their caretaker; lakhs of *muhajirs* are lying on the streets, victims of all kinds of illnesses, and the employment situation is such that for twelve or thirteen clerk positions there are 700 applications, which means that all that respect and peace that you are going for, that much hardship you will have to face.[57]

When 350 Muslim families returned to Delhi as a result of the Nehru-Liaqat Pact, *Al-Jamiat* reiterated its point that "*apna ghar apna hi hota hai* [one's own home is one's own]." It argued that if "it is well known that grain is very cheap in Pakistan, then why are these people coming back? . . . It is wrong to think that Pakistan is there for Muslims in their difficult times . . . it is only for the Muslims who belong there but not for those in India, Iran, or Egypt."[58]

If Pakistan was not going to be a refuge for Muslims in India, then *Al-Jamiat* would try to give hope of a better future in India itself. In one article it argued that there were two views of life for Muslims in India. In the first, murderers of Muslims were not being punished, communalists were not being stopped, those harassing Muslims were not being controlled, those attacking Islam were not being reprimanded, the government was biased, and the doors of employment were closed to Muslims, and they were being removed from their jobs. However, *Al-Jamiat* argued, this view was making Muslims afraid of living in India; it was making them hopeless for the future and so they were heading to Pakistan. *Al-Jamiat* offered an alternative perspective. India was where their roots were, and these roots were strong. The future, too, it argued, was "to a great extent bright" because they lived in a democracy in which all citizens were equal. Moreover, "even though this is not being implemented right now, how long can this state of affairs go on. Any system must eventually, in ten years or so, take effect." Thus noting a frustrating reality, *Al-Jamiat* asked Muslims to be patient.[59]

Al-Jamiat tried to respond to exclusionary denunciations that all Muslims in India were Pakistanis, particularly by the recently established Bharatiya Jana Sangh, an ally of the Rashtriya Swayamsevak Sangh on the Hindu right. Taking on their calls to reverse Partition, one article argued that such a demand imagined the territory of Pakistan as not foreign but still part of India. It quibbled with the semantics of *Pakistani* by arguing that "we are happy that Hindustan's Muslims are being called Pakistani because Pakistani was defined by them [the Jana Sangh]. I mean that a person who thinks Pakistan is a foreign country is *not* a Pakistani, and those who think it is not is a Pakistani. Thus by this definition, Jana Sangh are Pakistanis for they think of Pakistan as their country and want to make it part of Akhund Bharat."[60]

After discussions of the passport system and the closing of the Khokrapar border crossing emerged in 1952, the same two poles of opinion were evident. On the one hand, articles and letters in *Al-Jamiat* called the system a new wall, "passport *ki diwar*," between the two countries, and argued for an ease of travel because "although India and Pakistan are politically two separate countries yet both countries have people that have a spiritual relationship with each other." In addition, closure of the Khokrapar border crossing would have dire consequences:[61]

> At first we had heard that after the passport system the Khokrapar route would not be closed. But now we are hearing that the Pakistan government wants to close the Khokrapar route since it thinks that unless it is closed the passport system will not work. But it should not close it immediately, but wait and see if the passport system fails or not. . . . If it is closed immediately it will have a ter-

> rible psychological effect on Indian Muslims and for some time the people [*awam*] will suffer a depression.[62]

On the other hand, *Al-Jamiat* also argued that a complete sealing of the border was necessary for Muslims in India to be accepted as citizens of India. But this should only be so if the same restrictions are applied to Hindus in East Bengal, so that they are forced to remain there (presumably as hostages). As one letter argued, "the real passport is that Pakistan breaks all links with Indian Muslims and India with Pakistani Hindus . . . they consider them the nationals of the other country and take no interest in them."[63] Similarly another editorial argued that

> if the Government of Pakistan does not want Hindustan's Muslims to put their foot on Pakistan's territory then the Government of India should also place the same restrictions on East Bengal's Hindus and not let them come to Hindustan, and going and coming on both sides be completely stopped. . . . I will go so far as to say that until Pakistan's Hindus and India's Muslims put mud [*maṭī*] on themselves and are not considered the full citizens of the two countries, until then the introduction of the passport system is ridiculous. When in Hindustan there is such an uproar over Pakistan's Hindus and when in Pakistan there is fellow feeling with India's Muslims, then what good is the damn passport system?[64]

In the next chapter we will see how contingent "the damn passport system" was in aligning citizenship in a landscape still in flux with other forms of belonging and relationships. And yet these two poles of opinion reflect the predicament Muslims in India faced; if passports institutionalized national identities, this was a severing that made them "foreigners" to the once-proclaimed Muslim homeland, and left them in a still uncertain place of national belonging in their own homes.

6. *The Phantasm of Passports*

PHANTASM *n and adj: a thing or being which apparently exists but is not real . . . a figment of the imagination. . . . A person who is not what he or she appears or claims to be.**

The shift from the technology of permits to that of passports for controlling the movement of people was an extraordinarily important one. If defining the nations of divided South Asia was to achieve categorical closure, the emergence of passports served to distinguish citizens from aliens, nationals from foreigners, in the midst of an historical mess and a landscape of shifting identities. However, as a successor to permits, the passport had to be made to function as a travel document *and* a certificate of citizenship. This relationship between passports and citizenship could not be taken for granted, for it had to be produced with considerable bureaucratic imagination and force.

The passport system for travel between India and Pakistan was introduced at the insistence of the Pakistani government, so that Muslims coming from India to Pakistan could be positively identified as Indian nationals and thus be distinguished and severed from the multitudinous claims on the body of the Pakistani nation. However, the new passports had to function

* From the *Oxford English Dictionary* (ed. J. Simpson) by permission of Oxford University Press.

in a context in which the relationship between Muslim and Pakistani was far from resolved, and Indian Muslim–*muhajir* remained transitive categories. Not only were Muslims in India continuing to be displaced through Khokrapar to become *muhajirs*, but many were also attempting to return to their homes in India. For instance, in 1950, Indian Muslims who had come to Pakistan wanted to return to their homes, and 95,000 had registered to do so after the Nehru-Liaqat Pact. Furthermore, in India, public debates and permit and evacuee property court cases continued to grapple with raging questions of whether Muslims could be loyal citizens, subjected to deportations, or were simply "evacuees" and "intending evacuees."

Thus the passport system that emerged for travel between India and Pakistan inherited all the anxieties of the permit system, along with many of its techniques of control (which continue with minor variations to this day). The No Objection Certificates (NOCs, also called "Endorsements," see figure 6.1) came to be required even before visas could be applied for, and visas were then issued for specific cities or towns which additionally required police reporting and/or registration at consulates (see figures 6.2 and 6.3). The array of different kinds of permits were similarly converted into different kinds of visas, so that instead of temporary permits and permanent permits for return, there emerged short-term and long-term visas.

And yet the passport was of a different order in written documents since it came to be used to mark distinct national identities. Behind the passport was a single issuing state, and in front of it was an individual.[1] The document could be imagined as standing between a state and an individual and establishing a relationship between them, albeit a contingent one. It was here that the passport acquired phantasmic qualities.

With the advent of passports, a Muslim in India could be deemed a "Pakistani national" who had thrown away his passport, concealed his passport, or not yet acquired one. The Pakistani passport thus became a specter between a state and an individual, and its apparition was used by the Indian state to mark Muslim identity in national terms. The official files I examine here on "controlling the entry of Pakistani nationals" and of "regularizing the stay in India of Pakistani nationals" were attempts to fix and substantiate the phantasmic passport. The phantasmic qualities of the passport were exacerbated when the Pakistani state refused to issue Pakistani passports to those deemed to be Pakistani nationals by the Indian state (particularly given that the rationale for the introduction of passports had been to limit claims to Pakistani nationality).

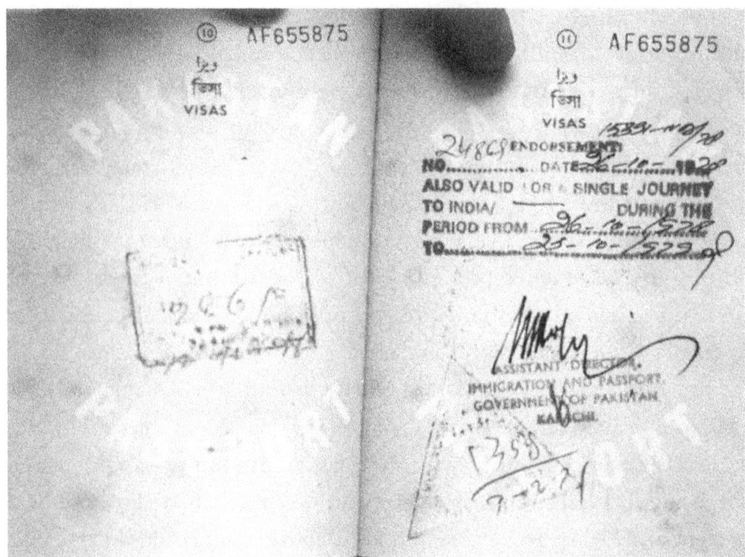

FIGURE 6.1 Endorsement from the government of Pakistan giving clearance to a Pakistani citizen to apply for an Indian visa.

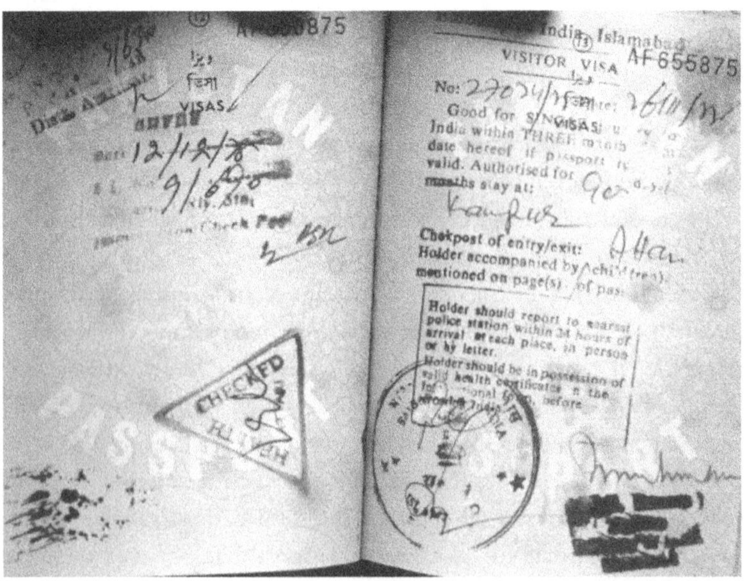

FIGURE 6.2 An Indian visa in a Pakistani passport, issued for only specific destinations within India, in this case Kanpur. An additional requirement: "Holder should report to nearest police station within twenty-four hours of arrival at each place, in person or by letter. . . ."

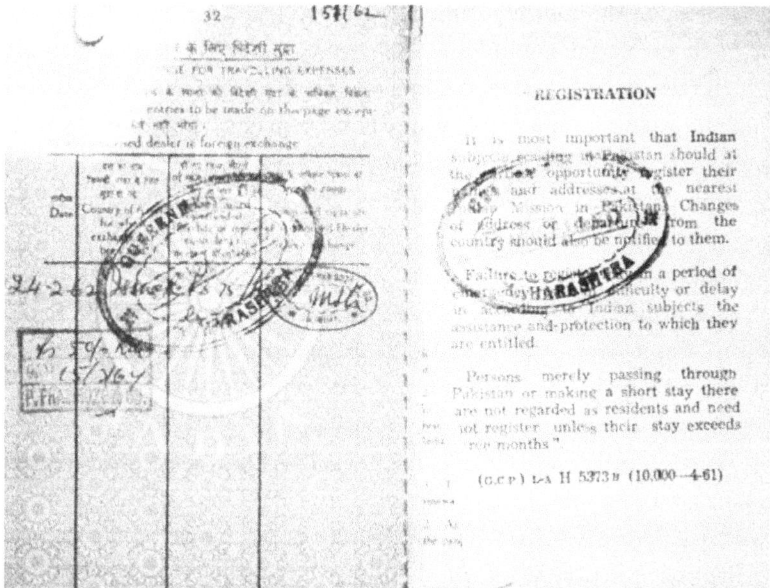

REGISTRATION

It is most important that Indian subjects [illegible] Pakistan should at the [illegible] opportunity [illegible]gister their [illegible] and addresses at [illegible] nearest [illegible] Mission in Pakistan. Changes of [illegible]ddress or departure from the country should [illegible] be notified to them.

Failure to [illegible] a period of [illegible] difficulty or delay in [illegible] Indian subjects the assistance and protection to which they are entitled.

Persons merely passing through Pakistan or making a short stay there are not regarded as residents and need not register unless their stay exceeds [illegible] months".

(G.C.P.) L-A H 5373 B (10,000—4-61)

FIGURE 6.3 India-Pakistan passport with notification requiring registration.

In this chapter I look at official writing "behind" the document, as the Indian state attempted to "fix" the "Pakistani," the emergence of the category of the "undefined," and the making of a "humanitarian" response to the bureaucratic violence of these spectral classifications of nationhood.

FORMS OF IDENTITY

Although many of the extraordinary restrictions that were part of the permit system were transferred to the Indo-Pak passport system, the passport was a fundamentally different kind of document and marks an important shift in technology and its inscriptional power. Therefore the very form of the passport deserves attention.[2]

To begin with, I asked almost every person I interviewed formally and informally if they still had a permit so I could look at it, but no one did. On the other hand, many people were able to pull out old and weathered passports. This ephemeral and transitory nature of permits distinguishes the documentary power of passports.

A person traveling under the permit system from Pakistan to India, for instance, would first obtain an NOC from the District Magistrate's Office, then apply to the Indian permit office for a permit for himself and family members traveling with him. The permit consisted of a piece of paper which was issued to a head of household for the entire family, and was for single journeys from a place of origin to a specific destination. Initially photographs were not required, but photographs were introduced later to improve its surveillance mechanism. Thus one person in the traveling group carried this paper, and at the check post of entry a part of the sheet was removed by the border official to form a counterfoil, which border officials mailed to the police of the district the person/group was traveling to. On arrival at the destination the person/group was required to report to the police station there, and if he failed to do so then the police could track the person with the counterfoil. For the return journey, if the person/group was making a temporary visit, the person had to go to the Pakistani permit office and present the NOC for obtaining a permit to return permanently to Pakistan. Before leaving he would report again to the police station to inform them that he was leaving, say within the period of the permit obtained from the Indian office. The process would be reversed if the journey was being made from India to Pakistan and back to India.

I have already suggested in chapter 3 the numerous ways in which people attempted to circumvent the permit system. Also there were repeated complaints that it was a complicated procedure to travel on permits, that there were mistakes made, officials at different stages of the paper trail demanded bribes, and a certain amount of confusion and harassment always accompanied the process. But here I present a normative account of a "permitted" journey to highlight two points. First, the life of the permit lasted only the duration of a single journey, and second, it did not require a declaration of citizenship.

With permits, there were Muslims in Pakistan who could not obtain permits for permanent return to their homes in India, and so obtained temporary permits, which they threw away or attempted to have converted for permanent stay. In addition, as I suggested earlier, there were Muslims who claimed to have never gone to Pakistan and were prosecuted for having returned via East Pakistan or having thrown away their permit. But the permits were ephemeral in nature, and though persons prosecuted, even deported, on permit regulations were deemed to have lost their Indian citizenship, they were not positively identified as "Pakistani nationals."

The NOC functioned alongside the permit and established the person's intention to return to his or her place of origin. It allowed for a presumption of citizenship but did not subject the person in those terms. This was in part because the permit system was brought into place before the citizenship laws were formulated for both of the new states, and because there was considerable ambiguity around questions of citizenship and mass displacement at the time. It was only when individuals were arrested, for instance for overstaying on temporary permits, that the disciplinary regime of permits engaged questions of national identity. Amid claims of having returned home, the juridical question centered on whether the person had *lost* the citizenship of birth and domicile by having "migrated" according to Article 7 of the citizenship provisions, and led to disputes over the meaning of *migration*.

However, the passport was a document issued by a single state to a single individual, and functioned like a book to carry its inscriptional authority. Even though passports were issued for only a limited period, their validity exceeded the period of a single journey. A person carried the document during and after a journey and could retain it after its validity had expired for purposes of renewal or reissue of a similar document. Therefore it had a potential lifespan that corresponded to the person's life, and could even exceed it as a commemorative document.

This relatively substantial and enduring character of the passport as a document between a state and an individual had important effects. An Indian government file on how to move the surveillance mechanisms of the permit system to that of the passport system is quite revealing. While discussing how to incorporate police reporting that was part of the permit system into the passport system, the Ministry of External Affairs and the Ministry of Home Affairs discussed how to prevent "undesirable elements from going underground and indulging in espionage activities." In the prior system, a counterfoil of the permit used to be sent to the superintendent of police of the district that the person was traveling to. But now the visa was lodged inside a passport that the traveler carried with him, and therefore it was suggested that the border post send an express letter to the district police warning them of "the entry of suspicious characters." However, it was argued that "absolute control is not possible," and that "[i]t is unlikely that our check-post will be able to know whether a particular Pakistani national is of suspicious character." Therefore a decision was made instead to stamp "Report to police station in person" inside

Pakistani passports, and thus mirror the practice of the Pakistani Mission in India. The police station at the person's destination would then note the arrival and subsequent departure of the individual beside the stamp. If an appropriate indication was not made beside the stamp then the person could be apprehended at the Indian border post.[3] This is the origin of the Indo-Pak police reporting visa as adapted from the permit system that is still in practice today. However, now the passport, required for all border crossings in the region, became a cumulative record of state-regulated movement, and the subjects of surveillance, previously identified as "Muslims," "Muslim refugees," or "Muslim repatriates," became positively identified by state-bound nationality—the passport allowed a categorical shift to "Pakistani nationals" in official Indian discourse.

Indeed there were still Muslim refugees who were trying to return home. But under the passport system, an inability to obtain a permanent permit translated into an inability to obtain an Indian passport. Thus instead of a temporary permit, Muslims who wished to return obtained a Pakistani passport and a short-term visa for their place of origin. This was particularly the case for Muslims who had come through Khokrapar to Pakistan; according to the Indian state they were deemed to have "migrated" and lost the right to Indian citizenship, while in a place like Karachi it was relatively easy to obtain a Pakistani passport for purposes of return travel, by declaring that the person had "migrated" before the commencement of the Pakistani citizenship laws (which did not require registration) or informally through a largely sympathetic *muhajir* bureaucracy. On reaching home, they discarded their passports (in a manner similar to the use of temporary permits), overstayed their short-term visas, or applied for a long-term visa, which became key to becoming "regularized" as an Indian citizen through fulfillment of residential requirements.[4]

Thus those carrying, as well as those *presumed* to be carrying, Pakistani passports came to be identified as "Pakistani nationals." In a governmental discussion on controlling the "illegal influx of Pakistani nationals," the joint secretaries of the Ministry of External Affairs noted that "some Pakistani nationals who had entered India with Pakistani passports were known to have thrown away their passports and to be staying on in India unauthorizedly." It was suggested that state governments "collect evidence proving the Pakistani nationality of the individual concerned." It is here that the presence and absence of the passport gave it phantasmic qualities. On substantiating the phantasmic passport, it was argued that

External Affairs should then ask the Pakistani High Commission "to provide travel documents to the Pakistani national." However, certain of the Pakistani government's reluctance to issue such passports, External Affairs issued the directive that if the Pakistani High Commission "should fail to provide a travel document, the state government should take steps to have the person deported."[5]

The phantasmic passport had grave consequences, and it encompassed not only Muslim refugees returning to their homes in India, but also Muslims who may have never left their homes. The Delhi administration conducted a considerable correspondence with the Ministry of Home Affairs about what to do with those "Pakistani nationals" who claimed that they had never migrated to Pakistan.[6] When a person (marked Muslim) applied for the issue of an Indo-Pak passport, the application instigated a police investigation into his or her "nationality." However, there were cases where the CID report showed that the applicant had "migrated" to Pakistan after March 1, 1947, but the applicant himself contested the report of the CID. The problem was exacerbated when there was "no documentary evidence" for the government's claim. This included not only those who were presumed to have gone to and returned from Pakistan before the permit system, but also those after it, since "they will hardly be willing to produce the same as it will definitely go against their interests."

The Delhi administration complained that there were also difficulties with individuals who were reported to have "migrated" to Pakistan *for a month or so*. If they only went to Pakistan for a short time then it was very difficult to assess whether it had been with the "intention" to permanently settle there. It may be that they originally went to Pakistan with the "intention" to settle there, but "after assessing their own chances of economic and social status they might have decided to come back to India."

Home Affairs replied to these queries by emphasizing that "mere suspicion" was not enough and that "reasonable evidence" in the form of witnesses or documents needed to be gathered. On the basis of this "evidence," the person would be required to prove otherwise. "Mere denial of the charge on their part will not be sufficient" and they would have to give "details of the places where they stayed and produce necessary evidence of receipts, postal communications received at those addresses, employment or profession pursued during the period, etc." Thus a simple application for an Indian Indo-Pak passport could have led to a fundamental challenge over nationality.

On the question of those returning from short visits, it was argued that no matter how difficult, the "intentions" had to be interrogated on the basis of the person's actions: "thus for instance, if the whole unit of family had gone to Pakistan without obtaining a No Objection to Return Certificate, or when there was no compelling circumstance like communal riots to justify a departure from India, the family will have to be treated as migrants. Where an individual member of a family had gone to Pakistan leaving other members in India, the plea that he had to go to Pakistan on account of communal riots . . . can hardly be accepted, and it will be a clear case of migration." Thus a visit to Pakistan for even a month could be interpreted as migration and result in the loss of Indian citizenship. Despite Home Affairs' offer to help improve the Delhi administration's power of deductive reasoning, the individual case files that I examine here reiterate the ambiguities of identity and nationality that governmental process attempted to secure.

MUSLIM DIFFERENCE

Not all "Pakistani nationals" *without* Pakistani passports were a problem for the Indian state. For example, Home Ministry wrote to the UP government without alarm about "persons" from Pakistan who entered India without travel documents.[7] It noted that these "persons belonging to the minority community in Pakistan who have come to India as displaced persons and did so with the object of making India their permanent home, should be registered as Indian citizens without any elaborate inquiries provided that they satisfy the residence qualifications." This is borne out in the file of Nevandmal, a "Pakistani national of the minority community." The case yielded only a brief correspondence, and required no elaborate inquiries and no attestations of loyalty.[8]

There were also "Pakistani nationals belonging to the minority community" who came to India *with* Pakistani passports, but there was a procedure by which they could "surrender" their Pakistani passports and acquire Indian citizenship. This procedure did not require obtaining a long-term visa and on completion of six months' residence in India they could be registered as Indian citizens. The Home Ministry noted that "[e]very month several hundreds of Pakistani nationals belonging to the minority community in Pakistan are being registered as Indian citizens by the various registering officers in accordance with the procedure."[9]

If Hindus had privileged access to Indian citizenship, an interesting comparison is with Jews who migrated to Israel and then wanted to return to India. The official policy is exemplified here:

> After reaching there they found conditions of living unsatisfactory and many of them expressed their desire to return to India. Considering that these persons had migrated to Israel without mature deliberations and without having full knowledge of the conditions there, the Government of India decided that they may be allowed to return to India.[10]

This sympathetic position on Jewish migrations from India to Israel was moderated later with a "dateline." Given that "now conditions there are better known," and after the Israeli nationality law which automatically gave citizenship to all Jews entering Israel went into effect on July 14, 1952, it was decided that they would not be allowed to return. However, Asher Reuben Moses, who left for Israel with his brothers in 1953 but now wanted to return to his mother in Bombay, was allowed to do so. His departure for Israel was noted as showing "he had more love for the new state of Israel. This is understandable as he is of Jewish faith." However, his love for Israel was not seen as irreconcilable with Indian citizenship. It was added that since both he and his father were born in India, "[h]e is therefore an Indian citizen for all practical purposes."[11]

Needless to say, such a sympathetic view was not extended to Muslims who went to Pakistan. For instance, a secretary in the Bihar government enquired from the Home Ministry about a few persons "numbering about a hundred or two, who had gone away to Pakistan and had become Pakistani nationals but who have now returned from Pakistan to their original homes in Bihar and now desire to become Indian citizens." The secretary argued that although a few of them might be Pakistani "spies," a majority of them "fled either from fear or from false notions of prosperity that might be awaiting them in Pakistan." He believed that they should not be deported, although it was possible to do that, and instead they should be given their Indian citizenship back, for "it may bring good by making loyal citizens of these people."[12] However, the Home Ministry ordered that each case be "laboriously" and individually examined because Indian citizenship was "a very valued privilege and cannot be conferred without full and proper examination of each case."[13]

It is noteworthy that although it was specifically "Muslims" who required careful scrutiny, the voice of the state used a universal vocabulary, eschewing religious markings. "Pakistani national," as we shall see, provided an adequate alternative.

PASSPORTS, LITERACY, PHANTASM

A group of five hundred unlettered coal miners in Bihar were "advised" to take out Pakistani passports, but then failed to get "F" visas to continue their employment in Bihar.[14] The correspondence began in 1954 when employers of these coal miners wrote to the Bihar government to inquire how to obtain "F" visas for them even though the last date for obtaining such a visa had expired. The query spawned a huge intergovernmental debate on ultimately who was a "Pakistani national," albeit with or without Pakistani passports, and lays bare the contingent character of documents amid forms of governmental writing.

The Damodar river valley, which stretches across Bihar and Bengal, is a major coal mining area in India, and some of the oldest coal mines in operation, dating as far back as 1815, are located here. According to a study of the coal mining labor force, the miners—drawn from lower-caste peasants, artisans, and tribal groups—originated largely from the districts surrounding the mines and maintained strong ties to their original villages, to which they returned for religious rituals, in the marriage season, and during harvests in the agricultural cycle. These ties were strengthened when women were no longer allowed to work in the mines in 1929, which forced women and children to remain in villages. Tracing their changing settlement and labor practices until 1947, the study argued that despite these changes the coal miners remained "close to the soil."[15]

When the Bihar government wrote to the Ministry of Home Affairs at the center about what to do with these "illiterate" coal miners who had been "advised" to take out Pakistani passports, the Bihar government placed the coal miners with passports as part of a larger problem of dealing with "Pakistani nationals" and their phantasmic passports:

> Instances have come to the notice of the state government in which Muslim Pakistani nationals who entered India on Pakistani passports and Indian visas have thereon *surrendered their Pakistani passports* to

> the Pakistan Mission in India. Presumably these Pakistani nationals consider that by surrendering their passports they acquire Indian nationality and may continue to live in India permanently . . . [further] *the erstwhile holder of a Pakistani passport,* if called on to regularize his stay in India, will express complete inability to do so. Nor can the state government apparently take steps to remove him from the country . . . no action is possible . . . A similar problem is presented by Pakistani subjects who came to India after October 1952 with valid travel documents but don't extend visas, or extend visas and stay beyond date of expiry. Such persons come up time and again on flimsy pretexts for extension of their visas. There are also Pakistani visitors who get visas for visits to specified places and then move about without prior permission from the state government. Yet again, there are Pakistanis living and working in India holding valid travel documents, whom the state government may consider undesirable to allow to remain in the country and whose early departure they would welcome. . . . The ordinary procedure for removal by repatriation (arranged by the Home Ministry) after conviction and sentence in court of law is a long drawn-out process and would be quite unsuitable in cases in which the state government desires to be rid of a Pakistani subject in a shortest possible time. (emphasis added)

A year later the Bihar government reiterated its frustrations with the "practical difficulties with the Indo-Pak passport system," as "[t]here are large number of Pakistani subjects *without valid travel documents* and the state government is powerless to get rid of them" (emphasis added). The Bihar government asked the central government how to "compel these recalcitrant Pakistanis to leave the country."

How did five hundred coal miners arguably "close to the soil" become "Pakistani nationals" who needed to be gotten "rid of," to be compelled to leave the country? The Ministry of External Affairs then began a correspondence with the Ministry of Home Affairs on the fate of these coal miners, as well as the general problem of fixing nationality on the basis of phantasmic passports. In this correspondence there emerged three points of view for "regularizing" those "playing about with their national status." There was the "legal" point of view, the "national" point of view, and "the humanitarian point of view."

The legal view was, simply put, that the coal miners were "aliens" without valid visas and therefore liable to deportation. The national view was that because of a "policy of nationalization of our industries" it was preferred that these people leave India and Indian nationals be recruited in their places.

But the matter was not so simple. There was an official realization that the meaning of the passport was contingent, and that therefore they may be dealing with a phantasmic/fictive classification of people. Had the coal miners acquired their "passport by mistake"? Were they duped, or had they "voluntarily declared themselves to be Pakistani nationals, and on this basis had taken out Pakistani passports"? Could an unlettered person be held accountable for written documents that they could not read or sign? Since they were "illiterate" could they be aware of the implications of what they had done? As these questions entered into official writing there emerged the "humanitarian" point of view.

Thus from the humanitarian point of view it was proposed that instead of declaring all the coal miners as "aliens," each case be reviewed "individually on merit," and that "[i]f they [the state government] find that a particular Pakistani national has made India his home and has no connection whatsoever with Pakistan and has taken a Pakistan passport by mistake then he may be allowed to stay in India even without a visa until the Citizenship Law is passed when their claim for Indian citizenship will have to be considered." However, "[i]n the case of other persons who have some connections with Pakistan, they should be asked to leave India."

However, from the case of the coal miners, two general issues arose. One was the question of how to "remove" those with "some connections with Pakistan," the "undesirable," and this was tied to the Bihar government's earlier frustrations. If they did not leave India "voluntarily" then a law needed to be formulated for deportation, because "repatriation" through the Pakistani High Commission would "lead to all kinds of protests and allegations." In the meantime "they may be threatened that they should leave India or suitable action may be taken against them." This led to the formulation of the policy that the "Government of India has decided that it is no longer necessary to refer cases to Pakistani Missions for repatriation. If they overstay the period of authorized residence they should be served with a notice to leave the country within a specified period. If they fail to comply with this order then they should be prosecuted and made to leave the country."

The other issue was the feeling that "we are not likely to hear the last of such cases. Ignorance, inconvenience, and unsympathetic attitudes of employers will continue to be trotted out as reasons for special consideration." Therefore it was decided that a new dateline be set for the issue of "F" visas, and that it be clearly announced that after June 30, 1957, those without visas would be dealt with under the Foreigners Act of 1946 as amended by the Foreigner Laws (Amendment) Ordinance of 1957. This was considered additionally "advantageous" because "all those who are still without Pakistani passports will be tempted to take out such passports. Thereafter we will be able to treat them as Pakistani nationals for all times to come."

This extension of the "dateline" led to disagreement with the Pakistani High Commission. The High Commission described this move as a unilateral extension on the previously agreed time limit of April 30, 1954, to take out Pakistani passports and relevant visas. It argued that "persons who did not take out Pakistan travel documents" by May 31, 1954, and were staying in India "beyond that date without Pakistani passports are no longer Pakistani nationals because they failed to exercise the final option given to them." External Affairs contested the Pakistani High Commission's position on the grounds that previously an extension had been made from the end of April to the end of May for the issue of Pakistani passports and visas for Pakistani nationals in India. On further dispute over the extended dateline, the high commissioner wrote to External Affairs on the larger question of who was a "Pakistani national," for this was at the core of the otherwise nominal contention:

> I feel that a certain amount of confusion and misunderstanding in dealing with this problem has arisen on account of the *lack of precision in the language* used in conversation and letters which has been somewhat loose on both sides hitherto. This was natural as the approach to the problem was based on *humanitarian grounds* rather than law or politics . . . The question, therefore, now is as to *who is a Pakistani citizen*. This as you will agree is a question of law and any view or opinion which does not conform to the law of the land will not be of any value . . . We have to see who is a Pakistani citizen before the question of granting him travel documents such as passports is taken into consideration. On this subject, the Pakistani Citizenship Act is the law which I have to follow. Under that law

only those persons living in India are Pakistani citizens who hold or have held or had obtained a valid Pakistani passport before April 30, 1954. Those persons who do not qualify under the provisions of our law are not Pakistani citizens.

There are approximately 3.5 crore of Muslims in India and they are Indian citizens under the laws of this country. If any one of them or even any Hindu in India is labeled as a Pakistani and asked to produce documents by the Indian authorities, that would not mean we can accept him as such. A person has to be qualified within the meaning of Pakistani Citizenship Act before we can give him travel documents or permit him to cross the border.

I therefore wish to point out that the intention of the note sent to you by this office was that we would recognize only those persons as Pakistanis who come within the definition of the Pakistan Citizenship Act, not anyone else whether Hindu or Muslim, including those who may wish to migrate to Pakistan now or whom the Government of India may wish to expatriate. I will continue to represent the cases of such Pakistani citizens about whose nationality there is no doubt, to you, but they should not be confused with the Muslim citizens of India or such others who cannot produce any evidence sufficient in the opinion of Indian authorities to prove their Indian citizenship. (emphasis added)

A considerable correspondence ensued to determine whether Pakistani Citizenship Laws stated May 31, 1954 as a final date for the becoming a Pakistani national or for the issue of a Pakistani passport. In turn, the Pakistani High Commission sent the Ministry of External Affairs the following cutting from *The Statesman* on a decision by the Andra Pradesh High Court on September 7, 1957, stating that a passport was not an identification of citizenship but rather merely a travel document:

A division bench of the Andra Pradesh court consisting of Chief Justice and Mr. Justice P.J. Reddy yesterday declared Rule 3 framed under the Citizenship Act of 1955 to be void on the ground that it infringed Article 14 of the constitution and enlarged the scope of Section 9 of the citizenship act. Section 9 of the act provides for the termination of the citizenship if a citizen of India voluntarily acquires the citizenship of any other country. Rule 3 lays down that

> obtaining of a passport from the government of any other country shall be conclusive proof of the voluntary acquisition of the citizenship of that country. The judges ruled that a passport could not be taken as evidence to establish the fact of citizenship. The judges were disposing of writ petitions filed by twenty-two residents of Kovvur who had been ordered by the state government to leave the country on their obtaining of passports from the Pakistani High Commission. The petitioners said that they had come from Baluchistan and settled in Kovvur before Partition. After Partition they acquired Pakistani passports under the belief that people born in the area now forming part of Pakistan were not citizens of India . . . The division bench ruled that a passport was not the basis on which the fact of citizenship could be established, but that it only embodied a request to another government to allow the bearer free passage and give him every assistance and protection. "A passport issued by a government to a citizen does not make it a document of title or a piece of evidence in a court of law to establish that fact. It is only a convenient link in the chain of international intercourse," they said.[16]

The Andra Pradesh ruling represented just one moment in continuing contests over the meaning and uses of passports. Finally, as we shall see, the Citizenship Rules of 1956 gave the central government, and not the courts, the authority to determine whether a person had acquired citizenship of another country. This ambivalence of passports and the Pakistani High Commission's reluctance to issue Pakistani passports to those presumed to be Pakistani nationals by the Indian state meant that a new category of people emerged—the "undefined."

THE UNDEFINED

In 1954 Ghafoor Khan, an unlettered millworker in Kanpur, received news that his daughter, who had migrated to Pakistan with her husband, was seriously ill and that he should be "by her bedside immediately." His petition noted that he was "advised by the laymen to whom I had referred about my difficulties that it would take months and months to secure a passport," and therefore he went through the Khokrapar Pass to

Karachi "without loss of time." However, after spending a month with his daughter, he found that return was not so simple:

> That after my visit to Karachi when I wanted to come back after a month or about I was told there that I would not be allowed to go back to India through Khokrapar Pass because the passage was one-sided and that I would not be allowed otherwise to enter into India unless I had obtained a passport from the Pakistan government. . . . That I felt and believed that it was just the necessary procedure to be gone through to be able to go back to my home, my country, and my people . . . I had gone there with the limited purpose of being beside the bed of my ailing daughter for whom I have great love and affection . . . I had gone alone, leaving my life-partner, my wife, my two sons, and daughter and grandsons in India.

It was the Pakistani passport that led to his arrest under the Foreigners Act after he had returned back home. He was thus forced to leave for Pakistan every time his passport and visa expired, to obtain a new one. Although he had great affection for his daughter in Pakistan, he tried to establish that "home" was where his wife, other children, and grandchildren were, and that to be declared a "foreigner" in his own "home" had caused him "intense mental anguish" which had shattered his health. He described himself as "an old, illiterate man of about sixty-two years of age" at his "journey's end," and "a humble illiterate person," and that he had been "a peaceful and faithful citizen of India," "an Indian national, entitled to remain here" with his family. He appealed on "humanitarian considerations" for his citizenship to be restored to him.

Ghafoor Khan's petition self-consciously established a relationship between the passport as a written document, literacy, and orality. Ghafoor Khan was an "illiterate" man who received oral information from "laymen" in his community that it was very difficult to obtain a passport, and he was "told" by people around him that a passport was his only means of return. To Ghafoor Khan, there was very little difference between the Indian and Pakistani governments issuing the written documents, for the landscape was foremost defined by a beloved daughter and his wife and other children and grandchildren. However, unable to remain at home with his wife, the Pakistani passport and Indian nationality acquired an unprecedented force.

The different official responses to Ghafoor Khan's Pakistani passport reflect the unsettled character of the written document, as a mere travel document or as tied to citizenship. When Ghafoor Khan was prosecuted for overstaying his visa he appealed to the courts, and the lower court adjudicated that he was not liable for prosecution under the Foreigners Act as he was not a "foreigner"; he had not ceased to be an Indian national. This judgment was based on the Andra Pradesh High Court decision that passports were not certificates of citizenship, but merely "convenient link[s] in the chain of international intercourse."

The police report on Ghafoor Khan was also sympathetic, and stated that he was "not dangerous from the security angle" and that he was an old man of fifty-six years who had "grown weak." In addition, all of his near relations, his wife, sons, and daughter were residing in India. "As such," the report added, "his stay in Pakistan might be a painful one." Another police inquiry stated that there was no conclusive proof (no written evidence) about the sickness of his daughter in Pakistan in November 1954, but according to other people in his locality "it was found that he went to Pakistan to see his daughter who was ill at that time in Pakistan."

Despite the lower court's decision and favorable police reports, the UP government rejected his claim to Indian citizenship as "untenable." It argued that Ghafoor Khan's version was "an afterthought and can hardly be accepted" because he worked as a fruit seller while he was in Pakistan, and did not approach the Indian Mission in Pakistan for help to return. His reason for now desiring Indian citizenship was that he "failed to establish himself in Pakistan" and was deemed to be "a full-fledged Pakistani national." The UP government refused to take into account that as a poor man, Ghafoor Khan needed to earn a living when he was in Pakistan, or that the Indian High Commission was unlikely to give an Indian passport to a Muslim man in Pakistan.

When the UP government forwarded Khan's file to the central government, the Ministry of Law wrote that it did not think Ghafoor Khan had "migrated" since he had compelling reasons for leaving on short notice without an Indian passport. Therefore he had not lost his Indian nationality, and the Pakistani passport had served as a mere travel document. On the other hand, the Ministry of Home Affairs insisted that his obtaining a Pakistani passport signaled that he had "voluntarily acquired the citizenship of Pakistan."

With conflicting views on Ghafoor Khan, the central government declared that "the fact of his migration" was not "conclusively established." But given Ghafoor Khan's illiteracy, old age, and mental anguish, a "humanitarian point of view" had to be taken to mitigate the violence of national categories. As a result, it was decided to allow him to remain in India "with undefined status, provided he does not come to adverse notice."[17]

The "undefined" then emerged as this category of moving people that became caught in the nationalizing order of the passport system. In the case of Basar Khan, an application for an Indian Indo-Pak passport to visit his ailing mother in Peshawar resulted in his being declared an "undefined person." Originally from Peshawar, Basar Khan came to work for a transport company in 1943 in Madras, where he met and married his wife, who was born there, and where they were resident at the time of application. He was, however, considered to have entered India before the permit system, and therefore his "status" was deemed to be "unclear." As he was considered "Possibly Pakistani," and there were "doubts about [his] Indian nationality," the Ministry of External Affairs raised the question of whether giving him an Indian passport would equal granting him citizenship.

Here again the "humanitarian point of view" had to be accommodated, for Basar Khan had left Peshawar and married and settled in Madras at a time, not just before the permit system, but well before Partition or Pakistan. Therefore instead of an Indian passport, a bureaucratic technique had to be found to accommodate him. Initially it was suggested that he be given an "emergency certificate" to be considered an Indian national. It was argued, however, that "emergency certificates" were granted to only "stateless persons, and he is still a Pakistani national." This led to a correspondence on whether he could "make an affidavit declaring his intention to stay in India permanently and renounce his Pakistani nationality," and thus become a stateless person who could then acquire Indian citizenship. However, allowing an individual to renounce his Pakistani nationality, in other words *choose* his own nationality, was to open a Pandora's box in this social and political landscape. There were immediately questions about whether this was "legally possible," as well as fears of others following suit. Therefore, it was finally decided to deny him an Indian passport to visit his mother, but allow him to remain in India in an "undefined status."[18]

DEPENDENT WOMEN, CHIVALROUS STATE

As I argued in chapter 3, women were not entitled to autonomous citizenship because of Article 5 of the citizenship laws by which their "domicile" was vested in that of their father or husband. Because permits were issued to both individuals and households, women, often incorporated in households, moved between the two states without directly engaging contestations of citizenship. However, with the onset of the passport system, when women applied as individuals for passports their legal status as "dependents" became of importance.

Karimunnisa's natal and conjugal home was in Nagpur, until her husband, Abdul Rahim, decided to go to Pakistan on December 28, 1947. She moved to Quetta with him and they lived there until he died. When he died, she decided to return to Nagpur on December 17, 1952, with her young children, as her entire kin network was based there and could provide her with the support she needed. She returned to India on a Pakistani passport and a "C" visa for temporary stay. Her visa was valid for only forty-five days and therefore she applied for an extension of her visa, while at the same time she made an application to the Indian High Commission for a permanent permit, and also applied through the state government to be admitted to the rights of Indian citizenship. When she received only a fifteen-day extension on her visa, she appealed to the courts so that she might not be prosecuted for overstaying after its expiration. She argued that "she did not *intend* to leave India permanently" and therefore had never lost her citizenship. According to Article 5 of the citizenship laws, which deemed place of birth and domicile as the basis of citizenship, her legal case relied on a particular definition of domicile from A.V. Dicey's *Conflict of Laws.*[19] Here "domicile" was defined as not only a permanent home where a person "resides with the intention of residence," but also "having so resided there, he retains the intention of residence, though he in fact no longer resides there." Therefore, she argued that her domicile of origin was revived when she had returned and that she was entitled to remain at Nagpur.

The High Court discussed the question of domicile at length, and concluded that Dicey's definition of domicile only applied 'to the case of a person who can exercise an independent volition so as to lose or acquire domicile." However, as a married woman her status was defined as a "dependent," and therefore she was not entitled to the use of that definition. Instead, "[t]he domicile of a legitimate infant is determined by, and changes with, that of his father while that of a married woman is the same as and changes with that of her husband. A domicile cannot be acquired by a dependent person through his own act." Thus on the basis of Article 5 of the citizenship laws, she was deemed to have lost her right to Indian citizenship by the "migration" of her late husband.[20] Denied autonomous citizenship, her argument that "although [she] had to leave India because her husband opted for Pakistan, she never intended personally to make Pakistan her home and anticipated early return to this country" was considered invalid. She was now to be considered as domiciled in Pakistan and could only acquire Indian citizenship on the basis of a migration certificate issued by the Indian High Commission. Since she did not have such a certificate, any stay beyond the expiration of her visa was a criminal offense.

Although the court did not rule in her favor, it nonetheless sympathized with her plight—not because the law denied her a right to independent mobility and residence, but because she was "helpless" and deserving of "Indian chivalry":

> We regret, therefore, that we cannot help the petitioner. We can only emphasize for the consideration of the authorities concerned that this is a hard and unfortunate case where a young and *helpless* woman is suffering for the act of another and deserves to be treated with that *sympathy which is characteristic of the best traditions of Indian chivalry*. This country has never been known to refuse an asylum to any person who, driven by circumstances, supplicated her protection. The case of a *helpless* widow who has young children to maintain and cannot live an independent existence without the support of her relatives in India deserves all the greater consideration. (Emphasis added)

Writing about Partition's abducted women, Veena Das pointed out that the state as *parens patriae* reified official kin codes amid more fluid and accommodating kinship practices.[21] Similarly, these citizenship laws, gendered rules of belonging in the nation-state, placed women's identity and belonging within a patrilocal familial order and did not allow for exceptions otherwise accommodated within unofficial kinship practices.

Furthermore, Partition's extraordinary and diverse displacements disrupted kin networks and the normative patrilocal family. There were women like Karimunnisa who left behind entire kin networks to accompany their husbands to Pakistan, but when their marriage ended, through estrangement, divorce, or death, they were left without the resources of kinship for material support within their natal families or social support for remarriage.

However, the court called upon the "sympathy" and "chivalry" of the bureaucratic state as a means to accommodate these spectral classifications of nationality, in much the same way the "humanitarian" perspective operated. In the archive there are long lists of case files bearing women's names. They include numerous cases of women who, at the end of their marriages, returned to their natal homes in India on Pakistani passports and the Indian state chivalrously accommodated them by granting them repeated visa renewals, albeit as Pakistani nationals. Once at home, one of the ways in which these women overcame restrictions on their continued residence in India was through remarriage with "Indian nationals." The cases of divorced women applying for recognition as Indian citizens through remarriage are equally numerous.

For instance, Mehrunnisa, from Pratapgarh, UP, married and then migrated with Mohd. Hasan to Pakistan in 1949. When she was divorced by her husband, she came back to her natal home on a Pakistani passport in 1956, and remained there on a one-year visa which was renewed every year. She then remarried in 1962 to Habibi from Allahabad, an Indian citizen, and this allowed her to register herself as an Indian citizen. Despite the fact that she had lived most of her life in UP, in her citizenship application she was not able to entirely shed the past with her first husband. Even though the Intelligence Bureau reported "no adverse notice" on her application, the UP government still considered her suspect because "she [wa]s the divorced wife of a Pakistani national and ha[d] lived in Pakistan for a number of years."[22]

Given cousin-marriage preferences among north Indian Muslims in particular[23] and proclivity to make marriage alliances through kin networks in general, as families found themselves divided across India and Pakistan there were, according to Omar Khalidi, 40,000 cross-border marriages a year in the 1950s, but which declined to only about 300 a year in the 1960s.[24] This is not surprising since such marriages not only made it difficult for women to return to their natal homes for social support and ritual purposes, they also made that separation almost permanent through loss of citizenship.

Ironically, because women's dependent status made patrilocal residence normative for citizenship, women could move through marriage while men could not move at all. Matrilocal arrangements, such as that of a *ghar-damad* (literally inhouse-son-in-law) found sometimes in cousin-marriage alliances when a woman had no brothers, was made impossible by these citizenship laws.

There were also women who chose not to leave their homes in India while their husbands went to Pakistan, but under these citizenship laws they lost their rights without ever leaving their homes. The case of Hidayathunissa Begum, along with her three daughters and a son, is one example. Her husband and their father, Fakhruddin, migrated to Pakistan in 1947 and acquired Pakistani nationality, but she and the children remained in their village in India. In 1958 they applied for an Indo-Pak passport to go to visit Fakhruddin, and then the question of their citizenship arose. On the basis of law, the state government declared that their very stay in India was "unauthorized" since "they were also Pakistani nationals in view of the fact that Shri Fakruddin had acquired Pakistani nationality," and therefore they should be deported to Pakistan.

However, "on humanitarian grounds" the state decided that it would not be "desirable . . . to compel them to leave for Pakistan against their will," as they had "all along resided here." They were allowed to stay in India, not as Indian citizens but as Pakistani nationals, "till they choose to go over to Pakistan." They thus acquired Pakistani nationality without ever going to Pakistan, and the home they had always lived in became officially only their temporary residence. Furthermore, when Fakhruddin died in 1960 they were left with no reason or relatives to go to in Pakistan, and had to initiate an application to be registered as Indian citizens.[25]

There were also numerous cases in which women chose to move while their husbands did not. Although the Ministry of Home Affairs stated that "normally it is not the policy of the Government of India to encourage members of the same family to have different nationalities,"[26] yet in the case of women "from the minority community in Pakistan" who came to India while their husbands remained in Pakistan as "Pakistani nationals," the government would evaluate each case "on its merits." If there were reasons whereby "the husbands of the applicants are precluded from coming to India and acquiring Indian citizenship by circumstances beyond their control it may not be justifiable to deny Indian citizenship to the ladies concerned."[27]

However, in the case of a Muslim woman who went to Pakistan while her husband remained in India, an important Supreme Court ruling decided that Article 7 on "migration" overruled Article 5 on domicile. Kumar Rani[28] went to Pakistan, and on her return argued that she had not lost her Indian citizenship because her domicile was vested in her husband, who had remained in India. She stated that she went to Karachi in July 1948 for medical treatment with a respected *hakim* there, leaving her husband in India. However, when she returned to India in December 1948 on a temporary permit her application for the permit noted that she was domiciled in Pakistan. She went back to Pakistan in April 1949 when her permit expired, and then applied for and obtained a permanent permit. However, when the permanent permit was cancelled after being issued to her, she appealed to the courts for adjudication. The government argued that it was entitled to cancel her permanent permit because the consent of the provincial government had not been obtained before the permit was issued, and that she made attempts to obtain a permanent permit only after her properties in Bihar were taken over by the Custodian of Evacuee Property. The question arose whether she could be deemed to have migrated to Pakistan under Article 7 of the citizenship laws, when under Article 5 her domicile and citizenship were dependent on those of her husband.

It was noted that Kumar Rani married Captain Maharaj Kumar Gopal Saran Narayan Singh of Gaya in 1920, according to Arya Samaj rites and subsequently also according to Muslim rites. She owned considerable properties, and in 1946 she created a *waqf-e-aulad*, or family endowment, of her properties consisting of 427 villages for the maintenance and support of herself, her sons, and her descendents. She became the *mutawalli,* or caretaker, of the *waqf* for her lifetime or until relinquishment, and appointed her three sons to succeed her as joint *mutawallis*. On June 21, 1949, the evacuee property laws were extended to Bihar through the Bihar Administration of Evacuee Property, and on September 2 her *waqf* estate was declared evacuee property. Kumar Rani then returned to Bihar on May 14, 1950, with a permanent permit from the Indian High Commission in Pakistan, and on July 5 of that year filed an application to the High Court at Patna challenging the custodian's office. However, her permanent permit was cancelled by the Indian High Commission on July 12 and the police issued her a notice to leave India by July 31. She then filed another application to the High Court against her deportation notice on July 28. On the basis of Article 5, whereby her domicile continued to be vested in her husband, the High Court at Patna ruled in Kumar Rani's favor.[29] However, when the case went to the Supreme Court, the High Court ruling was overturned on the basis that "Article 7 clearly overrides Article 5;" she was deemed to have "migrated" to Pakistan, and therefore lost her Indian citizenship.

It is difficult to disentangle to what extent the contestation over property influenced Kumar Rani's case, and to what extent her husband's non-Muslim status allowed her travel to Karachi to be interpreted as "migration," but it set a precedent giving Muslim women autonomy to "migrate" and lose Indian citizenship, but not to acquire it. It is clear that women's lives changed with Partition's displacements, but the ways in which mobility and citizenship affected Muslim women and their location in divided families, as well as the making of two nations, require much more careful study.

FLIGHT OF YOUTH

There were many teenage sons who went to Pakistan on their own, as youthful rebels and on journeys of adventure and discovery, or were sent to Pakistan by their parents as employment for Muslims became extraordinarily difficult in these years after Partition. However, as familial circumstances changed, they themselves or their parents wanted them to return. If he was an only son the imperative to negotiate the return was heightened. Here establishing the "minority" of the youth was of crucial significance, to claim by law that the youth's domicile as the basis of citizenship remained vested in his father's. To establish minority two facts played a role—one was the date of birth (not an uncommon variable in records) and the other was the majority age, which was eighteen in Indian law, but twenty-one in Pakistani.

Shah Mohammad of Kanpur claimed that he was an intermediate-level student when in October 1950, at the age of fifteen, he was persuaded by two Muslim youths to accompany them on a trip to Pakistan. He left with them for Pakistan "without the knowledge and consent of his father," who was an engine driver in the West Indian Railway and had opted to work and remain in India. Shah Mohammad and his family argued that he had gone to Pakistan only for a temporary visit and without any intention to settle there permanently, that he did not take his wife with him, and that during his stay in Pakistan he acquired no interest or property of any kind but made efforts to return which were unsuccessful. It was only after all other efforts to return failed that he obtained a Pakistani passport, and returned on a short-term visa for India. After his return home he applied to the state government for permission to live in India permanently but was refused, and now he was being asked to leave India before the expiration of his visa. Therefore he now turned to the courts to be allowed to remain in India.

The Indian government argued that Shah Mohammad went to Pakistan without obtaining an NOC from the district magistrate of Kanpur. Instead, he returned to Kanpur on July 22, 1953, on a Pakistani passport and visa, which was extended until July 20, 1954. On July 16, 1954, he applied for resettlement to the UP government, but was instead asked to leave the country. The government's case emphasized that during the three years Shah Mohammad lived in Pakistan "he earned his livelihood there," and that by obtaining a Pakistani passport he had acquired a "foreign nationality." The lower court, however, ruled in the young man's favor on the argument that he was a minor when he obtained a Pakistani passport; his minority was based on the Pakistani age for majority, which was twenty-one.

However, the Indian government appealed to the High Court on a different kind of contention. It made the case that the recently formulated Citizenship Rules gave the central government complete authority to determine whether an individual had acquired Pakistani citizenship, and therefore the civil court could not adjudicate on the matter. Despite this contention, the Allahabad High Court ruled on December 11, 1963, again in Shah Mohammad's favor. The judgment stated that Shah Mohammad had not lost his Indian citizenship because he was a minor at the time and that his departure did not constitute "migration" since he did not shift with the intention of permanent resettlement. The High Court ruling set a precedent that the Pakistani majority age of twenty-one was admissible to establish minority, and this broadening of the age within which return could be established was significant for other pending cases of Muslim youths who wanted to return to their parents.

However, Shah Mohammad's battle did not end there, for the case went on to the Supreme Court, and six years later, on March 13, 1969, it ruled against him. This final judgment relinquished to the central government the right to determine whether a person had acquired another nationality, and this ultimately placed bureaucratic verdicts beyond legal contestation.[30] Shah Mohammad's legal battle was an important one for it was followed in the press, and marked a coming closure to the many kinds of displacements of this long Partition.[31]

Rafiq Husain's case suggests the many different ways an appeal was made to the government, outside the rubric of the court itself. Rafiq Husain was from Bareilly, UP, but was studying in Sahranpur when he left with his friends for Pakistan. He claimed in his petition that he left due to "communal disturbances" in 1950, but then returned to his parents in 1953 on a Pakistani passport. He applied for Indian citizenship on the basis that he was a "minor" and therefore his citizenship was still tied to that of his father, who had continued to reside in Bareilly.

The very narrative of his petition was written to draw out a "humanitarian" response from the state. He argued not only that his parents and siblings lived in India, but also "all other near paternal and maternal relations" were Indian citizens. Furthermore, he argued that after "my going to Pakistan the condition of my mother who is an old patient of pleurisy grew worse and began to deteriorate every day because of the grief of separation. On my return to India she showed signs of improvement and recovered a great deal, and in case of my repatriation to Pakistan it is almost certain that her illness will take a serious turn."

His first application was rejected on the grounds that his birth date in his school certificate stated June 9, 1933, which made him a "major" on his return from Pakistan. However, he reapplied on the basis of a village birth certificate, which showed his birth date to be June 11, 1936. In addition, he filed a civil suit in the court of the *munsif* or subordinate judge in Bareilly to contest his claim to Indian citizenship. In case the courts failed, his family also used a patron in government to support their case. Thus Satish Chandra, the deputy minister of commerce and industry, wrote to Home Affairs to review Husain's case favorably, for the father of the applicant was known to him personally:

> As far as I am aware the entire family is living in the ancestral village. Rafiq Husain, who was a minor and student at Shahjahanpur during the communal riots of 1950, migrated without knowledge of his parents to Pak in the company of some other people. He

> came back to his parents in August 1953 on a Pakistani passport after failing in his attempts to obtain an Indian permit to return to India. This is a very hard case which I understand has been rejected by the Ministry of Home Affairs. I shall be grateful if the matter can be reconsidered with due regard to the facts and circumstances . . . sending the boy back to Pakistan will mean the disruption of a loyal family. To the best of my knowledge the boy does not possess any property and no other complications are involved.

It is noteworthy that Chandra's letter emphasized "loyalty" and a lack of property (and therefore no issues with the Custodian of Evacuee Property) as strengthening Husain's case. As a result, Rafiq Husain became a case for "reconsideration on humanitarian grounds." Although Home Affairs agreed in principle to grant him a long-term visa, they withheld it since he had filed a suit against the government. They did not want other petitioners to get the impression that filing suit could get the government to grant long-term visas. It was possibly intimated to him that this was why his long-term visa was being withheld, for he dropped the civil suit soon after, and was granted the long-term visa, which allowed him to eventually register as an Indian citizen.[32]

POLICING MUSLIM POLITICS

Permits and passports were used to discipline Muslim political participation in the public sphere. Passports made it difficult for Muslims in India to talk about the discrimination that they were facing in parts of north India, or to have an open political discussion about the bureaucratic and juridical struggle for inclusion and citizenship in the newly carved nation-state. For example, when Mohammad Hashim of Lucknow applied for an Indo-Pak passport, a CID report described him as "an old Muslim Leaguer and has pro-Pakistan views." He was considered a "political" person, as his activities included criticizing the government on the imposition of curfew, interviewing Chaudry Khaliquzzaman, and attending "a secret meeting . . . for the betterment of Muslims." The CID report concluded that "he is sure to vilify India in foreign countries," and on the basis of this report the UP government stated that he was "the type of person who seldom fails to take advantage of a situation in which he can rouse the

Muslim feeling against the government and the authorities." Therefore the Ministry of External Affairs decided not to issue him a passport.[33]

Shah Mohammad, the youth whose application for Indian citizenship had been rejected, leading to a court case on the basis of his minority, was also similarly "blacklisted" because he "along with other Pakistani nationals" had taken part "in the agitation over the book *Religious Leaders* in UP in 1956."[34] Simply taking part in an agitation was sufficient to produce the censure of the state. Therefore in petitions for Indian passports and citizenship, as in evacuee property cases examined earlier, it became important to align politics and sentiment with that of the government to prove loyalty to the nation.

APPEALING LOYALTY

The application of Zikar Yusuf of Sindewahi in Bombay State to register as an Indian citizen was a particularly messy one. He had gone to Pakistan before the introduction of the permit system and had returned to his home in Sindewahi on a temporary permit. Then he had traveled to East Pakistan after the introduction of the passport system and had returned to India on a Pakistani passport, which he claimed to have "surrendered."

However, when his application was refused he submitted a number of reasons for it to be reconsidered. In his petition he argued that he was "an unfortunate victim of the circumstances" because he believed that the government's decision to refuse his earlier application may have been influenced by the fact that he owned land and a house worth a large sum of money, which had been declared evacuee property. He feared his application had been rejected so that the custodian would not have to restore these properties to him. Therefore "he beg[ged] leave to submit that he gives up all his claims thereto and does not seek any relief in regard to them." We have seen in the cases of Kumar Rani and Rafiq Husain that ownership of property, which had become or could become evacuee, was at least taken into account. So Yusuf's belief that divesting himself of all claims to his property would help his citizenship case was not unfounded.

However, in addition to giving up his property, he also provided extensive evidence of his loyalty to nation. This included:

1. an oath of allegiance, dated May 10, 1957;
2. a certificate from M. D. Tumpalliwar, the president of the Nagpur Pradesh Congress Committee and member of the Rajya Sabha, dated May 20, 1957;
3. a letter from Hifzur Rehman, member of the Lok Sabha, dated May 23, 1957;
4. a certificate from V. N. Swami, member of the Lok Sabha, dated July 22, 1957.

If a formal oath of allegiance was not enough, the certificates and letter from recognized parliamentary figures were attestations meant to appeal to the state by aligning political affiliation, nationalism, and loyalty. M. D. Tumpalliwar, of the provincial Congress, wrote that "Zikar bhai . . . is well known to me for the last twenty years as a good and sincere Congress Worker . . . In 1949 he came into trouble because he went once to Pakistan when the permit system was not in force and had to return on a temporary permit. . . . He is a good and loyal citizen and I am of the opinion that his case deserves to be considered kindly and considerably." V. N. Swami of the Lok Sabha stated that Yusuf "never migrated to Pakistan" and was a "well-known Nationalist Muslim of the district and never had pro-League leanings." Furthermore, he was a "loyal citizen of Bharat but came into trouble owing to his ignorance and having once taken a temporary permit." These attestations had the desired effect, and this is evident in the official comment that "the certificates issued in favor of his loyalty toward India . . . and his continued efforts to return to India go in his favor."

However, what "swung the balance against him" was the Pakistani passport he acquired for return from his second trip to East Pakistan. He submitted a memo from the Pakistani High Commission that he had "surrendered" his passport, and also included a letter from the Pakistani high commissioner which stated that Zikar Yusuf had renounced his Pakistani nationality and was therefore "not eligible for entry into Pakistan." The letter was severe as it warned Zikar Yusuf that "[a]ny attempt at entry into Pakistan, crossing the border without travel documents will mean a great risk and you may thereby lose your life." In sum, Zikar Yusuf agreed to give up his land and his house, made claims to loyalty and corroborated those claims with attestations from those in provincial and national office, *and established that he had nowhere else to go*, in order to be recognized as an Indian citizen.

However, Ministry of Home Affairs, reviewing his reapplication, noted that the letter from the Pakistani high commissioner was "rather peculiar" in threatening his life, and cast doubt on its authenticity. His proclaimed "surrender" of his Pakistani passport was viewed with equal skepticism, and did not shed his status as a "Pakistani national." We have seen earlier that permitting the surrender of a Pakistani passport, in even "humanitarian" cases, was feared as setting an unacceptable precedent for the numerous Muslims attempting to return home at this time. Here too Home Affairs noted that accepting such a surrender would "bring in numerous similar cases." With *and* without a Pakistani passport, the Indian government held that "[a]s far as we are concerned the applicant remains a Pakistani national." Even if Yusuf could no longer return to Pakistan, or obtain Pakistani citizenship, he was denied Indian citizenship and "it [wa]s the concern of the applicant to make arrangements for his leaving India." Despite his being described as a "well-known Nationalist Muslim" and a "good and loyal citizen," the bureaucratic verdict, beyond legal adjudication, that Zikar Yusuf has been "posing as a Pakistani national and claiming Indian citizenship as it suited him," forced his ultimate expulsion.[35]

SYMPATHY OF THE STATE

Saeeduddin Khan of Fatehpur, UP, went to Pakistan in November 1952. He claimed that he went to Karachi "on hearing of the serious illness of his aunt" there, although he remained for about a year and was employed as an accounts clerk in the Power and Works Department in Karachi. When he contracted tuberculosis, he returned to his mother, wife, and children in Fatehpur in July 1954 on a Pakistani passport. When he applied for registration as an Indian citizen, he argued that he had no one to look after him in Pakistan, and needed to stay with his family in India.

Although he was granted a long-term visa "on compassionate grounds," the UP government rejected his application for citizenship because he had an uncle in the Pakistani military, and because the CID reported that he had "strong anti-government and anti-Indian views, which he propagated secretly." Although normally this could provide sufficient grounds for being dismissed as "disloyal," his petition noted that he came from "a respectable family" with "an illustrious record of public service in the field of education"—it was "a loyal family."

His familial background coupled with his serious health condition to make him a "sympathetic" case. He was under treatment for his tuberculosis in Fatehpur, and his illness had "considerably weakened [him] and incapacitated him for any sort of strenuous work." Because "the lightest strain aggravates his trouble and confines him to bed for several weeks," he could not "undertake any journey or physical or mental work in this state of illness to earn his living."

Like Zikar Yusuf, Saeeduddin's petition was buttressed with a number of letters to establish both his loyalty as well as his plight, and thus induce the sympathy of the state. Ansar Harvani, a member of the Lok Sabha, wrote to Home Affairs that Saeeduddin was "very well known to me" and was from "the most respectable family of my district." He argued that "it will be an act of injustice if he is forced to leave the land of his birth. I strongly recommend that the Home Ministry should reconsider its decision and save this ailing young man from being forced to leave his wife and children and old mother for some technical mistakes of his which made him go to Pakistan." In addition Harvani wrote to Nehru himself and offered his personal guarantee. This led the prime minister's office to also write to Home Affairs. In addition, Mohammad Ajmal Khan, a former personal secretary to Maulana Azad, the minister of education, wrote to UP's chief minister, G. B. Pant, that Saeeduddin was his niece's son-in-law, and requested that he be treated "as a case of mercy."

Home Affairs responded to these appeals from various levels of political leadership by insisting that they had already taken "a compassionate view" by allowing him to stay in India on a long-term basis. However, they could not grant him citizenship, which was "a very valued privilege and is granted only when it is fully established that the person concerned will make a good and loyal citizen."[36] As we have seen, this valued privilege and proof of loyalty was required mostly of Muslims, and was not demanded from "Pakistani nationals of the minority community" who could "surrender" their Pakistani passports and register as Indian citizens without any interrogation. It was also not demanded of Jews who left for Israel, but then decided to return. Saeeduddin could remain on "compassionate" grounds with his family in Fatehpur as a "foreigner" with a long-term visa, but not as an Indian citizen with a right to his home.

DIVIDED FAMILIES

In disputes over Indian citizenship, Muslims attempted to establish through the location of their nuclear-family ties the necessity to return to India, and wives, mothers, and fathers formed important relationships through which returning "home" was given meaning. At the same time, however, showing "no connections whatsoever with Pakistan" was equally important, as the location of extended family became subject to surveillance in passport and visa applications. Thus while long-term visa applications came to require "details of family members or near relations in Pakistan" alongside details of "near relations in India,"[37] the need to conceal relationships of brothers and sisters, uncles and aunts in Pakistan acquired significance.

An important discussion ensued in the Indian government on whether the term "family" in forms was sufficient for purposes of surveillance.[38] "It is quite clear," it was argued, "that we must have full information about all the near relatives of the applicant in Column 14 [on family in Pakistan] . . . It is only then that we can fully determine whether the applicant has severed ties with the country of his origin and can be expected to make a loyal and useful citizen."

While one official argued that "the family when strictly interpreted will not include parents unless they are dependent on the applicant," another official disagreed, suggesting that "this term has been used in a wider context so as to include all members of family and not only wife and children etc. entirely dependent on the applicant." On examination of various policies and laws it was found that "the term 'family' has been defined in different ways for different purposes" and the citizenship rules did not define the term either. Because it was feared that the general definition of the term "family" might not include parents and other near relatives, the intentions of Column 14 would be defeated. Therefore it was suggested that the words "*and near relations*" be added to the column.

The Law Ministry concurred by arguing that the legal meaning of "family" is really children, but its wider meaning is "controlled by the context and is in itself a word of a most loose and flexible description." Therefore it interpreted "members of family" in Column 14 to "normally embrace only the members of his family i.e. his wife and children," and perhaps parents if they are dependent on him. In order to inquire into relations like uncles, nephews, or nieces, the term "*and other relations*" needed to be added to the form.

However, the draftsman at the Law Ministry inserted "*near*," instead of "*other relations*," for he argued that the intention was to find out more about "*near relations*." This enlivened the correspondence further on whether it was only "*near relations*" in Pakistan that the government needed to ascertain, or whether a wider net needed to be cast. "*Other relations*," one official argued, "will make it necessary for the applicant to furnish information about *all his relatives* outside India," and therefore it may be a "more desirable" term. A similar broadening of the term "family" was not considered necessary for relatives in India, since the CID provided "detailed police reports giving full particulars about the applicant's relatives and other ties with India." Another official, however, argued that "[w]e cannot expect an applicant to give an exhaustive list of *all* relations," and therefore suggested "*other near relations*" as adequate.

Finally it was decided that "*other relations*" was necessary to obtain "all the information desired by the term." Anything less would leave "doubts," for "an applicant may very well claim that his uncles, cousin brothers, etc. are not near relations."

As extended kin were brought under surveillance, the now-divided family came to be seen as an obstacle to "loyalty"—a pollution and a danger that needed to be contained. This development is evident in the file on Muslim government servants in the Delhi administration. In keeping with this sense of danger, by the 1960s the disciplining of Muslim government servants came to require of them a declaration of "family and other relations."[39] In addition, their visits to Pakistan, as well as all visitors from Pakistan, came to be monitored. Table 6.1 is an excerpt from the file.

The lists, although minimal in information, are quite important tabulations of familial ties and attempts by the state to monitor and contain them through accounting forms. In content, they document the various stages of Muslim displacement from India, as well as continued relationships between "family and other relations" across the Indo-Pak divide.

They also show the indeterminacy of the categories of "family" and "relations" that government officials had earlier been concerned about. On the one hand, many reply in the negative to "Family in Pakistan," but list parents and siblings in Pakistan under "Relations." On the other hand, others list their brothers and sisters as "Family." Further, "cousin brothers" and "brother-in-law" are listed as "Relations." Certainly, these

TABLE 6.1 Family on the Other Side

Name	*Family in Pakistan*	*Relations in Pakistan*	*Date of Their Migration*	*Visited Pakistan?*	*Purpose and Periods of Visit*	*Family Visited in India, Number of Times and Why*	*Duration of Each Visit*
S.M.	No	Yes	Mother, sister, brother—Sept. 1947	Yes	Two months in 1949, 3.5 months in 1950	Family, none; Relations, yes: mother, 5 months in 1955–1956	Brother and family, week in July 1961
M.A	No	Yes, one married brother and two married sisters;	Brother, Sept. 1947; sister, Feb. 1951 sister, Dec. 1955	No		Brother, three times; sister, twice; sister, once to visit parents in Delhi	1–2 months each, 3–4 first time, 5–6 months second time, 6 months
M.K.	Yes, one widowed real sister with her two minor sons (migrated with her husband in Sept. 1947)			Yes	Sept. 1960, due to illness of brother-in-law, Sept. 9–30. In Dec. 1960 owing to demise in Oct. 1960, stayed until Jan. 27, 1961, to make business arrangements since sister was purdah-nashin	No. Both of the above visits were made with your kind permission.	No
M.K.N.	Only family of dead sister Nafisa in Wah (died Nov. 1958)		Migrated to Pakistan in 1952	Yes	To see special cricket match on special permit for seven days	Nafisa visited in 1954 and 1957, 2 months each to visit her parents	
M.A.	Yes	Mother, brother	Sept.–Oct. 1947	Yes	In 1954 to visit mother who was ill, for 3 months	Yes, my mother came to see me in 1960—4 months	

Note by M.K.N.:Younger sister Anisa Begum was married to a Pakistani national in 1957, but due to differences with her husband she came back to India in 1960 with her two-year-old son and is living with me. She is still an Indian national though her son is Pakistani, and visa is extended every year.

Name	Family in Pakistan	Relations in Pakistan	Date of Their Migration	Visited Pakistan?	Purpose and Periods of Visit	Family Visited in India, Number of Times and Why	Duration of Each Visit
M.Y.	Yes, please		1947 disturbances, sisters	Yes	1955 and 1957–58 to see relations	Yes, two times to attend marriage of my younger sister in 1955 and to look after my father in 1961, 6 months each	
K.A.K.	No	Yes	Since 1947	No	No	Visits made, but don't remember since they did not stay at our house	
A.S.	No	No		No			
A.A.	No	Cousin brother, brother-in-law, nephews	1947	Yes	In 1957 to see my ailing mother, 1958 to attend marriage of cousin sister	Rashid once, Jabir Mirza twice, Aijaz Ali twice, Masood Mirza twice	A month or so
M.H.	Two brothers		1949, 1959	No		Once in 1955: brother who left in 1949 came to the wedding of other brother	1 month
F.A.S.	No	Brother-in-law went in 1950		No			

variations can be read as strategies for establishing proximity or distance of consanguineous ties, depending upon the perception of Muslim government servants of their place within the state. If they felt secure in their job, perhaps declaring proximity may not have been so threatening, but if already uncertain about the consequences of being marked as a Muslim and a Muslim with ties in Pakistan, the description of distance might have been the preferred choice.

No matter how strategically negotiated, these forced declarations and surveillance of familial ties in Pakistan had effects for Muslims in the Indian government service which cannot be readily quantified. The very requirement of tabulating ties as "Family in Pakistan" and "Relations in Pakistan," and the reporting of all visits by and to them, as well as justifying those visits in ritual terms (for marriages, illnesses, funerals, etc.), made them by their very inscription in government ledgers a subject of suspicion.

The very ways in which one came to be marked as Muslim were transformed by the process of this long Partition, of dividing, categorizing, and regulating people, places, and institutions for bounding two distinct nations, and they accrued new meanings, for alongside citizens there emerged the "undefined," the "stateless," and a landscape of divided families.

In Conclusion

7. Moving Boundaries

We are communal histories, communal books . . .
All I desired was to walk upon such an earth that had no maps.[1]

In some sense we know much more about the ways in which colonial institutions and knowledge shaped "Hindu" and "Muslim" identities, and constructed communalism as an essentialized character of India. But what are the ways in which Partition drew the categories of "Hindu" and "Muslim" (and "Sikh") into the vortex of nation-state formation? I have tried to track some of the institutional sites in which "Hindu and Sikh refugees" and "Muslim refugees" folded into the distinction of "India" and "Pakistan," and the considerable labor of two postcolonial states to map identities, geographies, and histories into bounded nations. We cannot understand the landscape of contemporary South Asia without taking account of this formative long period in the making of two nation-states and the ways in which the "Muslim question" at the heart of Partition shaped them.

Economic, bureaucratic, and juridical institutions and inscriptions of both states asserted themselves into a ravaged landscape of people displaced from old ties, and permits, evacuee property legislation, and passports were techniques that sought to secure uncertain and contested relationships between refugees, religious minorities, and citizenship. People who were forced to leave and lost their homes, and people who never left their homes, were both unsettled as new nation-states and their margins came to be formed.

This book has tried to draw Ghulam Ali out of the margins of insignificance, to show how much his story was shaped by this long Partition, and the logic of making modern nation-states. But his story does not end in the Hindu camp in Lahore. It began there in the camp as he wrote petitions to the state, a limb fitter's ordinary prayer against the claims of nation, setting off the paper trail that has brought him into this very history. By way of a conclusion, let me return to Ghulam Ali in the folds of this past.

THE LIMB FITTER

Ghulam Ali's arrest and deportation for entering India, at first without a permit, and then on a Pakistani passport, as well as his arrest and incarceration for entering Pakistan without any passport, were not, as we have seen, exceptional events in themselves, albeit their coincidence in one lifetime was—as would be repeatedly noted in the numerous governmental and judicial files that mark him—most "unfortunate."

After his final arrest in 1957 by Pakistani border officials, Ghulam Ali was subjected to rigorous interrogation (presumably for being an Indian spy) but was found "innocent" and was placed in the "Hindu camp" at DAV College in Lahore. It was from here that Ghulam Ali began writing petitions to the Indian high commissioner, as well as the prime minister and the president of India, to appeal for permission to return to his home and family in Lucknow:

> Now I am here in Pakistan in great trouble without any hearth or home, kith or kin and living a life of complete destitute in Hindu Camp, quite penniless with any arrangements even for a single meal, although I was trained abroad as a specialist in Artificial Limb Fitting on Government expense. . . . [Mine is] a story of long suffering with the humble prayer that early decision be made in my case with honorable reinstatement to my original position in the Indian Army and be allowed to enter India and join my service and thus live with my family in my own motherland peacefully. . . . The 101

difficulties in which I am at present fixed—homeless, resourceless, and confined to the life of camp.

I want to trace here the centrality of Ghulam Ali's vocation as an artificial-limb fitter to his predicament, not only because it is so evocative for a history of severing, but also because of its subjective importance to Ghulam Ali himself. Of his 101 difficulties, Ghulam Ali particularly described himself as "trained abroad as a specialist in Artificial Limb Fitting on Government expense." This was so important to who he was that he began his case history not with his birthplace or kin ties, but rather thus: "I was recruited in the Indian Army in June 1943 at Allahabad. In 1945 I was sent to U.K. on Government Expenses for training in Artificial Limbs. When I returned from U.K. after completing my training I was posted at Kirki Artificial Limb Center."

More than the fact that he was recruited as a *havildar* in the British Indian Army, it was the distinction of being sent to Britain for technical training that was a source of considerable pride for him. I do not know what his experience in the United Kingdom was like toward the end of the Second World War, or how he was treated there as an Indian man (although here I am reminded of Kip, the Sikh sapper, in Michael Ondaatje's *The English Patient*).[2] Yet his technical skill for the rehabilitation of severed bodies (not unlike the skill of de-mining for the rehabilitation of land) was important enough to him that when he was offered a place in the Pakistan Army in another capacity, he refused. This recalcitrance sealed his fate.

The Pakistani judge who declared him an Indian national in 1956 noted that when information was received from the Indian government that India was unwilling to accept Muslims who had opted for India but had not yet joined their duties, his supervising officer asked him if he would like to "re-opt" for Pakistan. He replied that he would only re-opt if he was accepted in the Pakistan Army as Havildar Limb Fitter. As there was no such post in the Pakistani Army, he refused to re-opt for Pakistan. Captain Abdur Rahman stated from the witness box that he called Ghulam Ali three or four times and asked him repeatedly whether he would re-opt for Pakistan. "He said he would not do so unless he was accepted as a limb fitter."

He made that decision back in 1949. In the ensuing seven years, he had tried to return to his family in Lucknow and had been deported, and was now in Pakistan facing further dispossession. Thus when the judge asked him if he was now willing to be taken as Havildar Saddler, the position which the Pakistan Army wanted to give him, he said he was. The judge noted that "[h]e may have at one time attached a condition to his opting for Pakistan, but now he has, finding that he will lose his job altogether, withdrawn that condition."

Although the judge stated that Ghulam Ali's predicament was "altogether for no fault of his own" and that his was "rather an unfortunate case," he was not reinstated into the Pakistan Army, nor was he awarded Pakistani citizenship. By placing him in the "Hindu camp," the Pakistani state simply disowned him. However, despite the direness of his situation in the camp, Ghulam Ali appealed to the Indian officials and leaders not just to be able to return to his "hearth and home." He stubbornly continued to ask for an "honorable reinstatement to my original position in the Indian Army," for this arguably may have remained for him the key to an honorable life.

On receiving petitions from Ghulam Ali and the camp commander, the Indian deputy high commissioner wrote to the Ministry of External Affairs in 1958 to allow him to return to Lucknow on "humanitarian grounds." This led to an extensive correspondence between the Ministry of Defense, Home Affairs, and External Affairs, as well as the UP government on the "question of deciding the nationality of this ex-NCO."

It was perhaps in the order of things that the Ministry of Defense could not locate its records on him, and his petition moved from official to official, gathering comments that would eventually constitute a decision on his employment and his national identity. As the Army could not locate Ghulam Ali's files, a similar case of Havildar Bhom (presumably a non-Muslim) from 1955 was referenced. In Bhom's case "it was decided that he should be treated as an Indian national but should not be taken back in the Army. It was however decided that a civilian job should be offered to him." Bhom's military employment and nationality were separated, and there was no debate about Bhom's nationality.

In Ghulam Ali's case, an officer in External Affairs initially argued that while there was "no difficulty in granting him an emergency certificate in order to enable him to come to India," if the Army could not employ him with his qualifications in artificial-limb making then "there will not be any point in allowing him to come to India." His national status was made dependent on his employment. Not surprisingly, the Ministry of

Defense refused to accept him back in the Indian Army because he had served in the Pakistan Army. It deemed Ghulam Ali to be a Pakistani national. And yet despite this official position, Ghulam Ali's story had an effect on bureaucratic discourse, and a consensus developed that he had suffered "for no apparent fault of his own," that "Ex-Havildar G. Ali is indeed a very unfortunate case," and that because he was "homeless" he needed to be "dealt with urgently and sympathetically."

This sympathetic consensus produced in sum the very "humanitarian" discourse that mediated the violence of governmentality, the fictions of national classification, and it was agreed that Ghulam Ali should be allowed to return to his home in India. However, bureaucratic process relied on technologies of control. Thus, allowing his return was not a simple matter, and questions arose of *how* to "regularize" his return and his stay in India. Home Affairs argued that because he had taken a Pakistani passport, he could not be regarded as an Indian citizen, and with "emergency certificates" no longer being issued by the Indian High Commission, the only possibility now was if he was granted a long-term visa for permanent resettlement; that would allow him to meet residential requirements to become an Indian citizen. However, to be granted a long-term visa he needed a Pakistani passport! The Pakistani government was not likely to issue a refugee in the Hindu camp a Pakistani passport, and since he was not considered to be an Indian citizen yet, he could not be issued an Indian passport either.

This quandary produced further correspondence on how Ghulam Ali should be allowed to return. As a result, at the end of 1959, a year after his case was taken up by the High Commission, and twelve years after Partition, the Indian government decided to allow Ghulam Ali to return to Lucknow on "a restricted Indian passport with an endorsement that it does not confer Indian citizenship," and the UP government was asked to keep a watch on his activities. The passport as a technology had to be adapted to serve here as a mere travel document, unhinged from claims of citizenship. In this way Ghulam Ali was able to return to his familial home, without the job he so valued, as a person with "an undefined status" and as a subject of surveillance.

On June 16, 1960, Ghulam Ali returned to India. When his "restricted passport" expired on July 7 he applied to the UP government for permanent resettlement, in order to be able to eventually regain Indian citizenship. If the Pakistani government had been unwilling to give him

Pakistani citizenship, the Indian government was equally hesitant to acknowledge him as an Indian citizen, despite its humanitarian discourse. He was denied resettlement facilities because they were granted only to Pakistani nationals, and Ghulam Ali was not a Pakistani national. Home Affairs replied to the UP government's query in 1961 as follows:

> G. Ali is neither regarded as a Pakistani national by the Pakistani government nor can be deemed to be an Indian citizen. He has already been allowed to come to India on a restricted Indian passport as a stateless person with the stipulation to allow him to stay on in this country. He can stay on here in this status and it is neither appropriate nor necessary to regulate his stay by a residential permit.

Although subsequently Ghulam Ali was granted a residential permit as a means to "regulate" and "maintain a check over his movements," the permit was drafted so that at no point was he to be allowed to presume Indian citizenship. Although the surveillance reports on him recorded "no adverse notice," he was not to think that "he would be free to stay in the country as long as he likes." The residential permit had to be renewed from year to year, and clearly marked his status as "undefined." According to official rationale by subjecting him to renewals every year "it would be clear that he is being treated as a foreigner in India."[3]

Thus up to the end of the material record on Ghulam Ali, he remained a stateless person, "undefined" and a "foreigner" in his home—disowned by the Pakistani state on the one hand, and a subject of continuous surveillance by the Indian state on the other.

DIVIDED TODAY

One of the arguments of this book has been that families became divided not because members of a family chose to live in one country or move to another. They became divided because of the way the Indo-Pak border came to be constructed as an outcome of a long, drawn-out process of Partition. I have tried to complicate the very notion of "choice" that north Indian Muslims seemingly faced between secular India and Muslim Pakistan, by placing it within a history of state controls on movement and property that became instrumental in the making of two modern nation-states.

Despite the removal of services at Khokrapar, a trickle of Muslim refugees continued to travel through this border post without any papers. However, the 1965 war between the two states led to the complete closing of the Khokrapar border, as well as train services that connected Karachi and Delhi via Jodhpur. Although the passport system also began to regulate travel across East Pakistan and West Bengal, the complicated geography of the eastern frontier made it in important ways harder to control and easier to cross.[4] As a result, the eastern frontier remained a route for those who wanted to return to their homes in India, or move to Pakistan. Even after 1965, travel from Calcutta to Dhaka remained relatively easier than travel across the western frontier. The 1971 war of liberation resulting in the creation of Bangladesh severed that route for those wanting to go to or from the remaining West Pakistan.

As citizenship became congealed, travel across the western border to visit family members became extremely difficult. It became hard even to obtain a police reporting short-term visa for a single city on the "other side." During my interviews I was repeatedly told stories about failed attempts to get a visa to visit loved ones, and here are two of them.

Yusuf bhai told me about a lottery system for visa application that had been introduced at one time. The large number of people who lined up outside the Indian High Commission in Karachi were issued numbers, and each day only a few numbers were randomly drawn. Some people would stand in line for days, and Yusuf bhai joined them when he received news that his brother was critically ill in Delhi . But then one morning, as he stood in line, he received the news that his brother had already died. He remembered with deep regret, "*Hum apne bhai se nahin mil sakae*" [I could not meet my brother].

Ansa apa narrated how her sister in Karachi was refused a visa to attend her own son's marriage which she had arranged with the daughter of a relative in Delhi:

> *To main kabhi bhul hi nahin sakti, jo family divide hoī hai un ke dil se puchhe kiya taklīf hai. Appa ne, bahut bimar thi. Un ne mujh se kaha ke passport le jāo aur visa le lo. Visa officer jo tha, mujh se kehne laga, beṭe ki shadi hai, us men jā rahe hai. To kehne laga, baṛe rudely ke marriage can take place without mother also. To main, donon ānkhon men ānson. Mujhe rote hue dekha . . . to Appa ko baṛī mushkil se bataya. [Appa] to kehne*

> *lagi, "ye kyon nahin kaha tha ke main apne mian ke qabar par fateha paṛhne jā rahi hun. Jab to shayad de deta mujhe visa."*
>
> I cannot ever forget. The family that is divided, ask their hearts, what are their pains. Appa, she was very ill. She told me to take the passport and get the visa. The visa officer there, he said to me, we are going to the son's wedding. He said to me, very rudely, that marriage can take place without mother also. Then I had tears in both my eyes. Seeing me cry . . . with great difficulty I told Appa. [Appa] began to say, "Why didn't you tell him that I wanted to go to pray on my husband's grave. Then perhaps he would have given me a visa."

Appa's husband was buried in Delhi. She still had relatives there, and it was through those kin ties that she had arranged her son's marriage, on the other side. She was refused a visa to cross a distance of some proximity, in both a geographic and emotional landscape, and this only makes sense because it is against this very proximity that this highly surveillanced border must function, to inscribe national difference where it becomes the most blurred.

In more recent years, the Indian and Pakistani consulates at Karachi and Bombay respectively have been closed, and people from those cities sometimes travel a greater distance to Islamabad and Delhi to apply for a visa than the distance to their desired destination on the other side. In 2003, for instance, all rail and air links between the two countries were suspended, additionally requiring circuitous travel through third destinations.

Therefore it is astonishing that long lines continue at Indian and Pakistani High Commissions in both countries, and divided families continue to actively maintain ties. In comparison, other political boundaries that came to be drafted in the twentieth century have arguably been more successful at eroding such relationships.[5] Amira apa described this sense of continued connection sustained across generations when she recounted the experience of her first trip to Karachi with her children, to visit her relatives there:

> *Balke bachche ek dosre ko jante bhi nahin the, woh bhī itnī achhī tarha ek dosre ko mile. Sab log yehī kehte the ke ye hota hai khun ka rishta. . . .*
>
> [later in the interview]

> *Mera khyāl hai jis din hum jate hue hai, agle din se un log kī itnī dostī ho gaī thī ke lagta hī nahin tha ke ye pehlī mullaqa't hai . . . [when their flight reservation to return was changed for a later date] is men jo bachche ek dosre se gale gale lag lag kar jo khoshī huī itna woh ho raha tha ke sālon ke ba'd in kī mullaqa't huī hai.*
>
> Even though the children did not know each other, even then they met each other so nicely. Everyone would say that this is [the depth of] a relationship of blood . . . [later in the interview] I think from the day we went, from the next day they became such friends that it didn't seem at all that this was their first meeting . . . [When their flight reservation to return was changed for a later date] the children started hugging each other and were so happy as if they were meeting again after years.

These ordinary consanguineous ties passed down through generations, and, subjected to surveillance and scrutiny by the two states, survive in a context when other kinds of ordinary relationships between people are foreclosed by these severe travel restrictions in the region itself. What kind of histories can take account of these kinship ties, to represent their claims of filial love and joyous exchange, without being burdened to carry the tag of "disloyalty" and "danger" within the bounds of nation? What are the ways in which we may have to write against nation and against state to make such histories possible?

MOVING BOUNDARIES

The Partition of 1947 in many senses is not over; it is not behind us. Since the destruction of the Babri mosque in Ayodhya, UP, on December 6, 2001, signaling the rise of the Hindu right in India, and the communal violence that followed when chants of "*Jao Pakistan, ya Kabrastan* [go to Pakistan or your graves]" rang alongside attacks on Muslim communities across north India, the invocation of Partition and Pakistan reacquired a sinister meaning for Muslim minorities in India. The Hindu right's repeated portrayal of Muslims as invasive outsiders to India tied to a militant monotheism and temple destruction combines with the notion that Partition represented an inevitable parting of ways of two incompatible religious communities. To this day a spectrum of political opinion, from those fighting for a secular vision of India to those who imagine it as essentially Hindu, continues to draw upon different understandings of and lessons from Partition to argue for Muslim inclusion or exclusion in their imaginings of modern India.

Similarly, the rise of the Muhajir Qaumi Movement (MQM) in Karachi and Sind and its violent confrontations with the Pakistani state in the mid-1990s also drew upon narratives of Partition. The MQM expressed *muhajir* disenfranchisement from political power in Pakistan by arguing that they had made the most sacrifices for the very creation of Pakistan by leaving their homes in India, and yet had failed to be completely accepted as Pakistanis. While Altaf Husain, the MQM leader, has questioned whether Partition should have even happened, different opinions on the two-nation theory and Partition continue to feed debates on the contested role of Islam in imaginings of modern Pakistan. Thus Partition, as David Gilmartin has argued, continues "to be played out at the nexus between high politics and everyday life . . . linking the state and the arenas of everyday conflict."[6]

In important ways, then, what actually happened at Partition, and the ways in which Partition is rhetorically invoked and socially remembered, are tied to each other to produce what could be called *Partition effects*. In other words, the Muslim predicament in India today and the making of contemporary *muhajir* politics in Pakistan must be understood as both a product of this history of the long Partition and of the ways in which this history has been narrated within the ideological frames of nation. Thus in order to understand these Partition effects, we need to know a lot more about Partition itself, *and* at the same time we need to interrogate and move the very boundaries of how we write these histories.

Partition is not behind us. As recently as August 19, 2003, the *Telegraph* ran a story about Ibrahim, which paralleled Ghulam Ali's travails with the nation in this divided South Asia. According to the newspaper account, Ibrahim is a Muslim from Kerala who boarded a boat in 1969 to go to work in the Gulf states; he was left stranded in Karachi instead. "There, he came in touch with Malayalees who had come to Karachi years ago and been caught on the other side of the border during Partition. They were engaged in small businesses or odd jobs. Like them, he secured a road pass in Karachi and, in 1978, got himself a Pakistani passport, the only legal means to return to India." On his return home, he threw away the passport, married, and settled down to raise three children. Then in 1996 he was served with a deportation notice, and was taken forcibly from his home to the Wagah border post. He is among 360 other such "stateless Indian-Pakistanis" awaiting "humanitarian" adjudication of their national status.[7]

By crossing the Indo-Pak border, then, a goal of this book has been not to argue for comparative histories, but rather to attempt such a moving of boundaries. Nation-state bound histories not only naturalize the nation, but also naturalize national difference of states-in-conflict. Thus in a now-nuclearized region like the subcontinent, writing carries a special burden to "rescue," in Prasenjit Duara's words, history from the nation.[8] It is the categorical order of the nation that produces "stateless Indian-Pakistanis," and at the same time renders invisible other forms of belonging and processes in our modern world. This is particularly true for writing about a diversity of Muslim communities and networks that cross boundaries through Urdu poetry, Sufi shrines, trade networks, and familial ties; we must therefore rethink the very boundaries of what we know to be "Muslim," as well as "Indian" and "Pakistani." Even as it becomes more difficult to move such boundaries, we need these alternative regional histories to make other forms of belonging and politics available to the rhetoric and memory of Partition—and thus shift the very possibilities of how its future unfolds.

Abbreviations in Notes

AICC	All India Congress Committee
AIR	All India Reporter
CAI	Constituent Assembly of India, Legislative Debates
CAP	Constituent Assembly of Pakistan, Legislative Debates
DSA	Delhi State Archives
GOI	Government of India
GOP	Government of Pakistan
IOR	India Office Records, British Library
MEA	Ministry of External Affairs
MHA	Ministry of Home Affairs
M/o R&R	Ministry of Relief and Rehabilitation
MP	Mountbatten Papers
NAI	National Archives of India
NDC	National Documentation Center
NMML	Nehru Memorial Museum and Library
PLD	Pakistan Law Digest
RPP	Rajendra Prasad Papers
SPAI	Sind Police Abstracts of Intelligence

Notes

INTRODUCTION

1. Saadat Hasan Manto, *Mottled Dawn: Fifty Sketches and Stories of Partition* (New Delhi: Penguin Books, 1997), p. 10.

2. See Ayesha Jalal, *The Sole Spokesman* (Cambridge, England: Cambridge University Press, 1994), p. 1, and more recently Gyanendra Pandey, *Remembering Partition* (Cambridge, England: Cambridge University Press, 2001), p. 15.

3. George Marcus, "Ethnography in/of the World System: The Emergence of Multi-sited Ethnography," *Annual Review of Anthropology*, no. 25 (1995): 95.

4. E. Valentine Daniel, *Charred Lullabies* (Princeton: Princeton University Press, 1996), p. 150.

5. There are many histories of the making of religious community and communalism in modern South Asia. For instance, see Gyanendra Pandey, *The Construction of Communalism in Colonial North India* (Delhi: Oxford University Press, 1990); Sandria Freitag, *Collective Action and Community* (Berkeley: University of California Press, 1989); Barbara Metcalf, "Presidential Address: Too Little and Too Much: Reflections on Muslims in the History of India," *Journal of Asian Studies* 54, no. 4 (November 1995); Mushirul Hasan, "The Myth of Unity: Colonial and National Narratives," in *Contesting the Nation*, ed. David Ludden (Philadelphia: University of Pennsylvania Press, 1996), pp. 185–209.

6. Choudhary Rehmat Ali coined the word *Pakistan* as an acronym for Punjab, Afghanistan, Kashmir, Sind, and Baluchistan, and it literally means the land of the pure. I draw here upon Ayesha Jalal's discussion, "Muslim Schemes of the Late 1930s Reconsidered," in *Self and Sovereignty* (London: Routledge, 2000), pp. 388–422. She gives an important account of the extraordinary map-making exercises of this time which I have called "fabulous" in the sense Sumathi Ramaswamy uses it to recover place-making that is not false but "unavailable outside the imagination." See *Lost Land of Lemuria* (Berkeley:

University of California Press, 2004), p. 6. My metaphoric use of maps is self-conscious, for, as Ramaswamy has argued, it is a modern form of knowledge that, like the census, has had an important role in shaping the political imagination of nation. The phrase "moth-eaten Pakistan" is attributed to Mohammad Ali Jinnah, as he accepted a division of the provinces of Punjab and Bengal as part of the Partition plan.

7. Since 1947, countless contentious studies have examined the question of *why* Partition happened. This book is part of a broad historiographical shift in which attention has now turned to examining *what* happened at Partition. For a review of the earlier historiography, see Asim Roy, "The High Politics of India's Partition: The Revisionist Perspective," in *India's Partition: Process, Strategy and Mobilization*, ed. M. Hasan (Delhi: Oxford University Press, 1993); D. A. Low, "Digging Deeper: North India in the 1940s," in *Freedom, Trauma, Continuities: Northern India and Independence*, ed. D. A. Low and Howard Brasted (Walnut Creek, Calif.: AltaMira, 1998), pp. 1–14.

8. David Gilmartin, "Partition, Pakistan, and South Asian History: In Search of a Narrative," *Journal of Asian Studies* 57, no. 4 (November 1998): 1081–83.

9. Partha Chatterjee, *Nationalist Thought and the Colonial World: A Derivative Discourse* (Minneapolis: University of Minnesota Press, 1993), p. 131.

10. Pandey, *Remembering Partition*, p. 1.

11. Michel-Rolph Trouillot, *Silencing the Past: Power and the Production of History* (Boston: Beacon Press, 1995), p. 110.

12. Maulana Abul Kalam Azad, *India Wins Freedom* (Delhi: Orient Longman, 1988), p. 216.

13. Sardar Patel to Parmanand Trehan, July 16, 1947, in Durga Das, *Sardar Patel's Correspondence 1945–50* (Ahmedabad: Navajivan Publishing House, 1973), p. 289. Quoted in Pandey, *Remembering Partition*, p. 626.

14. CAP, March 6, 1948.

15. Mushirul Hasan, *Legacy of a Divided Nation: India's Muslims Since Independence* (Delhi: Oxford University Press, 1997), p. 173 and n.; Census of Pakistan, 1951, p. 84.

16. Tai Yong Tan and Gyanesh Kudaisya, *Aftermath of Partition in South Asia* (London: Routledge, 2000), p. 197. See also Dr. Salahuddin, *Dilliwallae* (Delhi: Urdu Academy, 1986); R. E. Frykenberg, ed., *Delhi Through the Ages: Essays in Urban History, Culture, and Society* (Delhi: Oxford University Press, 1986).

17. Sayid Ahmad Khan (1817–1898) wrote *Asar-us-Sanadid* and *Silsilat ul-Mulk* about Delhi's architecture, leading families, and rulers. *Asar-us-Sanadid* was written a decade before the Revolt of 1857, but was republished in different versions several times in the ensuing decades. See also A. H. Hali's *Hayat-i-Javed: A Biography of Sir Sayyid*, trans. David Mathews (Delhi: Rupa & Co., 1994).

18. The Jamiat-e-Ulema-e-Hind, Anjuman-e-Taraqi-e-Urdu, Jamia Millia Islamia, the Muslim League *Dawn* newspaper, the *Jang*, and *Anjam* are some of the institutions that were located in Delhi.

19. V. N. Datta, "Punjabi Refugees and the Urban Development of Greater Delhi," *Delhi Through the Ages*; Veronique Dupont, "Spatial and Demographic Growth of Delhi since 1947 and the Main Migration Flows," in *Delhi: Urban Space and Human Destinies*, ed. Veronique Dupont, Emma Tarlo, and Denis Vidal (Delhi: Manohar, 2000), p. 229.

20. See Ajmal Kamal, ed., *Karachi ki Kahani,* 2 vols. (Karachi: Aaj Magazine, 1996); Hamida Khuhro and Anwer Mooraj, eds., *Karachi: Megacity of Our Times* (Karachi: Oxford University Press, 1997).

21. Census of Pakistan 1951, vol. 1, GOP, p. 83.

22. Tan and Kudaisya, "Capital Landscapes: The Imprint of Partition on South Asia's Capital Cities," in *Aftermath of Partition*, pp. 163–203; Ian Talbot, *Divided Cities: Lahore, Amritsar and the Partition of India* (Karachi: Oxford University Press, 2006).

23. On the postcolonial state, see in particular Partha Chatterjee, "The National State," *Nation and Its Fragments: Colonial and Postcolonial Histories* (Princeton: Princeton University Press, 1994), pp. 200–219; Gyan Prakash, "Technologies of Government," *Another Reason: Science and the Imagination of Modern India* (Princeton: Princeton University Press, 1999), pp. 159–200.

24. D. A. Low estimated that 5.2 million refugees moved from West Pakistan into India, and about 5.8 million in the reverse direction, and this just between 1947 and 1948, and not taking into account the displacements from Delhi and Uttar Pradesh, or across the East Pakistan/Bengal border. See D. A. Low, "Digging Deeper," p. 1. Another attempt to enumerate deaths and displacements at the time of Partition can be found in C. Embdad Haque, "The Dilemma of 'Nationhood' and Religion: A Survey and Critique of Studies on Population Displacement Resulting from the Partition of the Indian Subcontinent," *Journal of Refugee Studies* 8, no. 2 (1995). The numbers for Partition's total displacements, however, remain speculative. In Europe, some 30 million people are estimated to have been displaced during the six years of war. See M. Proudfoot, *European Refugees, 1939–52: A Study in Forced Population Movement* (London: Faber & Faber, 1956).

25. Liisa Malkki, "Refugees and Exile: From Refugee Studies to the National Order of Things," *Annual Review of Anthropology* no. 24 (1995): 498.

26. See Vazira Fazila-Yacoobali, "Rites of Passage: The Partition of History and the Dawn of Pakistan," *Interventions: International Journal of Postcolonial Studies* 1, no. 2 (1991): 183–200.

27. See Ritu Menon and Kamla Bhasin, *Borders and Boundaries* (Delhi: Kali Press for Women, 1998); Veena Das, "National Honour and Practical Kinship: Of Unwanted Women and Children," *Critical Events* (Delhi: Oxford University Press, 1995), pp. 55–83; Urvashi Butalia, *The Other Side of Silence: Voices from the Partition of India* (Delhi: Penguin Books, 1998); Gyanendra Pandey, "The Prose of Otherness," *Subaltern Studies VIII* (Delhi: Oxford University Press, 1994), pp. 188–221.

28. Chatterjee, *Nation and Its Fragments*, p. 205.

29. See in particular the speech by Diwan Chaman Lall at this debate.

30. H. T. Sorley, "The Refugee Problem and Rehabilitation, Development and Social Welfare," *West Pakistan Gazetteer 1959*, GOP, pp. 751–55.

31. V. K. R. V. Rao, "India's First Five-Year Plan—A Descriptive Analysis," *Pacific Affairs* 25, no. 1 (March 1952): 3–23.

32. A conscious decision by the Indian government to rename refugees to this effect can be seen in "Decision that Refugees shall be termed 'Displaced Persons' and Refugee Camps 'Relief Camps' in all Governmental Communications," NAI MEA 1949 44(32)-A.D. This shift in terminology is also evident in Pakistani legislation.

33. Chatterjee, *Nation and Its Fragments*, p. 219.

34. See Gerard Noiriel, *The French Melting Pot: Immigration, Citizenship and National Identity* (Minneapolis: University of Minnesota Press, 1996); John Torpey, *The Invention of Passports* (Cambridge, England: Cambridge University Press, 2000); Radhika Viyas Mongia, "Race, Nationality, Mobility: A History of the Passport," *Public Culture* 11, no. 3 (1999): 527–56.

35. I draw this notion of "internal borders' from Etienne Balibar, who explains it as the "nonrepresentable limit of every border," drawing together all the ambivalence of marking "insiders" and "outsiders," such that the "inside" is ever polluted by that which

is "outside." In "Fichte and the International Border: On Addresses to the German Nation," *Masses, Classes, Ideas: Studies on Politics and Philosophy Before and After Marx* (New York: Routledge, 1994), p. 63.

36. Gyanendra Pandey, "Can a Muslim Be an Indian?," *Comparative Studies in Society and History* 41, no. 4 (October 1999): 608–29.

37. See, for example, Peter Sahlins, *Boundaries: The Making of France and Spain in the Pyrenees* (Berkeley: University of California Press, 1989); Pamela Ballinger, *History in Exile: Memory and Identity at the Borders of the Balkans* (Princeton: Princeton University Press, 2003); Kate Brown, *A Biography of No Place: From Ethnic Borderland to Soviet Heartland* (Cambridge, Mass.: Harvard University Press, 2004). In a review essay, Willem van Schendel and Michel Baud have valuably emphasized examining the two sides of a border and the "paradoxical character of borderlands." They consider the containment of a border as mediated by face-to-face cross-border interactions. "Toward a Comparative History of Borderlands," *Journal of World History* 8, no. 2 (1997): 211–42. See also Willem van Schendel, *The Bengal Borderland: Beyond State and Nation in South Asia* (London: Anthem Press, 2005).

38. http://www.upperstall.com/films/garamhawa.html

39. Shahid Amin, *Event, Metaphor, Memory* (Berkeley: University of California Press, 1995), p. 5.

40. Dipesh Chakrabarty, "Remembered Villages: Representations of Hindu-Bengali Memories in the Aftermath of the Partition," in *Inventing Boundaries: Gender, Politics and the Partition of India*, ed. Mushirul Hasan (Delhi: Oxford University Press, 2000), p. 318. Chakrabarty points out this sense of not consciously knowing what we remember until something "jogs our memory," and it is here that the temporality of speech allows for surprise.

41. The Hindu right has repeatedly victimized Muslims in India by representing their ties to people in Pakistan as part of the project of the Pakistani state. During the Kargil conflict in the summer of 1999, a Bollywood box-office hit got a government tax break, as it created an archetypal villain who had a *dil ka rishta*, ties of the heart, with both countries. Instead of portraying him as a sympathetic figure whose historical predicament required understanding, he was represented as a figure to fear and despise. See my essay on the film, "Yeh Mulk Hamara Ghar: The 'National Order of Things' and Muslim Identity in Mathew Mattan's Sarfaroosh," *Contemporary South Asia* 11, no. 2 (2002): 183–98. *Muhajir* ties to India have also been regarded with suspicion, heightened in Karachi by the emergence of the Muhajir Qaumi Movement since the 1980s. For instance, a statement by Benazir Bhutto, the former prime minister of Pakistan, that the people of Karachi would help the Indian Army if it were to attack Sind, led to staunch declarations that *muhajirs* had "burnt all their boats" when they came to Pakistan. See Sultan Rafi, "Muhajir ke nām ka istehsal," *Jang*, November 25, 1998.

42. I do not have statistics for divided families, although the long lines at Indian and Pakistani embassies on both sides are clear indications that against all odds, divided families are still common and still tied to each other. Many well-known public figures in the subcontinent became members of divided families, although this is usually a less acknowledged fact of their lives. For instance, Zakir Husain, the third president of India from 1967 to 1969, had a brother, Mahmud Husain, who went on to become a minister in the Pakistani government and for whom the Karachi University library is named. The *unani* practice of the famous Hamdard Dawakhana of Delhi also became divided when one brother, Hakim Mohammad Saeed, moved to Karachi, while his older brother Hakim Abdul Hamid remained in Delhi, and both brothers expanded the *unani*

practice into significant educational institutions, the Hamdard Universities, in both cities. The Imams of Jama Masjid in Delhi have come from the Bukhari family, which is also divided between the two cities. Please note that all names given with excerpts from interviews are pseudonyms.

43. Mushirul Hasan, "Introduction," *Invented Boundaries*, p. 39.

44. Allen Feldman, "Ethnographic States of Emergency," in *Fieldwork Under Fire: Contemporary Studies of Violence and Survival* (Berkeley: University of California Press, 1995), p. 228. See for example, Trouillot, *Silencing the Past* (1995); Shahid Amin, *Event, Metaphor, Memory* (1995); Shail Mayaram, *Resisting Regimes: Myth, Memory and the Shaping of a Muslim Identity* (Delhi: Oxford University Press, 1997).

45. Trouillot, *Silencing the Past*, p. 47.

46. See Pervez Hoodbhoy and A. H. Nayyar, "Rewriting the History of Pakistan," in *Islam, Politics and the State: The Pakistan Experience*, ed. M. A. Khan (London: Zed Books, 1985); K. K. Aziz, *The Murder of History in Pakistan* (Lahore: Vanguard Press, 1993).

1. MUSLIM EXODUS FROM DELHI

1. Trouillot, *Silencing the Past*, p. 149.

2. E. Valentine Daniel and John Chr. Knudsen, eds., *Mistrusting Refugees* (Berkeley: University of California Press, 1995), p. 1.

3. Julie Peteet, "Transforming Trust: Dispossession and Empowerment among Palestinian Refugees," in *Mistrusting Refugees*, p. 171.

4. "Nehru's tryst with destiny," *Indian Express*, August 15, 1947, p. 7.

5. Dipankar Gupta suggests that 10,000 Muslims were killed in this violence. Dipankar Gupta, "The Indian Diaspora of 1947: The Political and Ethnic Consequences of Partition with Special Reference to Delhi," in *Communalism in India: History, Politics and Culture*, ed. K. N. Panikkar (New Delhi: Manohar, 1991). Gyanendra Pandey's more recent account of the Delhi violence puts the figure of Muslim casualties as between 20,000 and 25,000. Gyanendra Pandey, "Partition and Independence in Delhi, 1947–48," *Economic and Political Weekly*, September 6, 1997, p. 2263. Quote is from "The Indian Situation: A Personal Note" by Lord Ismay, October 5, 1947, as reported in Pandey, *Remembering Partition*, p. 128. The chapter "Folding the National into the Local: Delhi, 1947–1948," pp. 121–51, in *Remembering Partition*, provides a different kind of account of the Delhi violence from the perspective of diverse observers.

6. *Annual Report on Evacuation, Relief and Rehabilitation of Refugees: Sept., 1947–August, 1948*, Ministry of Relief and Rehabilitation, GOI, New Delhi, 1949, p. 1. Maulana Azad praised Mountbatten for applying his military training to swiftly deal with the crisis by setting up the Emergency Committee. Azad, *India Wins Freedom*, p. 230.

7. See Deborah Poole, *Unruly Order: Power and Cultural Identity in the High Provinces of Southern Peru* (Boulder: Westview Press, 1994); Daniel, *Charred Lullabies* (1996); Fernando Coronil and Julie Skurski, "Dismembering and Remembering the Nation: The Semantics of Political Violence in Venezuela," *Comparative Studies in Society and History* 33, no. 2 (1991): 288–337; Allen Feldman, *Formations of Violence: The Narrative of the Body and Political Terror in Northern Ireland* (Chicago: University of Chicago Press, 1991); Pandey, "The Prose of Otherness" (1994); Butalia, *The Other Side of Silence* (1998).

8. Timothy Mitchell, "Society, Economy and the State Effect," in *State/Culture: State Formation after the Cultural Turn*, ed. G. Steinmetz (Ithaca: Cornell University Press, 2000), p. 90.

9. In particular, see Coronil and Skurski, "Dismembering and Remembering," pp. 296–99; and Pandey, "The Prose of Otherness," p. 189.

10. *Forthnightly Reports,* Chief Commissioner Sahibzada Khurshid to R.N. Bannerjee, Secretary, MHA, September 25, 1947, DSA CC 1/47/C, p. 78.

11. Azad, *India Wins Freedom*, pp. 228–29.

12. Percival Spear, *A History of India* (Delhi: Penguin, 1992), p. 238.

13. Datta, "Punjabi Refugees and the Urban Development of Greater Delhi," p. 442. Although I found some suggestions that the RSS were responsible for the "disturbances" or that it was "organized," yet these suggestions are not part of standardized accounts of the September violence. See, for instance, Sahibzada Khurshid to Deputy Commissioner M. S. Randhawa, October 17, 1947, DSA CC 60/47-C, p. 4.

14. On the civilian police, see CAI, November 19, 1947, Q102. For partisanship of the police, see K.T. Shankara, President, New Delhi District Congress Committee to Acharya Kripalani, President, AICC, September 22, 1947, AICC G-7, 1946–7, pp. 113–16. It was suggested that the deserters had taken refuge in Purana Qila in the belief that they would get safe passage to Pakistan as well as employment there, and despite attempts to assure their safety, as well as inform them of a lack of available jobs in the Pakistan police, they could not be convinced to return to their duties. Meeting of ECC, September 17, 1947, MP File 131A, pp. 21–22.

15. Writing about torture, Elaine Scarry and E. Valentine Daniel have both shown how the experience of extreme physical pain not only resists language but actually destroys it. Their work on silence produced by terror helps us understand the inability to put an experience of intense violence into words. Elaine Scarry, *The Body in Pain: The Making and Unmaking of the World* (New York: Oxford University Press, 1985); Daniel, *Charred Lullabies* (1996).

16. Khurshid to Bannerjee, September 25, 1947, DSA CC 1/47/C, p. 78.

17. Meeting of the ECC, September 24, 1947, MP File 52B, p. 39.

18. Tan and Kudaisya, *Aftermath of Partition in South Asia*, p. 199.

19. On perceived Muslim League propaganda, see Meeting of the Emergency Committee of the Cabinet (ECC hereafter), MP File 52B, p. 34. On Zakir Husain's visit, see Meeting of the ECC, September 17, 1947, MP File 131A, p. 20. This is also noted in Khurshid to Bannerjee, September 25, 1947, CC 1/47/C, p. 78. A number of cases where officials sent Muslims to camps were reported in the ECC. For instance, Sir Robert Lockhart noted that "many people of all types had been ordered to go to these camps." Meeting of the ECC, September 12, 1947, MP File 131A, p. 41. Mr. Patel reported that forty truckloads of Muslim refugees had been sent to the camps from Gurgaon by the superintendent of police there. Meeting of the ECC, October 3, 1947, MP File 131C, p. 69. For instance, Major General Cariappa "was led to believe that a very large number of those who had gone to the camps would return to their homes if some measures to ensure their security were taken." Meeting of the ECC, September 17, 1947, MP File 131A, p. 20. Requests for safety by various groups of Muslims was discussed on October 3, 1947, MP File 131C, p. 69. This also included appeals for supplies of food rations, as Muslims were unable to get food supplies, and when ration shops did open some shopkeepers refused to sell supplies to Muslims. Meeting of the ECC, September 20, 1947, MP File 131A, p. 2, and September 22, 1947, MP File 52B, p. 52.

20. See Meeting of the ECC, September 17, 1947, MP File 131A, pp. 21–22; September 18, 1947, MP File 52B; September 20, 1947, MP File 131A, p. 2; September 24, 1947, MP File 131B, p. 65.

21. Meeting of the ECC, September 18, 1947, MP File 52B.

22. The categorical term the Census of 1951 used was "displaced persons," for by this time the shift in nomenclature had taken place. This figure probably underestimates the number of displaced persons, as there were probably many who did not register themselves as such.

23. Meeting of the ECC, September 24, 1947, MP File 131B, p. 66.

24. *Annual Report on Evacuation, Relief and Rehabilitation of Refugees: Sept. 1947–August, 1948*, M/o R&R, GOI, New Delhi, 1949, p. 21.

25. Khurshid to Bannerjee October, 11, 1947, DSA CC 1/47/C, p. 83.

26. Meeting of the ECC, September 20, 1947, MP File 131A, p. 2.

27. "Buzdali ya bebasi," *Jang*, August 30, 1948.

28. CAI, February 11, 1948, Question 239.

29. CAI, November 29, 1947, p. 867; p. 920; p. 872.

30. Ibid., p. 872.

31. CAI, February 11, 1948, Question 239.

32. "Confidential," Randhawa to Bannerjee, October 13, 1947, DSA CC 60/47-C, p. 8; November 26, 1947, CC 60/47-C, p. 33; December 20, 1947, CC 60/47-C; October 17, 1947, CC 60/47-C, p. 4. See also Khurshid to Randhawa, October 17, 1947, CC 60/47-C, p. 4.

33. Randhawa to Khurshid, December 22, 1947, DSA CC 60/47-C, p. 46.

34. Randhawa to Bannerjee, December 20, 1947, DSA CC 60/47-C; November 26, 1947, CC 60/47-C, p. 33; March 23, 1948, CC 60/47-C, p. 84; Randhawa to Khurshid, December 14, 1947, CC 60/47-C, pp. 42–43.

35. Maulana Habibur Rehman to Deputy IG Police, January 14, 1948; "Misc Complaints: Alleged Harassment of Muslims in the Sadar Bazar Area on January 13, 1948," DSA File No PXI(50)/genl.

36. Randhawa to Bannerjee, October 13, 1947, DSA CC 60/47-C, p. 8.

37. Abdul Ghafoor to Rajendra Prasad, n.d., AICC G-7, 1946–47, pp. 5–6.

38. Pandey, "Partition and Independence," p. 2263.

39. Although these camps received some government assistance by way of food and medical supplies, their "management" remained with voluntary Muslim organizations.

40. Meeting of the ECC, October 7, 1947, MP File 131C, p. 62; October 17, 1947, MP File 131C, p. 46; October 31, 1947, p. 20. For analysis of attacks on trains, see Swarna Aiyar, "August Anarchy: The Partition Massacres in Punjab, 1947," in *Freedom, Trauma, Continuities*, pp. 15–38.

41. Meeting of the ECC, September 17, 1947, MP File 131A, p. 20. One tap, see Meeting of the ECC, September 20, 1947, ibid., p. 16. Indian government takes over camp, see Meeting of the ECC, September 11, 1947, MP File 52A, p. 78; September 17, 1947, MP File 131A, p. 20. Muslim guard, see Meeting of the ECC, September 12, 1947, MP File 131A, p. 41.

42. Malkki, "Refugees and Exile," p. 498.

43. Meeting of the ECC, September 17, 1947, MP File 131A, p. 20.

44. Anees Begum Kidwai, *Azadi ki Chaon Mein* (New Delhi: National Book Trust, 1990), p. 56.

45. Meeting of the ECC, September 12, 1947, MP File 52A, p. 84.

46. Muslim policemen in camp, see Meeting of the ECC, September 18, 1947, MP File 52B. On controlling movements, see Meeting of the Delhi Emergency Committee, September 29, 1947, MP File 131B, p. 8. It was noted that the numbers of refugees in Purana Qila and Humayun's Tomb remained the same since "refugees are not permitted to leave the camps except with a permit which is rarely issued." For discussion of "no

return movement" possible from camps to the city, see Meeting of the ECC, September 20, 1947, MP File 131A, p. 2; September 21, 1947, MP File 52B, p. 20; October 3, 1947, MP File 131C, p. 70. There were cholera epidemics in almost all refugee camps in Delhi and in both sides of the Punjab.

47. Pandey, "Partition and Independence," p. 2263.

48. Meeting of the ECC, September 20, 1947, MP File 131A, p. 15; and September 17, 1947, MP File 131A, p. 20.

49. John Knudsen, "When Trust Is on Trial: Negotiating Refugee Narratives," in *Mistrusting Refugees*, p. 22.

50. Daniel and Knudsen, *Mistrusting Refugees*, p. 3.

51. On arranging census, see Meeting of the ECC, September 12, 1947, MP File 52A, p. 84; and September 12, 1947, MP File 131A, p. 41. For K. C. Neogy's remarks, see Meeting of the ECC, September 21, 1947, MP File 52B, p. 21. On estimations, see Meeting of the ECC, September 24, 1947, MP File 131B, p. 65; October 17, 1947, MP File 131C, p. 46; "Meeting of the Ad Hoc Committee of the ECC to report on evacuation of refugees," September 25, 1947, MP File 131B, p. 35; "Appendix 'A' to the ECC," September 23, 1947; Item "Muslim Refugee Camps," MP File 131C, p. 33.

52. Sumit Sarkar, *Modern India, 1885–1947* (Madras: Macmillan India Ltd., 1983), p. 437.

53. Khurshid to Bannerjee, October 11, 1947, DSA CC 1/47/C, p. 83.

54. 'Azadi!-Aman!-Zindagi!: Jama Masjid ke munbr se Maulana Abul Kalam Azad ki ek dardnak cheekh: Sitare ṭuṭ gaye, suraj chamak raha hai, uṭho aur us ke kirane chuo," *Medina*, Bijnor, November 2, 1947, No. 80, p. 32.

55. Khurshid to Bannerjee, November 10, 1947, DSA CC 1/47-Conf C. See also interview with Mr. M.N. Masud by Hari Dev Sharma, NMML Oral History Transcript 218, November 19, 1973, p. 8. Masud was Azad's secretary and here remembers Azad's efforts to convince Muslims to stay in Delhi.

56. Azad, *India Wins Freedom*, pp. 236–37.

57. G. D. Khosla, *Memory's Gay Chariot: An Autobiographical Narrative* (Allied, 1985), as quoted in Pandey, "Partition and Independence," p. 2262.

58. Meeting of the ECC, MP File 131C, p. 19.

59. The Cabinet was aware of conditions for Muslims in Delhi, as an officer of the Pakistan government brought back reports of Muslim exodus into camps, the occupation of their homes, the desertion of the Muslim policemen, and so on. I mention this here to emphasize that the Pakistan government's position on Muslims from Delhi was formulated with this knowledge. Meeting of the Emergency Committee of the Cabinet (PECC hereafter), September 16, 1947, NDC File No. 58/CF/47, p. 7-A.

60. It was the perception of the PECC that the violence in the Punjab was entirely propelled by the Sikhs since they had the intention of forming a Sikh state based on Jullundur. This is repeated in almost all the Pakistani documents on the Punjab violence.

61. Report by Ghazanfar Ali Khan on the Punjab situation. He considered the Boundary Force the "root of all the trouble" because of "its present composition." Cabinet meeting, August 20, 1947, NDC File No. 23/CF/47.

62. Cabinet meeting, August 28, 1947, ibid.

63. PECC, September 14, 1947, ibid.

64. Cabinet meeting, September 5, 1947, ibid.

65. Cabinet meeting, August 28, 1947, ibid.

66. PECC, September 22, 1947, NDC 93/CF/47, p. 16. Liaqat, after his tour of Punjab with Nehru, reported that "[h]e had asked Pandit Nehru what precisely the India

government's policy was on the question of minorities. The latter told him that they wanted the minorities to stay where they were but events in the Punjab had developed in such a way that it was impossible to give a sense of security either to the Muslims in the East Punjab or the non-Muslims in the West Punjab. Consequently, so far as the Punjab was concerned, there appeared to him [Nehru] to be no alternative to the mass evacuation of minorities on either side."

67. CAI, November 18, 1947, Question 11. See also Bhaskar H. Rao, *The Story of Rehabilitation* (Delhi: Department of Rehabilitation, 1967), p. 26. Although the displacements in the Punjab came under the rubric of "planned," this did not mean that they were always necessary or voluntary. For instance, Muslim refugees in a camp in Ambala refused to be "evacuated" and pleaded with government officials for protection to remain there. This incident came up in the ECC, and is just one case which I came across. Yet the fact that there was an "agreement" meant that the Ambala Muslims had to leave, whether they wanted to or not. And in turn they *had to be* received by the Pakistani government.

68. The Pakistani Emergency Committee of the Cabinet was established on September 9, 1947, and it too created a Portfolio for the Evacuation and Rehabilitation of Refugees at this time. See S. Osman Ali, Deputy Secretary to the Cabinet, September 20, 1947, NDC File No. 31/CF/47.

69. PECC, September 15, 1947, NDC File No 58/CF/47; September 16, 1947, ibid., p. 7-A; "Reply to the Aide Memoire," NDC File 93/CF/47, pp. 27–43.

70. PECC, October 8, 1947, NDC File No 58/CF/47, p. 9.

71. Meeting of the ECC, October 7, 1947, MP File 131C, p. 62.

72. Associated Press, October 7, 1947.

73. Meeting of the ECC, October 7, 1947, MP File 131C, p. 62.

74. "Maghribi Izla ke Musalman," *Medina*, Bijnor, October 17, 1947, No. 76, p. 32.

2. HINDU EXODUS FROM KARACHI

1. Kishwar Naheed, "Censorship," in *We Sinful Women: Contemporary Urdu Feminist Poetry*, ed. and trans. Rukhsana Ahmad (New Delhi: Rupa & Co., 1994), p. 51.

2. Since the emergence of the Muhajir Qaumi Movement (MQM) in the 1980s, *muhajir* has acquired a new political charge as a category of identity. However, in its early usage it operated as a governmental category alongside other categories of identity like "panaghir," "Hindustani," "Dilliwalle," "UPwalle," "Hyderabadi," etc.

3. *Hijra* was also not supported by most of the north Indian ulam'a, who were largely opposed to the creation of Pakistan. For a discussion on *hijra* see Muhammad Khalid Masud, "The Obligation to Migrate: The Doctrine of *Hijra* in Islamic Law," in *Muslim Travellers: Pilgrimage, Migration, and the Religious Imagination*, ed. D.E. and J. Piscatori (Berkeley: University of California Press, 1990), pp. 29–39.

4. Census of Pakistan, 1951, vol. 1, pp. 87–89. Omar Khalidi argues that the 1951 Census underrepresents the numbers of *muhajirs* in Sind because many *muhajirs* attempted to evade this categorization. Khalidi, "From Torrent to Trickle," pp. 40–41.

5. "Census of 1951," NDC 133/CF/48.

6. *Fortnightly Reports*, Francis Mudie to Lord Wavell, March 7, 1947, and June 7, 1947, IOR MSS E 164/42, pp. 75, 101.

7. *Jang*, January 10, 1948.

8. Ghulam Husain Hidayatullah to Jinnah, September 11, 1947, NDC D.O. No. C-611, p. 117.

9. Arif Hasan, "The Growth of a Metropolis," in *Karachi: Megacity of Our Times,* p. 174. See all the other essays in this edited collection. Kamal's edited collection in Urdu, *Karachi ki Kahani,* has a number of essays by former Hindu residents of Karachi, but none examine the question of this massive exodus.

10. Sarah Ansari, "Partition, Migration, and Refugees: Responses to the Arrival of Muhajirs in Sind during 1947–48," *South Asia* 18, special issue (1995): 95–108. This essay is now part of a monograph, *Life After Partition: Migration, Community, and Strife in Sindh, 1947–1962* (Karachi: Oxford University Press, 2005).

11. Dr. Choithram P. Gidwani to Rajendra Prasad, December 3, 1947, NAI RP Papers 11-P/49, p. 1; Gidwani to Nehru, October 4, 1947, AICC G-16, 1947–1948, p. 228. See also CAI November 27, 1947, p. 790, and "What Is Happening in Sind—Weekly Diary," n.d., NAI RPP Papers 11-P/49, p. 5.

12. Harijan departures, see SPAI, November 1, 1947, p. 496. Hindu businesses, see SPAI, September 27, 1947, No. 39, p. 445, and October 11, 1947, p. 467.

13. Syed Hashim Reza, *Hamari Manzil: An Autobiography of Syed Hashim Reza* (Karachi: Mustafain & Murtazain Ltd., 1991), p. 80.

14. SPAI, September 27, 1947, No. 39, p. 461.

15. CAP, April 6, 1951, p. 907.

16. Ansari, "Partition, Migration, and Refugees," p. 100.

17. *Fortnightly Reports,* Mudie to Mountbatten, June 7, 1947, IOR MSS E 164/42, p. 101. Also in SPAI, September 6, 1947.

18. *Fortnightly Reports,* Mudie to Wavell, February 24, 1947, IOR MSS E 164/42, p. 72.

19. Ibid., p. 76.

20. On Sind University Bill, *Fortnightly Reports,* Mudie to Mountbatten, March 25, 1947, and June 26, 1947, IOR MSS E 164/42; Sind Landholders Mortgage Bill, ibid., April 7, 1947, pp. 85–86.

21. The pamphlet was written by Parsam V. Tahilrami, secretary of the Sind Assembly Congress Party, and was published in November 1947 to persuade the Indian state to intervene in Sind.

22. Reza, *Hamari Manzil,* pp. 95–96.

23. "Unrealities," *Hindustan Times,* March 27, 1948. In India there were debates on "whether the fears of Sind Hindus are real or wholly imaginary."

24. Liaqat Ali Khan's speech in CAP on December 16, 1948, pp. 4–5. Ansari also outlines similar problems through other sources. Sind Maintenance of Public Safety Ordinance, in NDC File 87/CF/47.

25. CAI, February 3, 1948, Question 55. Nehru's statement of policy was a reply to Giani Gurmukh Singh Musafar. The "Sind question" on whether the Indian government should do more for the Hindus who wanted to leave Sind came up several times for discussion in the CAI. See February 3, 1948; February 11, 1948; and April 6, 1948.

26. It was argued in a note to the Pakistani Cabinet that the Indian High Commission was distributing money to halis, dhobis, and sweepers, to pay their fare by ship to Bombay. However, the Indian High Commission denied this as a matter of practice. In Ahmad Ali, "Summary to Cabinet Ministers," December 18, 1947, NDC 217/CF/47. The issue of free passages is mentioned by Ansari, and in my interviews in Bombay with a few former residents of Karachi, one of them recalled the availability of such free passages, although none of them had traveled on one.

27. High Commissioner of India in Pakistan to Ministry of Foreign Affairs and Commonwealth Relations, December 3, 1947, NDC 217/CF/47.

28. Patel to Parmanand Trehan, July 16, 1947, in Durga Das, *Sardar Patel's Correspondence, 1945–50* (Ahmedabad: Navajivan Publishing House, 1973), p. 289. As quoted in Pandey, *Remembering Partition*, p. 626.

29. Rao, *The Story of Rehabilitation*, pp. 22–26.

30. *Annual Report on Evacuation, Relief and Rehabilitation of Refugees: September, 1947–August 1948*, M/o R&R. GOI, New Delhi, 1949, p. 5. It needs to be noted that, unlike the Punjab, this "planned" evacuation was not based on intergovernmental agreement and did not include an "exchange" of people.

31. SPAI, August 23, 1947; October 4, 1947; October 11, 1947; September 27, 1947; September 20, 1947.

32. Homi K. Bhabha, "By Bread Alone: Signs of Violence in the Mid-Nineteenth Century," in *The Location of Culture* (London: Routledge, 1994), p. 286.

33. SPAI, September 8, 1947; November 8, 1947; December 27, 1947.

34. SPAI, September 13, 1947.

35. M. U. Abbasi, *New Sind*, AICC G-16, 1947–1948, p. 208.

36. Choithram P. Gidwani to Liaquat Ali Khan, September 13, 1947, AICC G-16, 1947–1948, p. 129.

37. Letter to Kripalani, October 10, 1947, AICC G-16, 1947–1948, p. 144.

38. Letter to Kripalani, n.d., AICC G-16, 1947–1948.

39. "What is happening in Sind," *Weekly Diary*, December 2, 1947, NAI RP Papers 11-P/49, p. 5, and AICC G-16, 1947–1948, p. 29.

40. CAP, April 6, 1951, p. 897.

41. Puj Hindu General Panchayat Shikarpur to Kripalani, November 4, 1947, and Piece Goods Merchants Association Ltd. to Kripalani, September 20, 1947, AICC G-16, 1947–1948, p. 77.

42. Shamdas s/o Dewan Dewandas Ajbani to Kripalani, n.d., AICC G-16, 1947–1948, p. 82; N. R. Malkani to Nehru, October 6, 1947, AICC G-16, 1947–1948, pp. 198–99.

43. The fate of Karachi Port Trust employees is discussed in CAI, November 27, 1947, p. 790.

44. Tuljaram Valammal Thadhani to Kripalani, Karachi, October 20, 1947, AICC G-16, 1947–1948, p. 113.

45. President Sarva Hindu Sind Panchayat to Kripalani, November 11, 1947, AICC G-16, 1947–1948, p. 85.

46. "Makanāt aur panaghir," *Jang*, October 18, 1947, p. 2.

47. Tan and Kudaisya, *Aftermath of Partition in South Asia*, p. 179. Tan and Kudaisya argue that although a number of cities were suggested as a possible capital for the new country, including Dhaka and Multan, Karachi was chosen because it was offered by the Sind Muslim League, and that the fact that it was Jinnah's birthplace was incidental.

48. *Fortnightly Reports*, Mudie to Mountbatten, July 29, 1947, and July 9, 1947, IOR MSS E 164/42.

49. Tan and Kudaisya, *Aftermath of Partition*, p. 179.

50. Reza, *Hamari Manzil*, p. 84.

51. See Hamida Khuhro, "The Capital of Pakistan," and Anwar Mooraj, "Being Young in the Fifties," in *Karachi: Megacity of Our Times*, pp. 95–112 and pp. 357–38; Zeenat Hisam, "Guzare din, guzarte din," in *Karachi ki Kahani 2*, pp. 151–58.

52. *Fortnightly Reports*, Mudie to Mountbatten, June 26, 1947, IOR MSS E 164/42.

53. "Ghamzadah gharib clerk ki kahani Pakistan mein," *Jang*, December 6, 1947.

54. *Fortnightly Reports*, Mudie to Wavell, March 19, 1947, IOR MSS E 164/42.

55. PECC, September 10, 1947, NDC File no. 69/CF/47.

56. SPAI, September 20, 1947, and September 27, 1947.

57. Ghulam Husain Hidayatullah to Jinnah, September 11, 1947, NDC File No. 69/CF/47, p. 117.

58. This image of footpaths of the city filled with people came up again and again in interviews. In 1954 it was estimated that 250,000 people were still living on the streets.

59. For instance, in "Nadān dost," *Jang*, December 28, 1947, and *Jang*, February 15, 1948.

60. Editorial, *Jang*, December 21, 1947.

61. *Jang*, October 26, 1947, p. 2.

62. "Rent controller Karachi ke daftar mein hungama," *Jang*, November 5, 1947.

63. *Jang*, October 24, 1947, p. 2.

64. "Pakistan mein gadaron ki hosala afzaī, kiya hukumat-e-Sind sun rahi hai," *Jang*, November 24, 1947

65. "Chand tajaweez," *Jang*, November 13, 1947, p. 2; letter to editor, *Jang*, October 26, 1947, p. 2.

66. "Nadān dost," *Jang*, December 28, 1947; "Makanāt aur panaghir," *Jang*, October 18, 1947, p. 2.

67. "Makanāt aur panaghir," *Jang*, October 18, 1947, p. 2.

68. Letter to editor, *Jang*, November 17, 1947, p. 2.

69. "Makanāt aur panaghir," *Jang*, October 18, 1947, p. 2.

70. "Makān," *Jang*, October 29, 1947.

71. *Jang*, December 12, 1947, p. 1.

72. *Jang*, January 10, 1948; *Jang*, January 13, 1948. In CAI February 3, 1948, Question 54. Nehru, reporting on the violence in Karachi, noted that although only seventy "non-Muslims" were killed, 70 percent of their homes had been completely looted. Khuhro's speech was reported in *Jang*, January 23, 1948.

73. See *Jang*, January 13, 1948; *Jang*, January 15, 1948, p. 1; "Aman" and "Mister Khuhro ka qabil-e-tehseen rawaiya," *Jang*, January 15, 1948; "Hinduon ka inkhila," *Jang*, January 16, 1948.

74. Ansari, "Partition, Migration, and Refugees," pp. 100–1.

75. E. de V. Moss, "Note for Cabinet on the transfer of surplus refugees from West Punjab to Sind," Ministry of Refugees, December 31, 1947, NDC File No. 80/CF/47, p. 6-A-D.

76. "A Note on Statistics of the Refugees and Evacuees Problem," which is a part of this larger file, has also been reproduced in *The Journey to Pakistan: A Documentation on Refugees of 1947* (Islamabad: National Documentation Center, 1993), pp. 15–18.

77. James C. Scott, *Seeing Like a State: How Certain Schemes to Improve the Human Condition Have Failed* (New Haven: Yale University Press, 1998), p. 3.

78. There are wide-ranging criticisms of "overpopulation" and "population control" in the literature on "development." However, for an engaging critique of concepts of "population" in the making of "national economy," see Timothy Mitchell, *Rule of Experts* (Berkeley: University of California Press, 2002), pp. 212–13.

79. Meeting of the Cabinet, January 27, 1948, NDC File No. 80/CF/47, p. 9-A; and M.A. Khuhro to Jinnah, January 28, 1948, NDC File No. 80/CF/47, p. 10–10A. This politics of entitlement can be located broadly in a history of Sindhi nationalism. Mudie noted that "Sind for the Sindhis" sentiment had already begun to emerge before Partition when Bihari refugees arrived in February 1947. On May 22, 1948, when Karachi was made a centrally administered area, Sindhi politicians complained that Sind was being beheaded, and embittered provincial relations with the center. See Ansari, "Partition,

Migration, and Refugees," p. 103; Tan and Kudaisya, *Aftermath of Partition*, p. 182; Ayesha Jalal, *The State of Martial Rule* (Lahore: Vanguard, 1991), p. 89; H. M. Kagi, *Administrative Responses to Urban Growth: Karachi, Pakistan* (Ph.D. diss., Syracuse University, 1964).

80. CAP, March 6, 1948. See also Shaista Suhrawardy Ikramullah, *Huseyn Shaheed Suhrawardy: A Biography* (Karachi: Oxford University Press, 1991), pp. 68–70. Ikramullah calls it a "Speech that Cost a Career." It led to a debate about his membership in the Constituent Assembly, and while some people suggested that he be debarred and his seat be declared vacant, others argued that there were no rules in place for debarring him, and that there were others with "Indian nationality" holding responsible posts in the Pakistan government. (I discuss the case of Mr. Ismail, the Pakistani high commissioner in Delhi, later in this book.) A resolution was passed that anyone who had not taken up residence in Pakistan within six months of the resolution would have to discontinue as a member of the Assembly. According to Ikramullah, a number of obstacles were placed in Suhrawardy's way, and ultimately he did not want to leave his ailing father in Calcutta, which resulted in his seat being officially declared vacant on March 2, 1949.

81. "Karachi ke fasadāt Hindustan ki Muslim aqliyat ki dushman hain," *Jang*, January 11, 1948.

82. "Hindustan mein Musalman qaidi," *Jang*, February 9, 1948.

83. Mashriqi Pakistan," *Al-Jamiat*, October 24, 1948.

84. *Al-Jamiat*, November 11, 1948, p. 2; *Al-Jamiat*, March 3, 1949; *Al-Jamiat*, June 14, 1948.

85. The exchange of populations was an idea circulated in many imaginaries of Partition, and not only Muslim imaginaries of Partition. That many clamored for such an exchange of people can be seen in enraged letters and schemes sent to AICC. See AICC CL –10 (1946–1947). An example is Jwala Prasad Singhal's "Prepare for Logical Consequences." See also Pandey, "Can a Muslim Be an Indian?," pp. 613–14.

86. "Tabadala-e-abadi ki zarorat," *Jang*, November 14, 1947.

87. "Aqliyaton ki hifazat," *Jang*, November 19, 1947.

88. "Muslim League ki taqseem ka asar," letter to the editor, *Jang*, December 23, 1947.

89. "Pakistan aur Hindi Musalman," *Jang*, August 18, 1948.

90. "Aqliyaton ke masle ka wahid hal," *Jang*, August 20, 1948.

91. See Ayesha Jalal, *Self and Sovereignty* (London: Routledge, 2000), pp. 388–422.

92. "Hindi Musalman," *Jang*, October 7, 1949.

3. REFUGEES, BOUNDARIES, CITIZENS

1. Pablo Neruda, "Goodbyes," *Fully Empowered*, trans. Alistair Reid (London: Souvenir Press, 2005), p. 57.

2. Trouillot has been in general the most productive for me in thinking through silences. For his discussion of "unthinkable," see Trouillot, *Silencing the Past*, p. 27.

3. See Torpey, *Invention of the Passport* (2000); Mongia, "Race, Nationality, Mobility" (1999).

4. The permit system was then put into effect on July 19, only five days after it was announced. See CAI, August 17, 1948, Question 266.

5. "Statement on Partition made by the Deputy Prime Minister in the Constituent Assembly of India on the 12th of December, 1947," MP File 104. This decision was probably taken by the Partition Council on the assumption that significant Hindu and

Sikh minorities would be living in Pakistan, as there would be Muslims in India, and unrestricted movement would be necessary to reassure minorities on both sides. Later I discuss how, as part of the Nehru-Liaqat Pact on religious minorities, "freedom of movement" was considered a necessary part of reassuring minorities.

6. CAI, August 10, 1948, Question 79; *Al-Jamiat*, September 25, 1948, p. 3. This ordinance was promulgated in September 1948 and subsequently passed as an Act by the Indian Parliament on April 22, 1949. For text of the ordinance see *AJR Journal*, 1949, pp. 102–3.

7. *Al-Jamiat*, October 2, 1948, p. 2; for text of the Pakistani Ordinance, see PLD, 1949, vol. 1, p. 14.

8. *Al-Jamiat*, October 2, 1948, p. 2.

9. Letter to the Editor, *Al-Jamiat*, September 6, 1948, p. 2. Maulana Ahmad Saeed of the Jamiat-e-Ulama-e-Hind issued a press note assuring Muslims that the permit system was only a temporary measure on July 24, 1948. In *CID Weekly Reports*, July 24, 1948, DSA 68/47-C.

10. "Aman," Editorial, *Jang*, January 15, 1948.

11. Azad, *India Wins Freedom*, pp. 238–40.

12. Pandey suggests that the question of Muslim loyalty and belonging found an uneasy resolution when "exhaustion" coupled with Mahatma Gandhi's assassination in January 1948 "brought a good deal of northern India back to its senses and marked a turning point in the debate between 'secular nation' and 'Hindu nation.'" Although this book makes the case that the "Muslim question" took a much *longer* time to resolve, I interpret this "turning point" as one of perception, which may have influenced the return movement.

13. United Kingdom High Commission, Delhi, to Commonwealth Relations Office, May 14–21, 1948, IOR L/WS/1/1599, Opdom 39, para. 14; May 21–28, 1948, Opdom 41, para. 10; July 2–9, 1948, Opdom 54, para. 22.

14. *Weekly Reports*, CID Delhi, May 1, 1948, DSA, 68/47-C; Randhawa to Khurshid, April 30, 1948, DSA F56/48-Conf C, p. 1; June 1, 1948, DSA CC 60/47-C, p. 170; July 17, 1948, DSA 68/47-C.

15. *Weekly Reports*, CID Delhi, May 1, 1948, DSA 68/47-C; Diary of Superintendent of Police, CID Delhi, March 27, 1948, DSA CC 60/47-C, p. 101; *Source Report*, Inspector-General of Police, Delhi, May 15, 1948, DSA CC 55/48-Conf C, p. 9 and May 10, 1948, DSA CC 55/48-Conf C, p. 6.

16. Hindu and Sikh feelings are described as "taxing the public mind" in *Weekly Reports*, CID Delhi, April 17, 1948, and as "agitat[ing] the public mind" in *Weekly Reports*, CID Delhi, May 1, 1948, DSA 68/47-C.

17. Police and deputy commissioner reports are replete with instances of agitation against the government. On one occasion a refugee leader declared that if the minister of Relief and Rehabilitation did not solve their housing problem he would fast unto death before his residence. In *CID Weekly Reports*, April 3, 1948, DSA, 68/47-C.

18. Randhawa to Khurshid, June 14, 1948, DSA 68/47-C.

19. Randhawa to Khurshid, June 1, 1948, DSA CC 60/47-C, p. 170.

20. Azad additionally notes that prior to August 15, 1947, there had been a suggestion to send Randhawa elsewhere, but the "leading citizens of Delhi, especially a large section of Muslims, requested that he be retained as he was perceived to be fair-minded and strong." Azad, however, claims that the communal violence of the time deeply affected Randhawa, so that "the very Muslims who had a year ago pleaded for his retention now

came and pleaded that he was not giving the necessary protection to the Muslim citizens of Delhi." Azad, *India Wins Freedom*, pp. 231–32.

21. Even though most of Khurshid's kin network, his brothers and sisters and their children, migrated piecemeal to Pakistan after Partition, he and his children chose to remain in India.

22. Randhawa to Khurshid, March 29, 1948, DSA CC 60/47-C, p. 86.

23. According to *Encyclopaedia Britannica*, "fifth column" refers to a "clandestine group or faction of subversive agents who attempt to undermine a nation's solidarity by any means at their disposal. The term is credited to Emilio Mola Vidal, a Nationalist general during the Spanish Civil War (1936–39). As four of his army columns moved on Madrid, the general referred to his militant supporters within the capital as his 'fifth column,' intent on undermining the loyalist government from within." See http://www.britannica.com/eb/article-9034225/fifth-column

24. Randhawa to Khurshid, April 30, 1948, DSA, F56/48-Conf C, p. 1.

25. *Source Report*, May 12, 1948, DSA CC 55/48-Conf C, p. 8.

26. Letter from G.V. Bedeker, Deputy Secretary, MHA, GOI, to Khurshid, June 19, 1948, DSA F56/48-Conf C, p. 2.

27. *Extract from a Secret Report*, Intelligence Bureau, MHA, June 11, 1948, DSA F56/48-Conf C.

28. *Fortnightly Reports*, Shankar to Bannerjee, March 10, 1948, and July 27, 1948, IOR L/P&J/5/288.

29. CAI, March 22, 1948, Question 922.

30. "Muhajireen ki hindustan wapasi," letter to the editor, *Jang*, March 27, 1948.

31. "Wapis ja rahe hai," *Jang*, March 29, 1948.

32. UKHC Pakistan to Commonwealth Relations Office, Inward Telegram, April 14, 1948, Opdom 29, para. 7; and April 17, 1948, Opdom 27, para. 5, IOR L/WS/1/1599.

33. CAP, May 20, 1948, Question 190.

34. CAP, May 25, 1948, Question 7.

35. "Note for the Cabinet," Ministry of Refugees, August 9, 1948, NDC 210/CF/48. This position is reiterated in Meeting of the Cabinet, August 19, 1948, ibid.

36. Meeting of the Cabinet, August 19, 1948, ibid.

37. Meeting of the Cabinet, July 18, 1948, repeated on August 11 and 19, 1948, ibid. The planned two-way traffic was also discussed in the Indian Constituent Assembly. See CAI, August 17, 1948, Question 266.

38. "Extract from J. S.'s note on a discussion held by H.M. Interior with the Premiers of West Punjab and NWFP on August 29, 1948," August 30, 1948, NDC 210/CF/48. Discussed in the Meeting of the Cabinet, September 1, 1948, ibid.

39. "Summary for the Cabinet," October 15, 1949, NDC 210/CF/48. On November 14, 1949, an amendment was made to the Pakistan (Control of Entry) Ordinance to require permits from persons coming from India via East Pakistan.

40. "Note from the Ministry of Interior," September 17, 1948, NDC 210/CF/48.

41. "Note for the Cabinet: India's permit system and consideration of the action to be taken by Pakistan," Ministry of Refugees, August 9, 1948, and Meeting of the Cabinet, October 6, 1948, NDC 210/CF/48.

42. See Willem van Schendel, "Stateless in South Asia: The Making of the India-Bangladesh Enclaves," *Journal of Asian Studies* 61, no. 1. (February 2002): 115–47. Schendel's study of the islands of "Indian" and "Pakistani" territory created by the border there shows the complexities of crossing from one village to another in this region.

43. Khwaja Shahabuddin to Liaquat Ali Khan, March 25, 1949, NDC 210/CF/48.

44. "Note," Ministry of Interior, January 7, 1949, ibid.

45. Ibid.

46. Rajendra Prasad to Pandit Nehru, August 10, 1948, NAI RPP, 14-C/48, pp. 244–45.

47. *Jang*, July 18, 1948.

48. *Al-Jamiat*, January 10, 1949, p. 3. See also *Al-Jamiat*, March 7, 1949, p. 4; and April 3, 1949, p. 4.

49. *Weekly Reports*, July 17, 1948, DSA 68/47-C.

50. The Pakistan High Commission also instituted parallel permit variations.

51. CAI, August 17, 1948, Question 266.

52. *Jang*, May 14, 1949, p. 5.

53. "Changeover from Permit System to Passport and Visa System," November 24, 1952, MHA 6/38/58-IC, p. 7.

54. *Jang*, April 8, 1949, p. 8.

55. *Fortnightly Reports*, Shankar Prasad to Mr. Iengar, August 24, 1948, IOR L/P&J/5/288; *Weekly Reports*, September 11, 1948, DSA 68/47-C.

56. *Jang*, October 2, 1951. In "Permit!," *Jang*, December 16, 1951, the writer recounts the hardships of the permit system, which have not been eased despite inter-dominion conferences, and demands that a "people's view" be taken.

57. "Note," Ministry of Interior, January 7, 1949, NDC 210/CF/48.

58. The ability to make arrests with this amendment is recorded in *CID Weekly Reports*, September 4, 1948, DSA 68/47-C.

59. See the case of *Rochomal Daryanomal v. The Province of West Pakistan PLD*, 1960 (W.P.) Karachi, 1950.

60. The remainder of the citizenship laws came into force on January 26, 1950, when the whole Constitution of India came into force. Later the Indian Citizenship Act of 1955 was passed. See S.K. Agrawala Rao and M. Koteswara, "Nationality and International Law in Indian Perspective," in *Nationality and International Law in Asian Perspective*, ed. K.S. Sik (Dordrecht: Martinus Nijhoff Publishers, 1990), p. 74.

61. See Candice Lewis Bredbenner, *A Nationality of Her Own: Women, Marriage, and the Law of Citizenship* (Berkeley: University of California Press, 1998); Suad Joseph, ed., *Gender and Citizenship in the Middle East* (Syracuse: Syracuse University Press, 2000); Mary Ann Tetreault, "Gender, Citizenship and the State in the Middle East," in *Citizenship and the State in the Middle East*, ed. N. A. Butenschon, Uri Davis, and Manuel Hassassian (Syracuse: Syracuse University Press, 2000); Kif Augustine-Adams, "She Consents Implicitly: Women's Citizenship, Marriage, and Liberal Political Theory in Late Nineteenth and Early Twentieth Century Argentina," *Journal of Women's History* 13, no. 4 (2002): 8–30.

62. AIR, 1955 Supreme Court 282, p. 285.

63. AIR (38), 1951 Allahabad 16, *Badruzzaman v. The State*.

64. AIR (39), 1952 Allahabad 257, *Shabir Husain v. State of UP and Others*.

65. AIR, 1954 Allahabad 458.

66. AIR (38), 1951 Kutch 38, *Mandhara Jakab Khalak Dana and Others v. Kutch Govt.*

67. AIR, 1954 Bhopal 9, *Iqbal Ahmad v. State of Bhopal*.

68. AIR, 1954 Supreme Court 229, *Ebrahim Vazir Mavat and Others v. The State of Bombay and Others*.

69. *Al-Jamiat*, November 26, 1952, p. 3.

70. CAI, August 18, 1948. Of the 16,090 that asked to be allowed to stay in In-

dia, 13,018 were noted as reabsorbed. In addition numerous Indian government files examine the question of Muslim employees who requested reemployment, and a desire to come back to India. See NAI MHA 30/45/48-Appts, MHA 60/257/48-Ests, MHA 70/9/49-Appts, MHA, 1949 70/9-DGS. Of those who "provisionally" opted for Pakistan and then changed to India, see NAI MHA 68/102/48-Adm and 23/59/48–Est.

71. "Office Memorandum," MHA, October 20, 1948, "Correspondence re: Government servants whose families are staying in Pakistan," DSA CC F95/48-C Vol.II.

72. "Memorandum," MHA, October 29, 1948, ibid.

73. Letter from Sahibzada Aziz Ahmad Khan, November 12, 1948, ibid.

74 Letter from Mubashir Ali, n.d., ibid.

75. Office of CMO to PHB Wilkins, MHA, GOI, September 27, 1949, ibid.

76. PHB Wilkins, MHA to CC, Delhi, June 17, 1949, ibid.

77. Azmatullah to Judge of Small Cause Court, June 3, 1949, ibid.

78. Office of Judge to PHB Wilkins, MHA, June 4, 1949, ibid.

79. Shankar Prasad replied on July 8, 1949, that he would see to it that "no injustice is done." Ibid.

80. Azmatullah to VD Dantyagi, JT Sec M/o R and R, July 15, 1949, ibid. He wrote to see him personally "to explain the whole case with a view to secure early permission to bring back my family." On July 27, 1949, he wrote to the home secretary with a list of all the paperwork he had completed. He argued that "she is only waiting for the grant of Permanent Permit to return to India." On August 19, 1949, Azmatullah wrote to the judge that he had not been able to bring his family and lists all the letters and meetings he had undertaken toward this effort.

81. Top Secret, January 12, 1950, ibid.

82. MHA to CC Delhi, September 26, 1950, ibid.

4. ECONOMIES OF DISPLACEMENT

1. Gaston Bachelard, *The Poetics of Space* (Boston: Beacon Press, 1994), p. 56.

2. A body of legislation on displaced persons and their claims also went into place alongside evacuee property legislation, such as the Indian Displaced Persons Claims Act of 1950 and the Displaced Persons (Compensation and Rehabilitation) Act of 1954. See Rao, *The Story of Rehabilitation*, p. 121.

3. See Sumathi Ramaswamy, *The Lost Land of Lemuria*, p. 8.

4. "The Property of Refugees," Minutes of the Joint Defense Council, August 29, 1947, MP File 128.

5. Jyoti Bhusan Das Gupta, *Indo-Pak Relations, 1947–55* (Amsterdam: Universiteit van Amsterdam, 1958).

6. Ibid., p. 191.

7. J.B. Schectman, "Evacuee Property in India and Pakistan," *Pacific Affairs* (December 1951): 407.

8. Sardar Hukam Singh, in CAI, August 11, 1952.

9. Peter van der Veer, *Religious Nationalism: Hindus and Muslims in India* (Berkeley: University of California Press, 1994), p. 106.

10. See Gupta, "Chapter VI: Evacuee Property," for details on Indo-Pak negotiations over evacuee property. For an Indian government view of these negotiations, see Rao, "Negotiations with Pakistan: Immoveable Property," *The Story of Rehabilitation*,

pp. 92–112. For a Pakistani view, see Mohammed Ahsan Chaudri, "Evacuee Property in India and Pakistan," *Pakistan Horizon* (June 1957).

11. "Rehabilitation Prospects," Ministry of Rehabilitation, GOI, 1957, p. 4.

12. CAP, April 6, 1951.

13. Officially "agreed areas" in Pakistan included all of West Pakistan except unadministered agency areas. In India they included East Punjab, Delhi, Himachal Pradesh, Patiala and East Punjab States Union, Alwar, Bharatpur, Bikaner, Ajmer-Merwara, Dholpur and Karauli states, Rajasthan Union, Saurasthra Union, Jaipur and Jodhpur, and districts of Sahranpur, Dehradun, Meerut, and Muzaffarnagar in UP.

14. CAI, February 11, 1949.

15. Minutes of the Inter-Dominion Conference at Karachi, January 10–13, 1949, NDC 29/CF/48-III. The Indian view is noted in an "Attachment" for a meeting of the Committee of the Cabinet for Relief and Rehabilitation on April 12, 1949, where it is noted that at the Karachi conference no agreement was reached on the definition of the term "evacuee." DSA 82/49-Conf B.

16. "Evacuee Property in India," Ministry of Rehabilitation, GOI, 1961.

17. Ministry of Rehabilitation, GOI, to Chief Commissioner, Delhi, August 24, 1949, DSA 227, 1947, p. 15; "Form for the application for temporary permit holder. . . ." NAI MHA 20/50/56-FIII.

18. Ibid.

19. In Bengal, an Evacuee Property Management Board was set up on both sides. It managed properties only on the request of property owners. Since my research only focused on Delhi and Karachi, I do not know how this board really functioned.

20. Evacuee Property Amendment Bill, CAI, August 11, 1952.

21. Hukamchand Goyal, *The Administration of Evacuee Property Act, 1950 and The Evacuee Interest (Separation) Act, 1951* (Allahabad: Ram Narain Lal Beni Madho Law Publishers, 1964), pp. 72–75.

22. The fact that evacuee property laws became tied to the rehabilitation of another set of displaced is borne out by the parallel fashion in which amendments were made to the Pakistan Rehabilitation (Amendment) Bill on April 9, 1951, and again every time changes were made to evacuee property laws.

23. CAI, June 4, 1951.

24. CAI, 1948, vol. 1, no. 159.

25. CAI, February 25, 1948, Question 474.

26. Goyal, *The Administration of Evacuee Property Act*, p. 2.

27. A.P. Jain's statement to the house, in CAI, October 5, 1951. Achhru Ram's letter to A.P. Jain, dated September 20, 1951, was presented at the debate.

28. A Web site www.enemyprop.org allowed for the registration of claims until the end of 2002 by those dispossessed by the British institution of the custodian.

29. Janet Abu-Lughod, "Israeli Settlements in Occupied Arab Lands: Conquest to Colony," *Journal of Palestine Studies* 11, no. 2 (1982): 22; Simha Flapan, "The Palestinian Exodus of 1948," *Journal of Palestine Studies* 16, no. 4 (1987): 18–20. For a more recent and fuller account, see Michael R. Fischbach, *Records of Dispossession: Palestinian Refugee Property and the Arab-Israeli Conflict* (New York: Columbia University Press, 2003), pp. 1–80. Fischbach points out that in 1949 it was stated in the Knesset that the Israeli regulations "had been based on laws in the Indian subcontinent that dealt with the land permanently left behind by Hindu and Muslim refugees from Pakistan and India, respectively, in 1947." Fischbach, *Records of Dispossession,* p. 22.

30. After 1954 no more properties could be declared evacuee property, but court

cases over those already encompassed by these laws continued, and some continue to this day.

31. CAI, August 11, 1952.

32. "Evacuee Property in India," Ministry of Rehabilitation, GOI, 1961.

33. S.J.S. Chhatwal, MEA to Indian Missions, September 7, 1961, NAI MEA 24(1) LT/61.

34. The brochure claimed that the Indian government had taken back all the Muslim migrants from UP who had left for Pakistan during the period from February 1, 1950 to May 31, 1950, and had restored their properties to them, as agreed in the Nehru-Liaqat Pact. However, as I discuss in the next chapter, according to newspaper accounts in Karachi an extraordinarily large number of Muslims registered to return but only a fraction were able to do so.

35. This is also the focus of Rao's narrative of evacuee property in *The Story of Rehabilitation*.

36. Most of the files on the Custodian of Enemy Property were also destroyed by the British government, which is why today a Web site invites claims to rebuild the record on this area of Second World War history.

37. Vas Dev Varma to K.C. Neogy, DSA DC 309/1948, p. 99.

38. *Al-Jamiat*, January 26, 1949, p. 5.

39. *Al-Jamiat*, January 29, 1949, p. 2.

40. *Al-Jamiat*, February 6, 1949, p. 2.

41. *Al-Jamiat*, June 16, 1949, p. 1. In addition to JUH, a number of Muslim organizations emerged to help with changing evacuee property regulations, such as Anjuman-e-Islah and the Muslim Relief Committee, and their announcements also appeared from time to time in *Al-Jamiat*.

42. "Musalman malkān-e-jāedād tawajo kare," *Al-Jamiat*, August 4, 1949, p. 6.

43. "Jāedād ka masla," *Al-Jamiat*, August 31, 1949, p. 3.

44. *Jang*, December 22, 1949.

45. "UP mein andhergardi," *Jang*, February 27, 1951.

46. U. S. Dikshit, Office of the Custodian, to Rameshwar Dayal, Chief Commissioner, Delhi, November 17, 1948, DSA File, "Measure to stop pugree system in Delhi."

47. "Pagree System in Mixed Areas," ibid.

48. *Al-Jamiat*, August 10, 1952, p. 1.

49. Goyal notes that "an evacuee is not the same as a person who has given up Indian citizenship. A person might not have lost his Indian citizenship but still may become an evacuee." Goyal, *The Administration of Evacuee Property Act*, pp. 6–7.

50. In Nehru, *Letters to the Chief Ministers, 1947–64* (1985), as quoted in Khalidi, "From Torrent to Trickle," p. 38.

51. AIR, 1952 Supreme Court 3, 19, *Ebrahim Aboobakar and another v. Custodian General of Evacuee Property, New Delhi*.

52. AIR, 1953 Supreme Court 298, *Ebrahim Aboobaker v. Tek Chand Dolwani*. The court decided that once a person is dead he cannot be declared an evacuee.

53. Ministry of Rehabilitation, GOI, to Custodian of Evacuee Property, Delhi, May 24, 1949, DSA CC 102/49-Conf C.

54. "Hakim Dilbar Hasan Khan's Property," DSA CC F70/50-Conf B.

55. "Misc.–Complaints," DSA DC309/1948, pp. 70–71.

56. "Declaration as Evacuee Property of the Property of Mr. H. Ibrahim in Bombay," NAI MEA File No. 62–4/50-Pak II.

57. "Naya tufān," *Jang*, January 13, 1952.

58. This had far-reaching effects on many Muslim institutions which were based on *awqaf*. For instance, many institutions of Urdu in Delhi were initially taken over by the custodian, but then given over to a body of Muslims constituted by the government. Although the politicization of *awqaf* has colonial antecedents, under evacuee property legislation they underwent changes that need closer examination. See Gregory C. Kozlowski, *Muslim Endowments and Society in British India* (Cambridge, England: Cambridge University Press, 1985).

59. AIR, 1952 Allahabad 813, *Ali Ahmad v. Deputy Custodian of EP.*

60. Like Delhi, until urban development schemes could expand the city's housing capacity, in the initial years the primary source of housing remained the limited houses "left" by Hindus, although as I have tried to show, many Hindu families did not leave entirely, in the possible hope of return. When evacuee property laws went into effect, this meant the dispossession of those who remained; even this meant only 2 lakh of the original 14 lakh of the region's minorities.

61. This was later replaced by the Pakistan (Economic Rehabilitation) Ordinance of 1949 in "General Summary of the Policy and Progress of Rehabilitation of Muslim Urban Refugees in West Pakistan (excluding West Punjab)," NDC 3/CF/47, and "Note for the Cabinet by the Ministry of Refugees & Rehabilitation," NDC 103/CF/48.

62. Report of the Committee on Evacuee Trust Properties Board, vol. 2, GOP, p. 13.

63. The maps of the city still bear names reminiscent of the city's departed. For instance, Jinnah's mausoleum is near Guru Mandir, but if you ask someone on the street where the Mandir is, no one really knows.

64. *Jang*, August 14, 1948.

65. SPAI, December 27, 1947, p. 570.

66. He also filed suit against the government for their apparent laxity on evacuee property. This is reported as PLD, 1956 (W.P.) Karachi 533, *Maulana Abdul Quddus Bihari v. Chief Commissioner of Karachi.*

67. It ran like a serial, from "Custodian ne . . . ," *Jang*, July 8, 1952, "Palace Hotel ka bank mein ek paisa nahin raha" *Jang*, July 16, 1952, p. 6; "Palace Hotel ke . . . ," *Jang*, September 23, 1952; "Palace hotel ka muqadama," *Jang*, September 25, 1952, p. 6 and so on.

68. "Matroka jāedād ka allotment," *Jang*, July 23, 1952, p. 3.

69. "Matrokah amlāk ke qanoon par puri tarha amal kiya jāe," *Jang*, September 19, 1952, p. 6.

70. CAP, January 3, 1950, p. 248, Question 93. The incident reportedly took place on September 13, 1949.

71. Sind Rent Restriction (Amendment) Bill, CAP, December 24, 1948.

72. The discussion on the bill continued on December 29, 1948.

73. *Mahram* is anyone who can enter the *haram* or women's compartments, while *na-mahram* is someone from whom *purdah* is maintained.

74. I spoke with only one person who had lived under such a scheme. He was housed in the apartment of an elderly Parsi lady and recalled the awkwardness he felt, for every time he wanted to go to his room he had to pass through her living room. He moved out as soon as he found a place of his own, a few months later.

75. *Jang*, August 14, 1948, p. 1.

76. *Jang*, August 25, 1948.

77. "General Summary of the Policy and Progress of Rehab of Muslim Urban Refugees in West Pakistan (excluding West Punjab)," NDC 53/CF/47.

78. Reza, *Hamari Manzil*, pp. 99–100.

79. "Matroka Amlāk," *Jang*, February 27, 1951.

80. As most of the city's Hindu residents left the city and the province, evacuee property ceased to have relevance as an appropriating institution, and demands were made that ownership be passed on to *muhajirs* who had been allotted these properties. I am uncertain when exactly that happened, for an Evacuee Property Trust came to be reconstituted in 1960 and to this day manages only charitable, educational, and religious trusts. It is part of the Ministry of Religious Affairs.

5. PASSPORTS AND BOUNDARIES

1. Faiz Ahmad Faiz, "Evening Be Kind," in *The True Subject: Selected Poems of Faiz Ahmad Faiz*, trans. Naomi Lazard (Lahore: Vanguard Books, 1988), p. 87.

2. S. C. Consul, *Law of Foreigners, Citizenship, and Passports* (Allahabad: Law Book Co., 1969), p. 1. See also John Torpey, "The Great War and the Birth of the Modern Passport System," in *Documenting Individual Identity: The Development of State Practices in the Modern World*, ed. Jane Caplan and John Torpey (Princeton: Princeton University Press, 2001), pp. 256–70.

3. Ibid., pp. 209–10.

4. There exists a rich literature on "gossip" in anthropology. However, here I simply draw upon the insight that "gossip" at "the interstices of respectability" is not only used to negotiate "a world of value and behavior," but also constitutes a moral community. See Max Gluckman, "Gossip and Scandal," *Current Anthropology* 4, no. 3 (1963): 307–16; Anjan Ghosh, "Symbolic Speech: Towards an Anthropology of Gossip," *Journal of Indian Anthropology*, no. 31 (1996): 251–56; Luise White, "Between Gluckman and Foucault: Historicizing Rumour and Gossip," *Social Dynamics* 20, 1 (Winter 1994): 75–92.

5. "Selab-e-Nu," *Jang*, May 20, 1951.

6. Why Muslims were coming through Khokrapar was repeatedly discussed in Constituent Assembly debates. See, for example, CAP, February 23, 1949, Question 23.

7. "Disturbances in West Bengal and Assam in February 1950," CAP, April 1, 1950, Question 143.

8. As I have not done any research on the eastern border I do not know if this in fact happened or not. But figures stated in the CAI and CAP subsequently suggest that the majority did return.

9. CAP, March 1949, pp. 100–1.

10. See Golam Wahed Choudhury, *The First Constituent Assembly of Pakistan* (Ph.D. diss., Columbia University, 1956). Choudhury examines the contending views on Islam and statehood that emerged in the first Constituent Assembly, and its various committees, which ultimately made the task of drafting a constitution a very difficult one for Pakistan. On November 2, 1953, the Pakistani state became the Islamic Republic of Pakistan.

11. "Delhi ki bātcheet," *Jang*, April 9, 1950. In the remainder of this dramatization, Nehru repeated his invitation to return to the "real problem." So Liaqat asked him what the "real problem" to be discussed was. Nehru asked if it wasn't Kashmir. Liaqat then pointed out that Kashmir was not the agenda of the Delhi conference. It turned out that the agenda of the conference had been made by Sardar Patel, and Nehru had forgotten to pick it up from him. This was probably meant as a commentary on the relationship between Nehru and Sardar Patel.

12. Parveen Begum, "Uprooted Millions Find a Home," *Pakistan Standard*, Independence Day Number, 1954. This article claimed that 230,819 persons had registered to

return but only 22,845 had been repatriated. Regardless of how many desired to return, the Indian official figure for those who did return under the Nehru-Liaqat Pact was 23,991. In A.P. Jain's statement, CAI, August 11, 1952.

13. UKHC to the Commonwealth Relations Office, Review of Events in Karachi and Sind for the Period May 7–21, 1950, L/P&J/5/331.

14. "Rehabilitation of Refugees in Karachi and Measures to Check Their Influx," CAP, February 23, 1949, Question 23.

15. For Sindhi contestations over Karachi's separation, see Ansari, *Life After Partition,* pp. 74–121.

16. For arguments regarding the strength of *muhajirs* in the early Pakistani state, see Khalid B. Sayeed, "The Political Role of Pakistan's Civil Service," *Pacific Affairs* 31, no. 2 (1958): 131–46; Hamza Alavi, "Nationhood and Communal Violence in Pakistan," *Journal of Contemporary Asia* 21, no. 2 (1991): 152–78.

17. "Khwaja Shahabuddin mash-e-rah," *Jang,* 10 May 1950; "Muhajireen kyon āte hein?" *Jang,* May 6, 1950; "Hukumat-e-Karachi," *Jang,* July 2, 1951.

18. "Rehabilitation of Refugees in Karachi and Measures to Check Their Influx," CAP, February 23, 1949, Question 23; UKHC to the Commonwealth Relations Office, April 23–May 6, 1950, L/P&J/5/331/22300/1949; "Yaktarfa hijrat," *Jang,* May 5, 1950.

19. "Yaktarfa hijrat," *Jang,* May 5, 1950.

20. "Hal," *Jang,* September 19, 1951.

21. "95 Thousand," *Jang,* December 23, 1950.

22. "Sharamnāk!," *Jang,* April 14, 1952.

23. "Wapas jane ke bād," *Jang,* June 20, 1951.

24. "UP ke muhajireen ki wapasi kyon?," *Jang,* June 10, 1951.

25. "UP ke musalman," *Jang,* September 21, 1951.

26. *Jang,* April 15, 1952, p. 3.

27. "Yaktarfa hijrat," *Jang,* May 5, 1950.

28. "Muhajireen kyon āte hein?," *Jang,* May 6, 1950.

29. "ābadkari kaise ho?," *Jang,* May 22, 1950.

30. "Naye muhajireen aur Pakistan," *Jang,* October 30, 1950.

31. "Tabadala-e-ābadi," *Jang,* December 5, 1951.

32. *Jang,* April 9, 1952, p. 1.

33. "Mazeed ilāqa," *Jang,* September 18, 1952.

34. "Hijrat!," *Jang,* April 10, 1952.

35. See Pandey, "Can a Muslim Be an Indian?"

36. There were repeated complaints in *Jang* about the removal of these services, and the hardship they were causing. One letter by Ahmad Ali of Mirpurkhas described the conditions as "equal to death" for women and children making the journey in the heat through the desert without camels. Furthermore, they had to wait for days at Khokrapar for a train to come to take them to towns in Sind. On the one hand, he argued, the Indian government was making life impossible for Muslims, and on the other the government of Pakistan was finishing them off in this way. *Jang,* April 2, 1952, p. 3.

37. Khalidi, "From Torrent to Trickle," pp. 32–45.

38. CAP, April 9 and 10, 1951, p. 1064.

39. Apparently a statement by him had been published in the *Tanvir,* a newspaper of Lucknow, that he was not a Pakistani national and that he had no intention to adopt Pakistani nationality. This led to a debate in the Assembly on its propriety, and Mahmud Husain defended the high commissioner on the grounds that until Pakistani nationality was

defined by law the question was a moot one. CAP, January 12, 1950, Question 236. Sardar Shaukat Hayat Khan raised the question of Ismail's citizenship at this debate as well.

40. It was also argued in this debate that the passport system was not a "normal" requirement for "entry from one country to another," and particularly in the case of neighboring countries this was even less common. Dutta pointed out, for instance, that passports were not required for travel between Commonwealth countries, or in the two Irelands, or between France and England or between the United States and Canada.

41. A parliamentary discussion on introducing permits between East and West Bengal appeared in *Jang*, April 26, 1952, p. 1. Shortly thereafter announcements for a uniform system for both East and West Pakistan were made in *Jang*, May 8, 1952, p. 1. Restrictions on movement in the east were a central point of contention, for according to reports in *Jang*, the Indian government threatened to renounce the Nehru-Liaqat Pact if the Pakistan government imposed a permit system on the eastern border. In *Jang*, May 8 and 9, 1952, p. 1. Nehru was quoted as stating that the Indian government opposed the passport system since it would badly affect minorities in East Pakistan, although the Indian government would do its best to help them in every way. In *Jang*, May 24, 1952, p. 1. On passport negotiations, see *Jang*, May 19, 1952, p. 2; "Passport system agreement is complete, although the problem has been Indian requests for special conditions for Bengal," *Jang*, June 11, 1952, p. 1.

42. "Bharat ke Musalmanon ko jasoos bana kar Pakistan bheja ja raha hai," *Jang*, August 1, 1952, p. 1, headlines; on illegal travelers, see *Jang*, May 7, 1952, p. 1.

43. *Jang*, July 12, 1952, p. 5.

44. "Influx from Pakistan (Control) Repealing Bill," CAI, November 27, 1952; "Motion re: Migration Between Pakistan and India," CAI, November 15, 1952.

45. *Jang*, July 5, 1952, p. 1; *Jang*, August 18, 1952, p. 2. Details of the different locations of visa offices as well as visa types were announced, for the system was to start from 15 October 15, 1952. For Khwaja Nizamuddin's visit, see "Amad-o-raft," *Jang*, October 17, 1952, p. 17.

46. *Jang*, October 15, 1952, p. 1.

47. Letter to the editor, *Jang*, June 12, 1952.

48. "Passport," *Jang*, May 6, 1952.

49. "Pakistani Passport," *Jang*, September 7, 1952, p. 3.

50. "Passport system ki nafiz," *Jang*, October 22, 1952, p. 1.

51. *Jang*, June 15, 1952, p. 1; "Muhajireen par hukumat ki nazar enayat," *Jang*, May 21, 1952; "Gair qanoni dakhla," *Jang*, November 12, 1952; "Aane wale," *Jang*, December 5, 1952.

52. Munzurul Haq, "A Review of Indo-Pak Relations 1947–54," *Pakistan Standard*, Independence Day Number, 1954.

53. "Muhajireen," letter to the editor, *Jang*, November 16, 1952.

54. Nehru noted in 1953 that 3,000–4,000 Muslims were going to Pakistan via Khokrapar and that "most of them appear to feel that there is no great future for them in India." He considered the evacuee property laws as the most significant reason for the displacement. Jawaharlal Nehru, *Letters to the Chief Ministers 1947–64*, vol. 3, ed. G. Parathasarathi (New Delhi: Oxford University Press, 1985), p. 463; Khalidi, "From Torrent to Trickle," p. 38.

55. "Pakistan jane ki afwah," *Al-Jamiat*, July 4, 1951.

56. "Khokrapar ka rasta," *Al-Jamiat*, June 23, 1951.

57. "Pakistan jane ki afwah," *Al-Jamiat*, July 4, 1951.

58. "Pakistan se muhajireen ki wapasi," *Al-Jamiat*, July 7, 1951.

59. "Pakistan jane wallon se," *Al-Jamiat*, September 11, 1951.

60. "Taqseem ko khatm karneka tareqa," *Al-Jamiat*, January 16, 1952; "Pakistani kon hai?," *Al-Jamiat*, January 18, 1952.

61. *Al-Jamiat*, May 23, 1952; "Passport System," letter to editor, *Al-Jamiat*, June 14, 1952, p. 3; "Khokrapar ka rasta," *Al-Jamiat*, June 23, 1951.

62. "Khokrapar band," first letter to editor, *Al-Jamiat*, July 14, 1952.

63. "Khokrapar band," second letter to editor, *Al-Jamiat*, July 14, 1952.

64. *Al-Jamiat*, July 14, 1952, p. 2.

6. THE PHANTASM OF PASSPORTS

1. I draw upon Brinkley Messick's formulation—"Behind a given document text is the law, in front of it is the world"—to understand a document as mediating between state and individuals in society. Brinkley Messick, *The Calligraphic State: Textual Domination and History in a Muslim Society* (Berkeley: University of California Press, 1993), p. 227.

2. See Noiriel, *The French Melting Pot;* Torpey, *The Invention of the Passport;* Mongia, "Race, Nationality, Mobility."

3. After a period of five years a person could apply for registration, under the Citizenship Rules of 1956, although "the registering authority" had discretion to accept or reject an application. "Citizenship Rules 1956 and the Citizens (Registration at Indian Consulates) Rules 1956," NAI MEA F40–18/55-PSP.

4. "Instructions to checkposts—Intimations regarding entry of Pakistani nationals to District authorities in India," NAI MEA F 31(2)/56 PSP.

5. "Illegal Influx of Pakistani Nationals into Indian territory and Measures to Prevent it," NAI MEA-PSP F31(7)56-PSP.

6. "Question Regarding Nationality of Persons in Disputed Cases," NAI MHA 20/96/59-IC.

7. "Regularization of Stay of Persons of Minority Community in Pakistan who Entered India Without Travel Documents," NAI MHA 1/20/58-FIII.

8. "Permanent Stay in India of Shri Nevandmal s/o late Pradhandas," NAI MHA 5/16/63-FIII.

9. "Rules for Minority Community in Pakistan . . . ," NAI MHA 10/1/59-IC.

10. "Jews who have immigrated to Israel—Return of—Policy regarding," MHA F6/55/58-FI.

11. "Mr. Asher Reuben Moses an Israeli national," NAI MHA 3/53/58-IC.

12. Government of Bihar, Political Department to Ministry of Home Affairs, GOI, February 7, 1958, NAI MHA 1/36/58-FIII.

13. "Express Letter," May 17, 1958, Ibid.

14. "Unauthorized stay in Bihar of about 500 Pakistani nationals who did not obtain 'F' visas," NAI MEA 30(10)/55-PSP.

15. Ranajit Das Gupta, "Migrants in Coalmines: Peasants or Proletariats: 1850s–1947," *Social Scientist* 13, no. 12 (Dec. 1985): 18.

16. "Passport not Proof of Citizenship, Article 3 of Act Held Invalid," *Statesman*, September 8, 1957.

17. "Shri Ghafoor Khan s/o Late Sri Wazir Khan—determination of his national status," NAI MHA 16/175/59-IC.

18. "Grant of an India-Pakistan Passport to Shri N. Basar Khan and his wife," NAI MEA File No. 41(61)55-PSP.

19. Albert Venn Dicey, *A Digest of the Laws of England with Reference to the Conflict of Laws* (London: Steven & Sons, 1896), p. 77.

20. AIR 1955 Nagpur 6, *Karimun Nisa and others v. Govt of Madhya Pradesh and Another.*

21. Das, *Critical Events,* p. 62.

22. SL Yadav, Asst. Sec. to Govt. of UP to MHA, January 11, 1963.

23. See S. M. Akram Rizvi, "Kinship and Industry Among the Muslim Karkhanedars in Delhi," in *Family, Kinship, and Marriage Among Muslims in India*, ed. Imtiaz Ahmad (New Delhi: Manohar, 1976), pp. 27–48; Veena Das, "The Structure of Marriage Preferences: An Account from Pakistani Fiction," *Man*, no. 8 (1973): 30–45; J. P. S. Uberoi, "Men, Women, and Property in Northern Afghanistan," in *India and Contemporary Islam*, ed. S.T. Lokhandwalla (Simla: Indian Institute of Advanced Study, 1971).

24. Khalidi, "From Torrent to Trickle," p. 43.

25. Hidayathunissa Begum, NAI MHA 4/43/61-IC.

26. K. D. Gupta, Under-Sec, GOI to Sec., Govt. of Rajasthan, November 20, 1958, NAI MHA 4/221/58-IC, p. 2.

27. "Question whether ladies coming to India on migration certificates but whose husbands are still in Pakistan as Pakistani nationals may be registered as Indian citizens," NAI MHA 4/221/58-IC.

28. AIR 1955 SC282, *State of Bihar, Appellant v. Kumar Amar Singh and Others, Respondents.*

29. AIR 1951 Pat 434.

30. "Shah Mohd. s/o Abdul Ghafoor," NAI MHA 8/207/58-FIV.

31. "Pak-returned national," *Hindustan Times*, March 14, 1969.

32. "Rafiq Husain s/o Reaz Husain—Revision application," NAI MHA 15/39/57-IC.

33. "Grant of Indo-Pak passport to Sri Mohd Hashim," NAI MEA 41(155)PSP-55.

34. "Shah Mohd. s/o Abdul Ghafoor," NAI MHA 8/207/58-FIV.

35. "Shri Zikar son of late Haji Yusuf—Appeal," NAI MHA 4/108/57-IC.

36. "Saeeduddin Khan s/o Late Abdul Rashid Khan—Revision application," NAI MHA 15/50/59-IC.

37. "Form for the application . . . ," NAI MHA 20/50/56-FIII.

38. "Interpretation of the term 'family' used in Column 14 . . . ," NAI MHA 10/3/58-IC.

39. "Correspondence re: Government servants whose families are staying in Pakistan," DSA 95/48-C vol. 2.

7. MOVING BOUNDARIES

1. Michael Ondaatje, *The English Patient* (London: Picador, 1993), p. 261.

2. Ondaatje, *The English Patient*, pp. 181–203.

3. "Repatriation of Hav. Ghulam Ali alleged to be an ex-Indian Army Personnel," GOI, NAI MEA F20(30)/58-PSP.

4. See Willem van Schendel, "Stateless in South Asia: The Making of the India-Bangladesh Enclaves," *Journal of Asian Studies* 61, no. 1. (February 2002): 115–47; and *The Bengal Borderland: Beyond State and Nation in South Asia* (London: Anthem Press, 2005).

5. See for instance Pamela Ballinger, *History in Exile: Memory and Identity at the Borders of the Balkans* (Princeton: Princeton University Press, 2003), on the Julian March and the Yugoslavia-Italy border.

6. Gilmartin, "Partition, Pakistan, and South Asian History," p. 1092.

7. I am indebted to Willem van Schendel for sending me this newspaper story. http://www.telegraphindia.com/1030819/asp/nation/story_2277155.asp#top

8. Prasenjit Duara, *Rescuing History From the Nation* (Chicago: University of Chicago Press, 1995), p. 27.

Selected Glossary

Appa/Apa	sister
Ansār	friend, helper
Bhai	brother, form of respect
Chacha	father's brother
Crore	100 lakh, 10 million
Dada	grandfather
Eid/idd	festival following the completion of hajj, and the end of Ramadan
Fateha	prayer for the dead
Hijra	migration
Hakim	a wise man, physician
Jama Masjid	the Great Mosque
Khala	mother's sister
Khandan/i	family/familial
Khutba	lecture after Friday prayers
Lakh	100,000
Makan	house
Mohalla	neighborhood
Mu'amlati soch	transactional, businesslike thinking
Muhajir	refugee/migrant
Mutawalli	caretaker
Naaptol	measuring and weighing
Na-mahram	one from whom *purdah* is maintained

Pagri	lump-sum payment made for transfer of tenancy
Panaghir	seeker of panah or refuge, refugee
Purana Qila	old fort
Purdah/Purdah-nashin	veil, veiled woman
Qurbani	sacrifice
Qabza karnā	to occupy, seize
Saheb	sir, form of respect
Sharanati	refugee (used for non-Muslim refugee)
Waqf-e-aulad	Muslim family endowment

Bibliography

Abu-Lughod, Janet. "Israeli Settlements in Occupied Arab Lands: Conquest to Colony." *Journal of Palestine Studies* 11, no. 2 (1982): 16–54.

Ahmad, Aijaz. *Lineages of the Present.* London: Verso, 2000.

Ahmad, Imtiaz. *Family, Kinship, and Marriage Among Muslims in India.* Delhi: Manohar Press, 1976.

Ahmad, Rukhsana, ed. and trans. *We Sinful Women: Contemporary Urdu Feminist Poetry.* New Delhi: Rupa & Co., 1994.

Aiyar, Swarna. "August Anarchy: The Partition Massacres in Punjab, 1947." In *Freedom, Trauma, Continuities: Northern India and Independence*, ed. D. A. Low and Howard Brasted, pp. 15–38. Walnut Creek, Calif.: AltaMira, 1998.

Alavi, Hamza. "Nationhood and Communal Violence in Pakistan." *Journal of Contemporary Asia* 21, no. 2 (1991): 152–78.

Amin, Shahid. *Event, Metaphor, Memory.* Berkeley: University of California Press, 1995.

Anderson, Benedict. *Imagined Communities: Reflections on the Origins and Spread of Nationalism.* New York: Verso, 1991.

——. "Western Nationalism and Eastern Nationalism: Is There a Difference That Matters?" *New Left Review* 9 (May–June 2001): 31–42.

Anderson, Malcolm. *Frontiers: Territory and State Formation in the Modern World.* London: Polity Press, 1996.

Ansari, Sarah. "Partition, Migration, and Refugees: Responses to the Arrival of Muhajirs in Sind During 1947–48." In *Freedom, Trauma, Continuities: Northern India and Independence*, ed. D. A. Low and Howard Brasted, pp. 91–104. Walnut Creek, Calif.: AltaMira, 1998.

Ansari, Sarah. *Life after partition: migration, community and strife in Sindh, 1947-1962.* Karachi: Oxford University Press, 2005.

Appadurai, Arjun. "Number in the Colonial Imagination." In *Orientalism and the Postcolonial Predicament*, ed. C. A. Breckenridge and P. van der Veer, pp. 314–40. Philadelphia: University of Pennsylvania Press, 1993.

Aretxaga, Begona. "What the Border Hides: Partition and the Gender Politics of Irish Nationalism." *Social Analysis* 42, no. 1 (1998): 16–31.

Augustine-Adams, Kif. "She Consents Implicitly: Women's Citizenship, Marriage, and Liberal Political Theory in Late Nineteenth and Early Twentieth Century Argentina." *Journal of Women's History* 13, no. 4 (Winter 2002): 8–30

Azad, Maulana Abul Kalam. *India Wins Freedom*. Delhi: Orient Longman, 1988.

Aziz, K. K. *A History of the Idea of Pakistan*. Lahore: Vanguard Press, 1987.

——. *The Murder of History in Pakistan*. Lahore: Vanguard Press, 1993.

Bachelard, Gaston. *The Poetics of Space*. Boston: Beacon Press, 1994.

Baillie, Alexander F. *Kurrachee: Past, Present, and Future*. Karachi: Oxford University Press, 1997.

Balibar, Etienne. "Fichte and the Internal Border: On Addresses to the German Nation." In *Masses, Classes, Ideas: Studies on Politics and Philosophy Before and After Marx*, pp. 61–86. New York: Routledge, 1994.

Ballinger, Pamela. *History in Exile: Memory and Identity at the Borders of the Balkans*. Princeton: Princeton University Press, 2003.

Basch, L., N. Glick Schiller, and C. Stanton-Blanc. *Nations Unbound: Transnational Projects, Postcolonial Predicaments, and Deterritorialized Nation States*. Langhorne, Pa.: Gordon & Breach, 1994.

Bhabha, Homi K. "By Bread Alone: Signs of Violence in the Mid-Nineteenth Century." In *The Location of Culture*. London: Routledge, 1994.

Bredbenner, Candice Lewis. *A Nationality of Her Own: Women, Marriage, and the Law of Citizenship.* Berkeley: University of California Press, 1998.

Brown, Kate. *A Biography of No Place: From Ethnic Borderland to Soviet Heartland*. Cambridge, Mass.: Harvard University Press, 2004.

Brubaker, Rogers. *Citizenship and Nationhood in France and Germany*. Cambridge, Mass.: Harvard University Press, 1992.

Butalia, Urvaishi. "Community, State, and Gender: On Women's Agency During Partition." *EPW*, no. 17 (1993): 12–24.

——. *The Other Side of Silence: Voices from the Partition of India*. Delhi: Penguin, 1998.

Chatterjee, Partha. *Nationalist Thought and the Colonial World: A Derivative Discourse*. Minneapolis: University of Minnesota Press, 1993.

——. *Nation and Its Fragments: Colonial and Postcolonial Histories*. Princeton: Princeton University Press, 1993.

Chaudri, Mohammed Ahsan. "Evacuee Property in India and Pakistan." *Pakistan Horizon* (June 1957).

Choudhury, Golam Wahed. *The First Constituent Assembly of Pakistan*. Ph.D. diss., Columbia University, 1956.

Consul, S. C. *Law of Foreigners, Citizenship, and Passports*. Allahabad: Law Book Co., 1969.

Coronil, Fernando, and Julie Skurski. "Dismembering and Remembering the Nation: The Semantics of Political Violence in Venezuela." *Comparative Studies in Society and History* 33, no. 2 (1991): 288–337.

Daniel, E. Valentine. *Charred Lullabies*. Princeton: Princeton University Press, 1996.

Daniel, E. Valentine, and John Chr. Knudsen. *Mistrusting Refugees*. Berkeley: University of California Press, 1995.

Das, Veena. *Critical Events: An Anthropological Perspective on Contemporary India.* Delhi: Oxford University Press, 1995.

——. "The Structure of Marriage Preferences: An Account from Pakistani Fiction." *Man*, no. 8 (1973): 30–45.

Datta, V.N. "Punjabi Refugees and the Urban Development of Greater Delhi." In *Delhi Through the Ages*, ed. R.E. Frykenberg. Delhi: Oxford University Press, 1993.

Devji, Faisal Fatehali. "Hindu/Muslim/Indian." *Public Culture* 5, no. 1 (1992): 1–18.

Dirks, Nicolas B. "Colonial Histories and Native Informants: Biography of an Archive." In *Orientalism and the Postcolonial Predicament*, ed. C.A. Breckenridge and P. van der Veer, pp. 279–313. Philadelphia: University of Pennsylvania Press, 1993.

Duara, Prasenjit. *Rescuing History from the Nation: Questioning Narratives of Modern China.* Chicago: University of Chicago Press, 1995.

Dupont, Veronique. "Spatial and Demographic Growth of Delhi since 1947 and the Main Migration Flows," in *Delhi: Urban Space and Human Destinies*, ed. Veronique Dupont, Emma Tarlo, Denis Vidal. Delhi: Manohar, 2000.

Faiz, Ahmad Faiz, *The True Subject: Selected Poems of Faiz Ahmad Faiz*, trans. Naomi Lazard. Lahore: Vanguard Books, 1988.

Fazila-Yacoobali, Vazira. "Rites of Passage: The Partition of History and the Dawn of Pakistan." *Interventions: International Journal of Postcolonial Studies* 1, no. 2 (1999): 183–200.

——. "Yeh Mulk Hamara Ghar: The 'National Order of Things' and Muslim Identity in Mathew Mattan's Sarfaroosh." *Contemporary South Asia* 11, no. 2 (2002): 183–98.

Feldman, Allen. "Ethnographic States of Emergency." In *Fieldwork Under Fire: Contemporary Studies of Violence and Survival.* Berkeley: University of California Press, 1995.

—— *Formations of Violence: The Narrative of the Body and Political Terror in Northern Ireland.* Chicago: University of Chicago Press, 1991.

Fischbach, Michael R. *Records of Dispossession: Palestinian Refugee Property and the Arab-Israeli Conflict.* New York: Columbia University Press, 2003.

Flapan, Simha. "The Palestinian Exodus of 1948." *Journal of Palestine Studies* 16, no. 4 (1987): 3–26.

Foucault, Michel. "Governmentality." In *The Foucault Effect: Studies in Governmentality*, ed. G. Burchell, C. Gordon, and P. Miller. Chicago: University of Chicago Press, 1991.

——. "Questions on Geography." In *Power/Knowledge: Selected Interviews and Other Writings, 1972–77.* New York: Pantheon Books, 1980.

Frankel, Francine R. *India's Political Economy 1947–77: The Gradual Revolution.* Princeton: Princeton University Press, 1978.

Frykenberg, R. E., ed. *Delhi Through the Ages: Essays in Urban History, Culture, and Society.* Delhi: Oxford University Press, 1986.

Ganguly, Sumit. *The Origins of War in South Asia: Indo-Pakistan Conflicts Since 1947.* Boulder, Colo.: Westview Press, 1994.

Ghosh, Anjan. "Symbolic Speech: Towards an Anthropology of Gossip." *Journal of Indian Anthropology* no. 31 (1996): 251–56.

Gilmartin, David. "Partition, Pakistan, and South Asian History: In Search of a Narrative." *Journal of Asian Studies* 57, no. 4 (November 1998): 1068–95.

Gluckman, Max. "Gossip and Scandal." *Current Anthropology* 4, no. 3 (1963): 307–16.

Goyal, Hukamchand. *The Administration of Evacuee Property Act, 1950 and The Evacuee Interest (Separation) Act, 1951.* Allahabad: Ram Narain Lal Beni Madho Law Publishers, 1964.

Gupta, Dipankar. "The Indian Diaspora of 1947: The Political and Ethnic Consequences of Partition with Special Reference to Delhi." In *Communalism in India: History, Politics, and Culture*, ed. K. N. Panikkar. New Delhi: Manohar, 1991.

Gupta, Jyoti Bhusan Das. *Indo-Pak Relations 1947–55*. Amsterdam: Universiteit van Amsterdam, 1958.

Gupta, Ranajit Das. "Migrants in Coalmines: Peasants or Proletariats: 1850s-1947." *Social Scientist* 13, no. 12 (December 1985): 18-43.

Hali, A.H. *Hayat-i-Javed: A Biography of Sir Sayyid* . Trans. David Mathews. Delhi: Rupa & Co, 1994.

Hansen, Thomas Blom. "Governance and Myths of State in Mumbai." In *The Everyday State and Society in Modern India*, ed. C.J.F. a.V. Benei. New Delhi: Social Science Press, 2000.

Haque, C. Emdad. "The Dilemma of 'Nationhood' and Religion: A Survey and Critique of Studies on Population Displacement Resulting from the Partition of the Indian Subcontinent." *Journal of Refugee Studies* 8, no. 2 (1995): 185–209.

Hasan, Mushirul. *Legacy of a Divided Nation: India's Muslims Since Independence*. New Delhi: Oxford University Press, 1997.

——. "The Myth of Unity: Colonial and National Narratives." In *Contesting the Nation*, ed. D. Ludden. Philadelphia: University of Pennsylvania, 1996.

——, ed. *India Partitioned: The Other Face of Freedom*. 2 vols. New Delhi: Roli Books, 1995.

——, ed. *India's Partition: Process, Strategy, and Mobilization*. Delhi: Oxford University Press, 1993.

——, ed. *Inventing Boundaries: Gender, Politics and the Partition of India*. Delhi: Oxford University Press, 2000.

Hodson, H.V. *The Great Divide: Britain, India, Pakistan*. London: Hutchinson, 1969.

Hoodbhoy, Pervez Amirali, and A.H. Nayyar. "Rewriting the History of Pakistan." In *Islam, Politics, and the State: The Pakistan Experience*, ed. M.A. Khan. London: Zed Books, 1985.

Husain, Mazhar. *The Law Relating to Foreigners in India and Citizenship Laws of India and Pakistan*. Lucknow: Eastern Book Co., 1967.

Ikramullah, Shaista Suhrawardy. *Huseyn Shaheed Suhrawardy: A Biography*. Karachi: Oxford University Press, 1991.

Jacobson, Doranne. "The Veil of Virtue: Purdah and the Muslim Family in the Bhopal Region of Central India." In *Family, Kinship, and Marriage Among Muslims in India*, ed. Imtiaz Ahmad, pp. 169–215. New Delhi: Manohar, 1976.

Jafri, A. B. S. *Behind the Killing Fields of Karachi: A City Refuses to Surrender*. Karachi: Royal Book Co., 1996.

Jalal, Ayesha. "Conjuring Pakistan: History as Official Imagining." *International Journal of Middle Eastern Studies* 27 (February 1995): 73–89.

——. *Self and Sovereignty: Individual and Community in South Asian Islam Since 1850*. London: Routledge, 2000.

——. *The Sole Spokesman*. Lahore: Vanguard, 1985.

——. *The State of Martial Rule*. Lahore: Vanguard, 1991.

Jan, Najeeb, and Vazira Fazila-Yacoobali. "The Battlefields of Karachi: Ethnicity, Violence, and the State." *Journal of the International Institute* (Fall 1996): 16–17.

Joseph, Suad, ed. *Gender and Citizenship in the Middle East*. Syracuse: Syracuse University Press, 2000.

The Journey to Pakistan: A Documentation on Refugees of 1947. Islamabad: National Documentation Center, 1993.

Kagi, H.M. *Administrative Responses to Urban Growth: Karachi, Pakistan*. Syracuse: Syracuse University Press, 1964.

Kamal, Ajmal, ed. *Karachi ki Kahani*, 2 vols. Karachi: Aaj Magazine, 1996.

Khalidi, Omar. "From Torrent to Trickle: Indian Muslim Migration to Pakistan, 1947–97." *Bulletin of the Henry Martyn Institute of Islamic Studies* 16, nos. 1–2 (January–June 1997): 32–45.

Khuhro, Hamida, and Anwer Mooraj, eds. *Karachi: Megacity of Our Times*. Karachi: Oxford University Press, 1997.

Kidwai, Begum Anees. *Azadi ki Chaon Mein*. New Delhi: National Book Trust, 1990.

Kozlowski, Gregory C. *Muslim Endowments and Society in British India*. Cambridge, England: Cambridge University Press, 1985.

Lari, Yasmin, and Mihail Lari. *The Dual City: Karachi During the Raj*. Karachi: Oxford University Press, 1996.

Low, D.A., and Howard Brasted, eds. *Freedom, Trauma, Continuities: Northern India and Independence*. Walnut Creek, Calif.: AltaMira, 1998.

Ludden, David, ed. *Contesting the Nation: Religion, Community, and the Politics of Democracy in India*. Philadelphia: University of Pennsylvania Press, 1996.

Malkki, Liisa. "National Geographic: Rooting of People and the Territorialization of National Identity among Scholars and Refugees." *Cultural Anthropology* 7, no. 1 (1992): 24–44.

——. "Refugees and Exile: From Refugee Studies to the National Order of Things." *Annual Review of Anthropology*, no. 24 (1995): 495–523.

Manto, Saadat Hasan. *Mottled Dawn: Fifty Sketches and Stories of Partition*. New Delhi: Penguin, 1997.

Marcus, George. "Ethnography in/of the World System: The Emergence of Multi-sited Ethnography." *Annual Review of Anthropology*, no. 25 (1995): 95–117.

Masud, Muhammad Khalid. "The Obligation to Migrate: The Doctrine of Hijra in Islamic Law." In *Muslim Travellers: Pilgrimage, Migration, and the Religious Imagination*, ed. Dale Eickelman and James Piscatori. Berkeley: University of California Press, 1990.

Mayaram, Shail. *Resisting Regimes: Myth, Memory, and the Shaping of a Muslim Identity*. Delhi: Oxford University Press, 1997.

Menon, Ritu, and Kamla Bhasin. *Borders and Boundaries*. Delhi: Kali Press for Women, 1998.

——. "Recovery, Rupture, Resistance: Indian State and Abduction of Women During Partition." *Economic and Political Weekly*, April 24, 1993.

Metcalf, Barbara. "Presidential Address: Too Little and Too Much: Reflections on Muslims in the History of India," *Journal of Asian Studies* 54, no. 4 (November 1995), 951–967.

Messick, Brinkley. *The Calligraphic State: Textual Domination and History in a Muslim Society*. Berkeley: University of California Press, 1993.

Mitchell, Timothy. *Colonizing Egypt*. Berkeley: University of California Press, 1991.

——. *Rule of Experts*. Berkeley: University of California Press, 2002.

——. "Society, Economy, and the State Effect." In *State/Culture: State Formation after the Cultural Turn*, ed. G. Steinmetz. Ithaca: Cornell University Press, 2000.

Mongia, Radhika Viyas. "Race, Nationality, Mobility: A History of the Passport." *Public Culture* 11, no. 3 (1999): 527–56.

Neruda, Pablo. *Fully Empowered*. Trans. Alistair Reid. London: Souvenir Press, 2005.

Noiriel, Gerard. *The French Melting Pot: Immigration, Citizenship, and National Identity*. Minneapolis: University of Minnesota Press, 1996.

Noman, Omar. *The Political Economy of Pakistan, 1947–85*. London: KPI, 1988.

Ondaatje, Michael. *The English Patient*. London: Picador, 1993.

Ong, Aihwa. "Cultural Citizenship as Subject-Making: Immigrants Negotiate Racial and Cultural Boundaries in the United States." *Current Anthropology* 37, no. 5 (1996): 737–62.

Pandey, Gyanendra. "Can a Muslim Be an Indian?" *Comparative Studies in Society and History* 41, no. 4 (October 1999): 608–29.

——. *Construction of Communalism in Colonial North India*. Delhi: Oxford Univesity Press, 1990.

——. "In Defense of the Fragment: Writing About Hindu-Muslim Riots in India Today." *Economic and Political Weekly* 26, no. 11/12 (1991): 559–72.

——. "Partition and Independence in Delhi, 1947–48." *Economic and Political Weekly*, September 6, 1997, pp. 2261–72.

——. "The Prose of Otherness." In *Subaltern Studies VIII*, ed. D. Arnold and D. Hardiman, pp. 188–221. Delhi: Oxford University Press, 1994.

——. *Remembering Partition*. Cambridge, England: Cambridge University Press, 2001.

Peteet, Julie. "Transforming Trust: Dispossession and Empowerment Among Palestinian Refugees." In *Mistrusting Refugees*, ed. E. Valentine Daniel and John Chr. Knudsen. Berkeley: University of California Press, 1995.

Philips, C. H., and M. D. Wainwright, eds. *The Partition of India: Policies and Perspectives*. London: Allen & Unwin, 1970.

Poole, Deborah. *Unruly Order: Violence, Power, and Cultural Identity in the High Provinces of Southern Peru*. Boulder, Colo.: Westview Press, 1994.

Prakash, Gyan. *Another Reason: Science and the Imagination of Modern India*. Princeton: Princeton University Press, 1999.

Proudfoot, M. *European Refugees: 1939–52: A Study in Forced Population Movement*. London: Faber & Faber, 1956.

Ramaswamy, Sumathi. *Lost Land of Lemuria*. Berkeley: University of California Press, 2004.

Rao, H. Bhaskar. *The Story of Rehabilitation*. Delhi: Department of Rehabilitation, 1967.

Rao, S., K. Agrawala, and M. Koteswara. "Nationality and International Law in Indian Perspective." In *Nationality and International Law in Asian Perspective*, ed. K.S. Sik. Dordrecht: Martinus Nijhoff, 1990.

Rao, V. K. R. V. "India's First Five-Year Plan—A Descriptive Analysis." *Pacific Affairs*, 25, no. 1 (March 1952): 3–23.

Reza, Syed Hashim. *Hamari Manzil: An Autobiography of Syed Hashim Reza*. Karachi: Mustafain and Murtazain Ltd., 1991.

Rizvi, S. M. Akram. "Kinship and Industry Among the Muslim Karkhanedars in Delhi." In *Family, Kinship, and Marriage Among Muslims in India*, ed. Imtiaz Ahmad, pp. 27–48. New Delhi: Manohar, 1976.

Roy, Asim. "The High Politics of India's Partition: The Revisionist Perspective." In *India's Partition: Process, Strategy, and Mobilization*, ed. M. Hasan. Delhi: Oxford University Press, 1993.

Sahlins, Peter. *Boundaries: The Making of France and Spain in the Pyrenees.* Berkeley: University of California Press, 1989.

Salahuddin, Dr. *Dilliwalle.* Delhi: Urdu Academy, 1986.

Sarkar, Sumit. *Modern India, 1885–1947.* Madras: Macmillan India Ltd., 1983.

Sayeed, Khalid. *Pakistan: The Formative Phase, 1857–1948.* Karachi: Oxford University Press, 1968.

Sayeed, Khalid. "The Political Role of Pakistan's Civil Service." *Pacific Affairs* 31, no. 2 (1958): 131–46.

Scarry, Elaine. *The Body in Pain: The Making and Unmaking of the World.* New York: Oxford University Press, 1985.

Schectman, Joseph B. "Evacuee Property in India and Pakistan." *Pacific Affairs* 24, no. 4 (1951): 406–13.

Schendel, Willem van. *The Bengal Borderland: Beyond State and Nation in South Asia.* Anthem Press, 2005.

——. "Stateless in South Asia: The Making of the India-Bangladesh Enclaves." *Journal of Asian Studies* 61, no. 1 (February 2002): 115–47.

Schendel, Willem van, and Michiel Baud. "Toward a Comparative History of Borderlands." *Journal of World History* 8, no. 2 (1997): 211–42.

Schendel, Willem van, and Mohammad Mahbubar Rahman. "I Am Not a Refugee: Rethinking Partition Migrations." Paper read at Conference on Displaced People in South Asia, Chennai, India, March 2–4, 2001.

Scott, James C. *Seeing Like a State: How Certain Schemes to Improve the Human Condition Have Failed.* New Haven: Yale University Press, 1998.

Selier, Frits, and Jan van der Linden, eds. *Karachi: Migrants, Housing, and Housing Policy.* Lahore: Vanguard, 1991.

Spear, Percival. *A History of India.* Delhi: Penguin, 1992.

Talbot, Ian. *Divided Cities: Lahore, Amritsar, and the Partition of India.* Karachi: Oxford University Press, 2006.

——. *Freedom's Cry.* Karachi: Oxford University Press, 1996.

Tan, Tai Yong, and Gyanesh Kudaisya. *The Aftermath of Partition in South Asia.* London: Routledge, 2000.

Tarlo, Emma. "Paper Truths: The Emergency and Slum Clearance Through Forgotten Files." In *The Everyday State and Society in Modern India.* New Delhi: Social Science Press, 2000.

Tetreault, Mary Ann. "Gender, Citizenship, and the State in the Middle East." In *Citizenship and the State in the Middle East*, ed. N. A. Butenschon, Uri Davis, and Manuel Hassassian. Syracuse: Syracuse University Press, 2000.

Torpey, John. *The Invention of Passports.* Cambridge, England: Cambridge University Press, 2000.

Torpey, John, and Jane Caplan, eds. *Documenting Individual Identity: The Development of State Practices in the Modern World.* Princeton: Princeton University Press, 2001.

Troll, Christian, and Gail Minnault, eds. *Abul Kalam Azad: An Intellectual and Religious Biography.* New Delhi: Oxford University Press, 1988.

Trouillot, Michel-Rolph. *Silencing the Past: Power and the Production of History.* Boston: Beacon Press, 1995.

Uberoi, J. P. S. "Men, Women, and Property in Northern Afghanistan." In *India and Contemporary Islam*, ed. S.T. Lokhandwalla. Simla: Indian Institute of Advanced Study, 1971.

Veer, Peter van der. *Religious Nationalism: Hindus and Muslims in India*. Berkeley: University of California Press, 1994.

Verkaaik, Oskar. *Migrants and Militants: Fun and Urban Violence in Pakistan*. Princeton: Princeton University Press, 2004.

——. *A People of Migrants: Ethnicity, State, and Religion in Karachi*. Amsterdam: VU Press, 1994.

Weinbaum, Marvin, and Chetan Kumar, eds. *South Asia Approaches the Millennium: Reexamining National Security*. Boulder, Colo.: Westview Press, 1995.

White, Luise. "Between Gluckman and Foucault: Historicizing Rumour and Gossip." *Social Dynamics: A Journal of the Centre of African Studies University of Cape Town* 20, 1 (Winter 1994): 75–92.

Index